T0322501

HOW BRITAIN BROUGHT FOOTBALL TO THE WORLD

How
Britain
Brought
Football
to the
World

STUART
LAYCOCK
AND
PHILIP
LAYCOCK

For Richard Laycock 1930–2021,
a gentleman and a gentle man.

First published 2022

The History Press
97 St George's Place, Cheltenham,
Gloucestershire, GL50 3QB
www.thehistorypress.co.uk

British Library Cataloguing in Publication Data.
A catalogue record for this book is available from the British Library.

ISBN 978 0 7509 9879 6

Typesetting and origination by The History Press
Printed and bound in Great Britain by TJ Books Limited, Padstow, Cornwall.

Trees for LYfe

Contents

Foreword

I knew world football came from here. I knew that much, but what I didn't know was how that happened. I was lucky enough to play football at the top level in this country, I watch lots of football, and I have been involved in the game all my life but even I really knew only a little about how football spread across the world. It's an amazing story, and something we can all be proud of.

Graham Stuart
Chelsea, Everton, Sheffield Utd, Charlton Athletic,
Norwich City, England U-21

Maps of the World

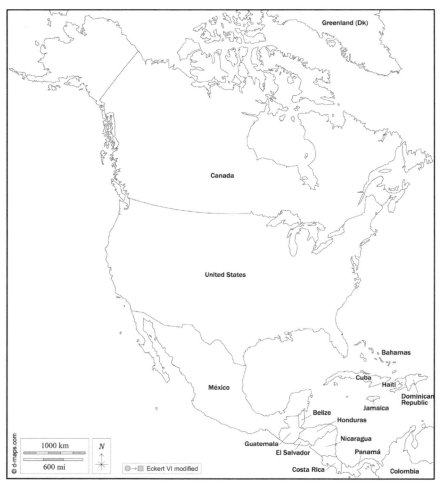

North America. (Courtesy of d-maps.com/carte.php?num_car=5083)

South America. (Courtesy of d-maps.com/carte.php?num_car=2319)

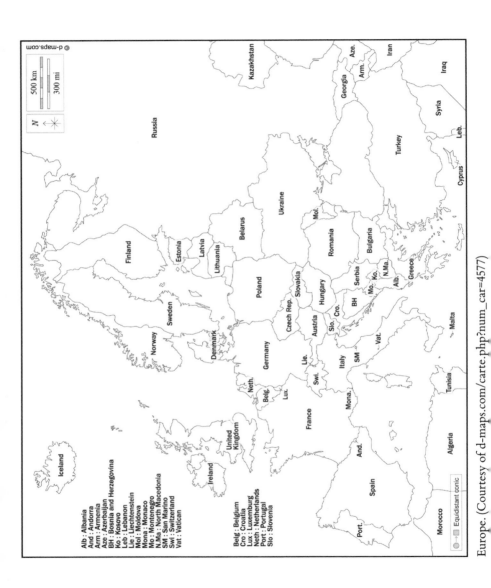

Europe. (Courtesy of d-maps.com/carte.php?num_car=4577)

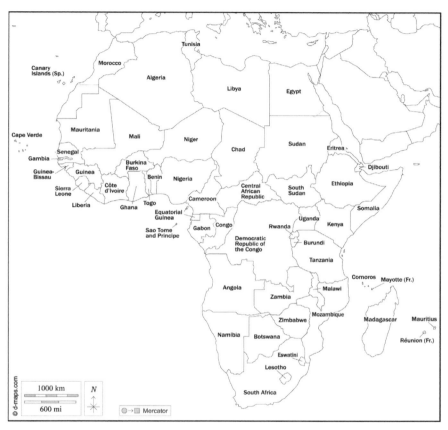

Africa. (Courtesy of d-maps.com/carte.php?num_car=4339)

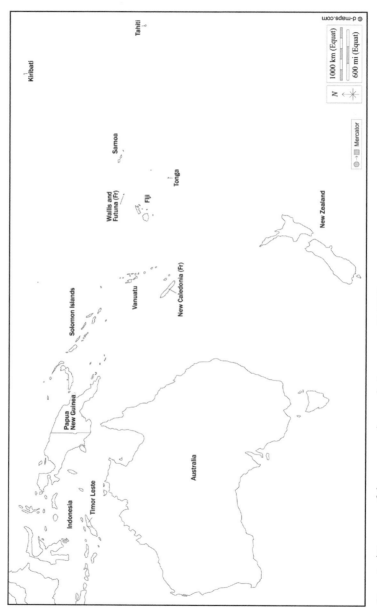

Oceania. (Courtesy of d-maps.com/carte.php?num_car=284583)

Asia. (Courtesy of d-maps.com/carte.php?num_car=5161)

Introduction

There is nothing quite like the global phenomenon that is football today. There has never been anything like it in human history; so many humans, from so many countries and cultures, enthusiastically participating in and watching a single developed sport, with shared rules. And there may never, ever again be anything like it, because with football occupying such a dominant position in the world's sporting passions, there is limited space for competitor sports to develop.

There are many reasons for the triumph of football, including its sheer playability in so many environments, with a ball, or anything that can serve as a ball, being about the only piece of essential specialist kit. We thought it would be fun to try to find out which countries got football directly from Brits and which got it indirectly. This book is about how a sport developed here in Britain, then spread across the globe to become the greatest sport in human history, bringing excitement and elation. Yes, there is occasional despair there too, but it is part of the positive genius of football that the despair is usually short-lived. There is always another match, another season, another tournament, giving the chance to replace defeat with victory.

When we set out to do the research for this book, we weren't entirely sure where it would lead. We knew, like most people, that football came from here and spread across the world, and we knew some key Brits had been influential in taking football to key countries like France, Italy and Brazil. By the time we had finished the research, we had found the amazing story of how Britons were directly involved in the beginnings of football in about 60 per cent (well over 100 of them) of the world's countries, and indirectly involved in the spread of football to the rest of the world's countries. There are football monuments to many of these figures in the countries they helped, but few here, the country from which they came. That's something that should and, we hope, will change.

To try to get as broad a picture of world football development as we could, the list of chapters is a hybrid. It contains all the UN member states (even those few who are not members of FIFA) but it also contains those entities that are not UN-recognised sovereign states, but are members of FIFA or a linked regional football association. The main chapters run in alphabetical order; however, to simplify the addition of some of the smaller of these entities, they have been added under a sovereign state chapter heading, where that might seem logical to the average British reader. So if you want to read something about football in Guadeloupe, look under France, if you want to read something about football in Guam, look under the USA.

Nobody is pretending that Britain's role in spreading football across the world is without its controversies. One of the ways it was spread was through the British Empire and through colonial administrations. Racist attitudes were widespread among such colonial administrations, and so was exploitation of those being ruled by them. Sport had a role both in enforcing imperial rule and in resisting it.

However, the Empire was far from being the only way Brits exported football. British trade spread the game well beyond the political restraints of the Empire, and the pioneers who did so came from many walks of life, not just from the ranks of the Empire's military and administrators. There were, for instance, sailors looking for entertainment on shore leave, miners and railway workers keeping fit, schools and missionaries aiming to build team spirit, and middle-class merchants extolling a British way of life. Many of the pioneers of football were Scottish.

Equally, nobody is pretending that the amazing world sport that is football today is solely the result of British talent and efforts. On the contrary, part of the genius of football is that in each country and culture, it has grown and flourished as a unique part of that country and culture.

Many different cultures have contributed to the way the game is played today. Brazil, Argentina, Italy, Spain, Hungary and Holland have, for instance, all helped develop our understanding of what makes good winning football. And even though it's not the main purpose of this book, we thought it would be fun also to take a little look at how Britain and the countries of the world have helped each other out with the progress of football in the years since it started and where football in each country is at today.

The story of how football spread across the United Kingdom is also a fascinating one, but one already dealt with superbly in a number of excellent books, so we won't be looking at that here. Current British Overseas Territories, like Gibraltar and Bermuda, come under the British umbrella, so you won't find those in here either.

People were, of course, kicking round objects around in various parts of the world long before association football turned up, and we will mention some of those games as we work our way across the world. There are also, of course, other forms of football, with the Americans, Irish and Australians developing separate games, some of which have affected the development of soccer. We will be making some mention of those as well.

Women's football deserves, and clearly has, a huge future. England's spectacular victory in the 2022 Euros will do huge amounts for the game in this country. Women across the world often look to British women playing during the First World War as the start of their game. Due to the history of the game and of society around the world, and due to the situation today, more of this book is about the men's game than the women's game, but if we get to do a second edition we hope that will have changed.

All in all, it's been great fun to write this book, and we hope it's great fun to read. Read it in alphabetical order, or in any order you fancy!

A Big Thanks

In compiling this book we have looked at a huge range of sources, both in print form and online. This is not, though, an academic history, so we didn't want to weigh it down with copious notes and a huge bibliography. We would, however, like here to pay tribute to and say thank you to some key sources and books we have found very useful.

We would like to make special mention, in no particular order, of *Origin Stories: The Pioneers Who Took Football to the World* by Chris Lee; *The Ball is Round* by David Goldblatt; *African Soccerscapes* by Peter Alegi; *¡Golazo!* by Andreas Campomar; *World Class* by James Ferguson; *A Journal of African Football History 1883–2000* by Barry Baker; *Mister* by Rory Smith; *Feet of the Chameleon* by Ian Hawkey; *The Trouser People* by Andrew Marshall; *Fathers of Football* by Keith Baker; *Contested Fields* by Alan McDougall; *Football: The First Hundred Years* by Adrian Harvey; *Historia Minima del Futbol en América Latina* by Pablo Alabarces; *Fear and Loathing in World Football* eds Gary Armstrong and Richard Guilianotti; *Sport and Diplomacy* ed. J. Simon Rofe; *The Blizzard: The Football Quarterly* ed. Jonathan Wilson; and the UEFA, FIFA and RSSSF websites. We would also like to thank Martin Weiler at Exeter City Football Club Museum Trust and The Grecian Archive, and Richard McBrearty and the Scottish Football Museum for their assistance.

The Countries

Afghanistan

It is not going to have escaped the notice of anybody here that the UK has fought in Afghanistan. A war in which we were involved there has just finished, and when football first really came to the country, a war there had also just finished.

The Third Anglo-Afghan War (yes, there were two even before that) started in 1919 and ended the same year in a bit of a draw really, but it did somewhat lessen British political and military influence over Afghanistan, and was regarded by many Afghans as a victory. The king who had led the war, Amanullah Khan, saw it as his mission to make Afghanistan more technologically sophisticated and more open to western cultural links. Part of that was football.

In the late nineteenth century, football was already well established a few miles to the south of Afghanistan, in Bannu, where English missionary Theodore Leighton Pennell had established himself in order to reach travellers to Afghanistan and where he had also established a local football team. In 1922, the Afghanistan Football Federation was founded, and in 1923 Amanullah Khan built the Ghazi Stadium in Kabul, which went on to become Afghanistan's main football stadium. Amanullah Khan founded schools in which, among other subjects, English was taught, and soon school football teams were playing competitions.

The realities of geography and politics meant that, despite the Third Anglo-Afghan War, the cultural and sporting influence of Britain remained strong in Afghanistan. The British Legation in Kabul played a number of sports against Afghan competition in the 1920s and '30s, including billiards, cricket and tennis, and also organised visits to Afghanistan from hockey and football teams from British India. In 1923, in the same year that the Ghazi Stadium was built, Amanullah Khan beat British civil servant Richard Roy Maconachie at billiards.

Amanullah Khan's rule would end in a terrible civil war (by no means the last of those in the country in the last 100 years) partly brought about by his attempts to change Afghanistan. Football was not, however, eradicated. By the 1930s proper football clubs were being established, with Afghan teams now going on tour in neighbouring British India.

In 1948, Afghanistan joined FIFA and the Afghan national football team travelled to Britain to play in the Olympics. They were beaten 6-0 by Luxembourg, but they were there and they were playing international football.

The decades after were pretty thin on international football success for Afghanistan. And worse was to come on other fronts. First there was the Soviet occupation, then warlords fighting warlords, then the Taliban took over for the first time. Under the Taliban, the Ghazi stadium saw public executions take place. In one incident a woman was made to kneel near the penalty spot before being shot. A visiting Afghan team were also arrested by the Taliban for wearing shorts and had their heads shaved. However, the Afghan passion for football continued.

After the Taliban were removed from power by international forces and their Afghan allies, there was a definite resurgence of football, which Britain did something to encourage.

The British Army was involved. For instance, the Taliban fled Kabul in November 2001 and by February 2002, a mainly British team from ISAF (International Security Assistance Force) were taking on Kabul United, a team assembled from the best players of four local sides. Kabul's national stadium was serving its intended purpose again. Kabul United scored first, but, in the end ISAF won 3-1.

And there was wider involvement from the British football community, too. British coaches, for instance, trained Afghan coaches.

An Afghanistan national women's side was also created. In 2013 the national men's side won the South Asian Football Federation Championship.

However, now the Taliban are in power in Afghanistan again. Many of Afghanistan's women footballers have fled the country, and the future direction of football in Afghanistan, and indeed of the country itself, is uncertain.

Albania

Under communist dictator Enver Hoxha, Albania was a bit of a mystery to much of Europe, but it has had a fascinating history and, yes, football is a key part of that history.

Football first reached Albania in the early twentieth century, and it seems to have been first played there in the northern city of Shkodër. By that time, due to the large British presence in Malta, the game had already been long firmly established there, and it is reported that it was an Anglo-Maltese monk who, in 1908, brought the game to Albania. Locals watched students playing at the Roman Catholic Xaverian mission school and began to take an interest.

Somewhere in there also, though, are other influences. Some players in Shkodër, for instance, had experience of playing football in Italy, just across the Adriatic from Albania.

As so often, football here involved an expression of local and national identity. Albania had declared independence from the Ottoman Empire that year and, in 1913, Independenca Shkodër took on a side selected from part of the Austro-Hungarian armed forces that happened to be stationed in the area to help guarantee the new country's borders. Despite the Albanians scoring, the Austro-Hungarians narrowly beat the team from the young nation, but still at least the young nation had a team.

And the Austro-Hungarian Empire shortly after suffered a much more serious defeat – in the First World War – and ceased to exist, while Albania, with its love of football continued. In 1919, KF Vllaznia Shkodër was founded and is still in existence today, one of the most successful clubs in Albanian football history.

The reign of King Zog, Italian occupation, the Second World War, and the creation of a communist state that would last until 1991 (or 1992 depending on how you look at it) were all to follow.

In 1946, Albania won the Balkan Nations' Cup and the national team has had a few other successes over the years. For instance, in November 1965, at home in Tirana, Albania managed a 1-1 draw against Northern Ireland, when the visitors needed a win to qualify for the World Cup. More recently, Albania qualified for the 2016 Euros.

In 2011, the Albania women's team played their first international, and Aurora Seranaj scored their first international goal, which was enough to give them victory in a friendly over FYR Macedonia.

Algeria

When you think of European connections to Algerian football, you tend to think of France. There is, of course, the football legend that is Zinedine Zidane, born in France to parents from Algeria. What a career! And what on earth happened in that World Cup final?

However, Britain too has strong links to Algerian football, and our involvement there started early.

Football was first played in Algeria in the 1890s by European expatriates, and prominent among those playing were, yes, the Brits. They even went as far as getting hold of *The Football Annual 1896/7* from Britain to help improve their Algerian version of the sport.

In 1897, the first football clubs were formed in Algeria, and in 1906 the Royal Navy arrived to help give football a boost. A team from HMS *Dreadnought* took on Sport Club d'El Biar in front of a large, local crowd.

Football in Algeria started as a European game, but soon the local Arab population adopted it with a passion and started to express their own identity through it, forming their own clubs. In 1918, the Algiers Football Federation was founded, in 1919 the Constantine Football Federation too, and in 1920 the Oran Football Federation came along.

British involvement continued. For instance, in 1923 a team from the English North Nottinghamshire League toured Algeria and received gold watches from their hosts for their troubles.

Algeria has, of course, become a leading African football nation. The men's national team have twice won the Africa Cup of Nations and have qualified for the World Cup four times. The women's national team have qualified for the Women's Africa Cup of Nations five times.

And people with Algerian heritage have, of course, made a big contribution to the sport in Britain. Look at Riyad Mahrez, for example.

Andorra

Andorra is a small principality in the Eastern Pyrenees and it has one of those nice national sides that rarely give British football fans a fright.

Andorra has a long history dating back to Charlemagne. Since the Middle Ages, its control has been shared between France and Spain. In 1993, it adopted a new constitution and joined the United Nations and the Council of Europe. These changes also led to the formation of the Andorran Football Federation in 1994 and Andorra joined FIFA in 1996.

While Andorra may be better known for its duty-free shopping and skiing, it has a reasonable football profile for somewhere with fewer than 80,000 inhabitants. The national team makes regular appearances in the qualifying rounds of World Cups and European Championships.

It's probably fair to say that Britain played little direct role in the early development of football in Andorra, which has been dominated by the Spanish and Catalonia. This is hardly surprising given the geography of Andorra and Catalan is the national language. However, as we will see, Britain played an important part in the spread of football to Spain and Catalonia, so it did have some influence in the background. There is an Andorran club called 'Rangers', which may be a link to the British heritage of football, and the Andorran side played in the first qualifying round of the Champions League in 2007–08.

The first proper football club in Andorra, named simply FC Andorra, was founded in 1942. Britain was not involved as, apart from anything else, it was rather preoccupied with fighting Germany and Japan at the time. FC Andorra is now the principality's major club, but it plays in the Spanish Second Division, rather than Andorra's national league.

Andorra introduced a Liga Nacional de Fútbol in 1995. It has given clubs like UE Sant Julià, Principat, Santa Coloma, Rangers and Constel·lació Esportiva the chance to play on the European stage. For Andorra this is like the FA Cup. It gives amateurs and their supporters an opportunity to compete against professionals and experience larger stadiums.

A 1-0 home victory for Santa Coloma against Maccabi Tel-Aviv in the UEFA Cup in 2007 was the first victory for an Andorran side in Europe.

The national side has not found a lot of international success, and its first victory only came in 2004, a 1-0 triumph against Macedonia.

Andorra also fields a women's team. In 1996, there were only a few female players in Andorra. There are now six teams playing in a league and there is a development programme to attract more girls and women to the game. So far, the women have beaten Gibraltar, in 2014, and Liechtenstein, in 2021.

Angola

Angola was a Portuguese colony when football arrived there, and it seems likely the sport arrived there via Portugal, rather than directly from Britain.

The first football in Angola seems to have been played around 1913–15, in, perhaps not surprisingly, its main port and capital, Luanda. Again, perhaps not surprisingly, considering the origins of football elsewhere in the world, both rail workers and military personnel seem to have been involved with the start of the sport in the country.

In the 1920s, close links between football in Angola and in Portugal led to the creation of clubs with strong attachments to some of Portugal's football giants. Sporting Clube de Luanda, with links to Sporting Clube de Portugal, Sporting, was founded in 1920 and Sport Luanda e Benfica, with links to Sport Lisboa e Benfica, Benfica, was founded in 1922.

After a long guerrilla war, Angola became independent from Portugal in 1975, and the Angolan Football Federation was created in 1979. The Angola national men's team qualified for the 2006 World Cup, and has qualified for the Africa Cup of Nations on a number of occasions, reaching the quarter-finals twice. The national women's team came third in the 1995 African Women's Championship.

Antigua and Barbuda

It's probably safe to say that the popularity of cricket in this country has somewhat held back the development of football. The cricket legend that is Viv Richards, after all, comes from Antigua.

However, there is still plenty of passion for the world's greatest sport in this Caribbean country – multi-talented Viv Richards has liked a bit of football. And, yes, football in Antigua and Barbuda does have a strong British football heritage.

The Antigua and Barbuda Football Association came into being in 1928 while the country was still a British colony, and some of the names of clubs in the country have a clear English flavour. There's Point West Ham, Aston Villa, Villa Lions, Empire and English Harbour, for example.

The men's national team came fourth in the Caribbean Cup in 1998, and in 2014 the women's national team qualified for the Women's Caribbean Cup.

And the traffic hasn't at all been one way. For instance, Mikele Leigertwood was born here and has played for a number of

English clubs, but he was also eligible to play for the Antigua and Barbuda national side, and did so.

Argentina

Yes, we gave Argentina football.

Of course, if the average England fan had to pick out any country, apart from Germany, as their bitterest football rivals, it would probably be Argentina.

Where do you start in describing that rivalry? Perhaps you start with the Falklands War of 1982, in the end a triumph for the UK and such a disaster for Argentina. But in football terms there was already something of a grudge. In 1966, England's 1-0 victory over a ten-man Argentina in the quarter-finals ended in controversy and bad feeling. That football rivalry only became fiercer after 1982 and was brought to a head four years later. In the 1986 quarter-final in Mexico there was the goal Maradona infamously attributed to 'the Hand of God', followed famously by his 'Goal of the Century', as his team won 2-1.

There is, it has to be said, still something special in the air every time England and Argentina take the pitch against each other. However, with Argentine managers like Pochettino and Bielsa having served in the Premier League and with a host of talented players, including, of course, Sergio Agüero, Willy Caballero and Carlos Tevez, having played for major clubs, there is perhaps also a more positive view emerging of Argentina as one of the world's great football nations.

The world's greatest sport came early to Argentina. The Argentine Football Association claims that British sailors were kicking a cow's bladder around with goals marked by stones in the 1840s. Certainly, Britain recognised Argentina as an independent country in 1825 and by 1831 there were enough

British residents in Buenos Aires to establish Buenos Aires Cricket Club.

The first official football match in Argentina took place in June 1867. This is still very early, as the Football Association rules had only been agreed in December 1863 and Buenos Aires is some distance from London. A copy of the rules was passed through various hands to Yorkshireman Thomas Hogg, who was a member of Buenos Aires Cricket Club. The result was the formation of Buenos Aires Football Club, which played its first game between the Blancos (White Caps) and the Colorados (Red Caps). The result was a decisive 4-0 victory for the Blancos. The match was played to Association rules with some additions, and seems to have been a fairly rough affair.

Alexander Hutton, often considered the father of football in Argentina, was born in 1853 in the Gorbals, Glasgow, and eventually went to Edinburgh University to study philosophy. To fund his studies, Hutton got a teaching job at George Watson College. It took him nine years to get his degree, which, in some senses was perhaps fortunate as it meant he was still a student when Edinburgh University Association Football Club was set up in 1878. When he arrived in Buenos Aires in 1882 to teach, he brought with him not only a football and something with which to inflate it (handy) but also a deep enthusiasm for the game, which he passed on to the students at the school he established.

Alec Lamont, another Scot teaching at St Andrews School, organised the first Argentine football competition in 1891, calling it the Argentine Association Football League. It had a distinctly British or perhaps even Scottish flavour; teams included Old Caledonians and St Andrews Athletic Club. In its inaugural year St Andrews and Old Caledonians finished level on points. The championship was settled by a play off, which Old Caledonians won.

Hutton relaunched the AAFL in February 1893, becoming its president until 1896. It is this body that is usually seen as South America's first national football association. Lomas, a club formed by Englishmen at Lomas Academy, won the first championship in 1893 and went on to win five of the first six titles before, inexplicably, switching to rugby. Another of those early clubs, Quilmes, started by the British as a rowing club, is now the oldest football club still competing in the championship.

Hutton left his mark on the league even after he ceased to be president. He formed the Club Atlético English High School for teachers and ex-pupils of his school. Known as the Alumni, they were to win the title ten times between 1900 and 1911. Thus the early years of the Argentine League were dominated by British teams and players.

The British can also lay claim to having started the spread of football beyond Buenos Aires. In Rosario, football began with the British-owned Central Argentine Railway Athletic Club, which Thomas Mutton formed in 1889. In 1903, Miguel Green led a move to change its name to Club Atlético Rosario Central and to allow locals who did not work for the railway to join. This created Rosario, one of the big teams of Argentine football.

Rosario's great rival, Newell's Old Boys, was also originally a British team. It is named after Isaac Newell. Newell was born in Kent, but in 1869, aged only 16, he accepted a job working for the Central Argentine Railway in Rosario. In 1890, he set up the Argentine Commercial School and later he founded Club Atlético Newell's Old Boys for teachers and ex-students of his college. The red of their strip is supposed to represent England and the black Germany, as Isaac's wife was German. By 1905, Newell's was strong enough to take the Rosario regional league title from Rosario Central. Newell's is now famous all over the world as the starting point for Lionel Messi's football career.

At the start of the twentieth century, Argentinians began to form their own football clubs. The oldest is Club de Gimnasia y Esgrima La Plata. Originally formed in 1887, it added football to its unusual combination of gymnastics and fencing between 1900 and 1905. One of Argentina's greatest teams, Club Atlético River Plate, emerged in 1901 from the merger of Santa Rosa and Las Rosales, and its great rival, Boca Juniors, was founded in 1905 by Genoese immigrants.

Visiting British sides also contributed to a growing enthusiasm for football in Argentina. Southampton FC was the first British club to tour in 1904 and they won all of their six games, scoring thirty-two goals. Nottingham Forest, Everton and Tottenham Hotspur all toured unbeaten before 1914. However, the speed with which Argentines were improving was evident when in 1914 Exeter City was defeated 1-0 by a select Buenos Aires XI.

By the 1920s, Argentine football was dominated by the locals, with a bit of help from their Spanish and Italian immigrants. The standard of the football was also improving, with a distinctive quick passing to feet style being developed on both sides of the River Plate in Argentina and Uruguay. Argentine supporters felt bitterly disappointed by their loss to Uruguay in the 1930 World Cup final. Their mood was not improved when Uruguay won the World Cup again in Brazil in 1950.

However, Argentine success on home soil in 1978 felt like an example of 'football's coming home'. It was a great display of Argentine talent and, on the back of it, Ossie Ardiles and Ricky Villa became early foreign imports for top British clubs. The 1986 Maradona-inspired World Cup triumph in Mexico confirmed Argentina's place as a leading football nation.

Although British influence on Argentine football faded rapidly after the First World War and the formation of so many Argentine teams, Britain can still take some pride in certain elements of its national success as there have been a number of

Brits or British families who have played for Argentina. Arnoldo Watson Hutton, the son of Alexander, scored one of the two goals in Argentina's triumph over Uruguay in the Copa Lipton (a trophy given by the Glasgow tea magnate Thomas Lipton to be contested between Argentina and Uruguay). In total, Arnoldo won seventeen caps and scored six goals for Argentina.

Jorge Gibson Brown, known as 'El Patriarcho' (The Patriarch), featured in all ten of Alumni's league titles between 1900 and 1911, and won twenty-three caps. There is also José Luis Brown, who scored for Argentina in their 3-2 victory over West Germany in the 1986 World Cup final. Even more recently, there is Carlos Javier Mac Allister, who earned three caps helping Argentina qualify for the 1994 World Cup.

Ultimately, the rivalry between England and Argentina is so intense, not just because of the obvious reasons, but also because for Argentines, as their captain, Roberto Perfumo, expressed it, 'Winning against England is like schoolkids beating the teachers'.

Argentine women have also played against the Lionesses. In the 2019 Women's World Cup, Phil Neville's England defeated Argentina 1-0, but in 1971 at an unofficial women's world cup organised in Mexico it was Argentina that emerged as 4-1 winners. Women's football came early to Argentina, with the first match recorded in 1913 when two teams from Club Fémina in Rosario played each other. Ten years later, 6,000 spectators turned up at the Boca Juniors ground in Buenos Aires to watch Argentina defeat the Cosmopolitos 4-3. In fact, women's football in Argentina in the 1920s became sufficiently popular that Andy Ducat, an English footballer, wrote to the sports magazine *El Grafico* to complain about women playing a man's game. Argentina never banned women's football, but it didn't do much to encourage it either; it just struggled along in the background for much of the twentieth century. However, in 2006 they won the Women's Copa América and they earned their first World

Cup points in 2019 by drawing with Japan. Maybe one day they will have the same star status as Messi and the men.

Armenia

Somewhat confusingly, the first Armenian teams may not have been in Armenia itself.

By the early twentieth century, Armenians were living widely across parts of the Middle East. In Turkey they played an important role alongside Britons, Greeks and locals in getting football started in places like Istanbul and Izmir. After expulsions and deportations and the deaths of huge numbers of Armenians during the First World War, however, the development of Armenian football in the 1920s mainly switched to Armenia itself, which from 1922 had been a part of the USSR. British footballing influence was swapped for Soviet footballing influence.

In 1935, a club named Spartak was founded in the Armenian capital, Yerevan. Like the rather better-known Spartak Moscow, this name is a typical Soviet-era one chosen in honour of Spartacus, the gladiator who led a slave rebellion against Rome. Yerevan's Spartak would go on to be one of Armenia's most successful clubs and to be renamed FC Ararat Yerevan. Yes, it's Mount Ararat from the Bible; you can see it from Yerevan. There's also now an FC Noah.

Armenia became independent again in 1991. Scot Ian Porterfield was coach of the Armenian national team in 2006 but sadly he died in 2007. Not long ago, Armenia was promoted to UEFA Nations League B. The women's national team has not had a lot of international success so far.

Henrikh Mkhitaryan is perhaps the best-known Armenian footballer of the modern era and, in May 2017, he scored in the Europa League final as part of the victorious Manchester United team.

Australia

Well, among other sports, we gave them cricket and we gave them football. It is, of course, a very long time since Australians were in any sense junior to us on the cricket pitch, but at least we are still bigger in football.

Football in Australia predates the Football Association in Britain. When European settlers first arrived, they found people playing some kind of ball game that involved kicking and catching. In 1859, Tom Wills, aided by his cousin Henry Harrison and journalists William Hammersley and James Thompson, drew up a set of rules for the game that was to become Aussie Rules football. Wills had been educated at Rugby School, where he captained the football team. His rules took influences from cricket, rugby, football and maybe even the old local ball game to create something fast-flowing and entertaining to suit Australian conditions.

Melbourne Rules Football, as Wills's game was called, developed rapidly. Consequently, when association football arrived in 1880, Aussie Rules already had a firm grip on the nation. Rugby and cricket were also firmly established, so soccer had tough competition.

School teacher John Fletcher founded the first soccer club, Wanderers FC, in Sydney, in 1880. Their match against a King's School team the same year has a strong claim to be the first proper association football game in the country. Fletcher then went on to start the New South Wales English Football Association in 1882 to administer the game. The name of the association made it clear that this game was English.

Australia became self-governing within the British Empire in 1901. By then football had spread a little. Balgownie Rangers FC, probably the oldest remaining football club in Australia, had been started by the Scottish miner Peter Hunter, and football associations had also been established in Victoria and Queensland.

Perhaps Australia's most significant contribution to world football was the introduction of numbered shirts. These first appeared in 1911 when Sydney Leichhardt took on the wonderfully named HMS *Powerful*. It was not until 1928 that numbered shirts reached the professional league in England.

As Australians volunteered to fight in Europe in the First World War, they met British Army football teams. Balgownie captain James Masters led an Australian Imperial Force football team in France. After the war, football flourished in Australia. In 1921, the Australian Football Association was formed and Australia played its first official internationals during a tour of New Zealand. Unfortunately, Australia lost two of the matches but drew one. In 1925, an English touring party arrived and won all its twenty-five matches. Football still had some way to go in Australia.

'Ladies' teams had appeared in New South Wales before the First World War. The first official game was in 1921, when North Brisbane defeated South Brisbane at the Gabba in front of a large crowd. However, Australia was not yet ready to let women play. As in England, the AFA discouraged women's football, arguing it was 'medically inappropriate'.

Australia emerged from the Second World War with a football system still dominated by Brits and under-developed compared to Aussie Rules. Mass immigration from Italy, Yugoslavia and Greece changed this. The new immigrants were used to playing football, while cricket and rugby were too British for them and Aussie Rules too strange. Team names like Brighton and Bexhill were replaced by Polonia, South Melbourne Hellas, Side Sydney Croatia and Slavia.

Immigration helped raise standards of the national team in international competition. In 1974, the 'Socceroos' qualified for the World Cup, and in 1977 a professional league was started. Since 2006, Australia has qualified for every World Cup including 2022. Slav Aussies have contributed to the improvements.

Women's football has also progressed, with a national league begun in the 1970s. Since 1995 the 'Matildas' have qualified for every FIFA Women's World Cup. In the 2020 Tokyo Olympics, Australia defeated England in the quarter-finals.

Soccer still lags behind other Aussie sports but it has grown and home-grown soccer talents, including, for instance, Mark Bosnich, Mark Schwarzer and Mark Viduka (a lot of Marks), have played their part in English football.

Austria

In some countries, football offers a sense of continuity that national politics can struggle to match.

There have been a lot of big changes in Austria in the years since the game was first played there at the close of the nineteenth century. Then, it was part of a large multicultural empire, stretching as far south as Montenegro and as far east as Ukraine and Moldova, which contained 52 million people. At its centre was Vienna, famed for its café culture, science, music and art. A city ready to adopt new ideas, including football.

While there was some football played in schools from 1876, which may have had a British connection, it was in 1894 that football really started. The first recorded game was in Graz between two teams organised by the Academic Technical Cycle Association in the spring of 1894, but it was in Vienna that the first two clubs were founded, within days of each other.

First Vienna FC was, as it happens, the first to register. Convenient that. The club developed from a little kick-around in the grounds of Nathaniel von Rothschild's large house. British gardeners took on the Austrians, with the Austrian Franz Joli, who had been educated in Britain, supplying the ball. The game was fun, the damage to Rothschild's lawn less amusing.

Their rivals, Vienna Cricket Club, were uniformly Brits, and although the club had actually been founded in 1892, two years later it also started playing football.

The first game between the two Viennese clubs was in November 1894, when the Cricket Club beat First 4-0. The local derby between the 'Gardeners' and the 'Bankers' was to become a feature of the Viennese social scene and in 1896 the British ambassador turned up to watch.

In 1897, John Gramlick (founder of the Cricketers) established a cup for the best teams in the Austro-Hungarian Empire and by 1911 a league had been established. Austria joined FIFA in 1905 and by 1907 Vienna had seventy football clubs, with about 300 in the Empire.

One feature of the expansion was tours by British teams and many of these were the work of Mark Nicholson. Nicholson had been a professional footballer in England and an FA Cup winner with West Bromwich Albion. In 1897 he became manager of Thomas Cook in Vienna, and he retained his enthusiasm for football alongside his passion for tours. He became the star of First Vienna and took on a mission to raise the standard of football in the city. He wrote articles about training and discouraged players from smoking and drinking in the days before a game. He also encouraged British teams to tour so that locals could see what top-class football looked like.

Oxford University toured in 1899. The following year Southampton FC, a professional side, were there. The Corinthians toured in 1904. However, the most influential visitors in

1904 were the Scottish clubs Rangers and Celtic. Rangers took home an Austrian goalkeeper, Karl Pekarna, but they left behind a concept of football as a skilful game with short passing, which was to shape the future of the Austrian game.

It was the combination of Austrian manager Hugo Meisl and the English coach Jimmy Hogan that was to refine the Scottish approach and produce the Austrian 'Wunderteam' of the 1930s. Jimmy Hogan played professional football for Burnley, Fulham and Bolton Wanderers, but it was as a coach that he really made his name. He was hired to prepare the Austrians for the 1912 Olympics in Stockholm. Hogan believed in possession football and saw ball control as the key skill and a craft that could be taught. Despite all his efforts, Austria was eliminated in the second round by the Netherlands.

Further development in Austria was halted by the First World War and Hogan was briefly interned before spending the conflict working with MTK Budapest in Hungary. It was not until he returned in the 1930s that the fruits of his labours became obvious.

Austria emerged from the First World War a very different country. Stripped of its empire, it was reduced to a population of only 6.5 million people. However, the world's best sport flourished. The new government reduced the working day to eight hours and many Austrians turned to football in their new leisure time. There was money in the game too, and in 1924 Austria became the first country outside the UK to host a professional football league. The first Austrian football celebrity was Rapid Vienna's Josef Urdil, nicknamed 'The Tank' (a comment on his stature rather than a military association). Made famous by exploits like scoring seven times in a game against Wiener AC, where Rapid had been 5-2 down at half time, he went on to endorse his own beer and have a song written about his exploits.

It was in the 1930s that Meisl, with some help from Hogan, was able to turn this domestic success into a national 'Wunderteam'. In 1931, Austria became the first team from outside the United Kingdom and Ireland to beat Scotland. The following year, Austria was narrowly defeated by England in an entertaining game at Stamford Bridge. However, they did beat England in Vienna, in 1936, in one of England's earliest defeats.

In the 1934 World Cup, Austria finished fourth after losing the semi-final to Italy, the eventual winners. In the 1936 Olympics, after a controversial quarter-final against Peru, Austria won the silver medal, again losing to Italy. Since the Second World War, Austria have qualified for the World Cup and the Euros on a number of occasions.

Women's football started in Vienna in the 1920s with the founding of the wonderfully named First Viennese Ladies Football Club Diana. Sadly, the club was short-lived; as well as the usual hurdles, Austrian women also suffered the Anschluss and Nazi occupation, which brought an end to their playing.

Women's football had been revived by the 1970s with unofficial international games and domestic competitions. A domestic league was begun in 1982 and in 1990 an official national team was formed. They have yet to qualify for a World Cup but did finish third in the 2017 Euros and went out against Germany in the 2022 Euros quarter-finals.

Among Austrians to contribute to British football have been Marko Arnautović and Christian Fuchs.

Azerbaijan

In recent years, Baku, the capital of Azerbaijan and a flourishing city on the western shores of the Caspian Sea, has become a major venue for international football. The 2019 Europa League final in Baku is a treasured part of Chelsea history, and a slightly less treasured part of Arsenal history. Many Welsh fans are also fond of Baku, after their side's draw with Switzerland and defeat of Turkey there during the Euros in 2021.

Football has a long history in Azerbaijan, and yes, we played a key role in its beginnings there. Asked to think of an early area of oil drilling and exploitation, many people might suggest somewhere like Texas. However, natural gas flares from the earth have long been a part of the geology of the Caucasus and one of the most important areas for the nineteenth-century oil industry was the land around Baku. The oil and gas industry remains a key part of Azerbaijan's economy today and the Flame Towers skyscrapers that you see in so many photos reflect the importance of fire in Azerbaijani culture.

Companies and workers from far afield flocked to Baku during the nineteenth and early twentieth century. Among the outsiders who turned up were Ludvig Nobel, elder brother of the man who created the Nobel Prizes, who would become one of the richest men in the world, and Joseph Stalin, who became famous (or at least infamous) for rather different reasons.

However, also among those who rushed to Baku were workers, who brought football and footballs with them. And a key element among those were the Brits. Teams were already being formed in the area in the first years of the twentieth century, and, in 1911, the first official championship was held in Baku. Winners? It was the British Club. And, to show it was no fluke, they won again in 1912!

Football has continued to be a passion in Azerbaijan since then. And there is one football connection that, in particular, forms a unique link between England and Azerbaijan. Yes, it's *that* goal in the 1966 World Cup final. With England and Germany 2-2 and in extra time, Geoff Hurst smacked the ball against the crossbar and it then hit the ground. But where did it land? The man sometimes described as 'the Russian linesman' was, in fact, born in Baku. Azerbaijani Tofiq Bahramov reckoned England had scored. The rest is football legend. There is now even a football stadium named after Bahramov in Azerbaijan and a statue. Geoff Hurst himself was, appropriately enough, there for its dedication. Perhaps we should have a Bahramov stadium or statue here.

The men's and women's national team have used the Tofiq Bahramov Republican Stadium for some of their home matches, although, since 2015, Baku Olympic Stadium has been Azerbaijan's leading football venue.

Bahamas

The islands are known for beautiful beaches, but rather less well known for football. However, there is a fascinating story of bravery behind the introduction of football to the country.

Soon after the start of the First World War, it became obvious to the British government that it was going to need all the manpower it could get in order to win the war. As well as making use of existing military forces from across the Empire, Britain looked to find new sources of recruits. There was already a regular West India Regiment, but in 1915, the British West Indies Regiment was also formed. In all, about 700 Bahamians would serve overseas in various units during the war. The soldiers served with bravery and distinction, both on the Western Front and in the Middle East. However, racist attitudes towards them were common among the British authorities, and in late 1918, after the war's end, resentment at unfair labour, pay and promotion led to some BWIR soldiers in Italy refusing to obey orders, and attacking officers. A lot of the veterans returned home determined to fight for equality and self-determination in their Caribbean homelands.

Some of the Bahamian veterans also returned home with a love of football and, presumably, with some footballs. By the 1920s, there were regular matches being played on New Providence, the main island in the Bahamas. As elsewhere, Royal Navy sides, from ships in the area, would sometimes drop in for games.

Leagues were organised in the 1950s and the Bahamas Football Association was eventually founded in 1967. Their record of international success has been somewhat modest so far, but the men's team did recently earn promotion from League C to League B in the CONCACAF (Confederation of North, Central America and Caribbean Association Football) Nations League. The Bahamas are very close to the USA and Bahamians have had rather more success in some other sports, like basketball.

Bahrain

Football first came to Bahrain when British influence over the country was strong. From 1926 to 1957, Sir Charles Dalrymple Belgrave was chief administrator to the rulers of Bahrain and had extensive power over developments in the country.

One of those developments was football. Already, by 1928, sports clubs were being founded, like the one that would become Al-Muharraq SC, one of Bahrain's biggest and most successful clubs. By 1931, there was a championship being competed for by RAF and company teams.

Bahrain was on the Allied side in the Second World War and actually got bombed on one occasion by long-range Italian bombers aiming at its strategically important oil industry. But not even Italian bombs could stop the advance of football in Bahrain (or indeed stop the oil industry).

The passion for the sport developed further in the country after the war. By 1957, there was a football association and by 1959, a national team. The team has received guidance from assorted British managers over the years and has had some successes. In 2019, for instance, Bahrain won both the West Asian Football Federation Championship and the Gulf Cup in the same year.

In 2014 the Bahrain women's national team made football history when they played Italy and became the first Arab and Gulf women's team to take on a European side.

Bangladesh

In 2021, Bangladesh celebrated a big birthday. It's fifty years since a period of terrible violence ended with what had been East Pakistan becoming independent.

While Bangladesh is young, football in the area is quite old. The sport was introduced by the Brits in Dhaka, now the capital of Bangladesh, in the nineteenth century and the 'beautiful game' was to play an important role in the formation of the nation.

When football began, Bangladesh was part of the British Raj. Its proximity to Calcutta (now Kolkata) meant that locals were aware of the sporting prowess of Mohun Bagan (see India) and its Bengali links.

The British Army introduced the game to Dhaka at the end of the nineteenth century. There were matches between Army units and also between locals and British Army teams. Dhaka's first team, the Wari Club, began in 1898. Between 1900 and the creation of Pakistan in 1947, football flourished. Club names show the influence of the Raj: there was the Victoria Club, founded in 1903, Dhaka Wanderers and East Pakistan Gymkhana Club. Other teams like Mohammedan Sporting Club were influenced by their namesakes in Calcutta. As early as 1915 Dhaka had a football league. Football skills improved rapidly. In 1910, Wari Club defeated a Royal Palace Team and in 1937 a Dhaka XI defeated the Islington Corinthians. Football success, in turn, encouraged local and national pride.

The partition of India in 1947 left India sandwiched between East and West Pakistan. East Pakistan had a real passion for football, with a wide variety of new clubs being formed. The old clubs, however, still dominated the league. Victoria Club won the First Division in 1948, 1960, 1962 and 1963, while Dhaka Wanderers were champions six times between 1948 and 1957. East Pakistan also had its own superstar, Abdul Ghafoor Majna, nicknamed 'Pakistani Pelé', who won trophies with both Mohammedan Sporting Club and Dhaka Wanderers.

When East Pakistan declared independence in March 1971, its provisional government was forced to flee to Calcutta. Players were recruited from the refugee camps in India to form a football team to be ambassadors for the new Bangladesh nation. 'Shadhin Bangla Football Dol' (Free Bengal Football Team) toured India to raise money and promote an independent Bangladesh. Before their opening game in July 1971 the team unfurled a green flag bearing a map of Bangladesh at its centre. The team played sixteen matches, winning twelve of them, but also raised large amounts of money and encouraged celebrities to side with the new nation.

While football is popular in Bangladesh and played a part in the formation of the nation, international success has been limited. In 2003 Bangladesh won the South Asian Football Championship and they were runners-up in 1999 and 2005. They have yet to qualify for a World Cup. The national team has had a number of English coaches.

Women's football in Bangladesh has had a much shorter history than the men's game there. A women's tournament was organised in 2007 for eight regional teams, and there was a school competition the following year. Sabina Khatun has emerged as one of the stars of the women's game in Bangladesh. She played for the national team at the South Asian Games in 2010, where she won a bronze medal, and has captained the side.

Barbados

This is another Caribbean country where football really got going in the early twentieth century when the country was part of the British Empire.

The Barbados Football Association was formed in 1910 and soon teams were competing for the Barbados FA Cup. The list of winners contains plenty of names that seem to speak of Barbadian football's British heritage. Wanderers was one of the first clubs in Barbados. Kensington Rovers was one of the biggest early clubs. Then there was Empire, which won the cup a few times. In recent years, Weymouth Wales has been having some good years.

The Barbados men's national football team, the Bajan Tridents, have not had a hugely successful international career, but have had occasional moments of glory, like their 2-1 win over Costa Rica in 2000. The women's national football team have had a fairly mixed track record as well.

Barbados has contributed a lot to football in Britain too. Walter Tull was born in Folkestone in 1888, the son of a Barbadian carpenter who had arrived in Britain in 1876 and of a woman from Kent.

Tull soon showed a huge talent as a footballer, playing for Clapton FC, so much so that in 1909 he signed for Tottenham Hotspur. He put in some impressive performances there but received racial abuse, for instance, in a 1909 match played in Bristol. In 1911, he signed for Northampton Town for a 'substantial fee', and would play 111 games for the club.

Tragically, however, the First World War would end his football career and his life, as it ended the careers and lives of so many others. He enlisted in a Footballers' Battalion of the Middlesex Regiment, and served with distinction both in France and Italy. He became an officer, before being fatally wounded on 25 March 1918 as the Germans threw all their reserves into a last desperate attempt to end the war on terms favourable to themselves. A monument to him now stands near the Sixfields Stadium, Northampton.

Among more recent footballers here with Barbadian heritage is Ashley Cole, of Arsenal, Chelsea and England.

Belarus

Britons were involved with the beginnings of football in a lot of countries close to Belarus, and, in the early twentieth century, it was part of the Russian Empire. Britons played a very key part in introducing football to Russia, so, all in all, it is possible Britons were there, in some sense at least, at the start of football in Belarus.

A football club is said to have been founded in 1910 in Gomel, in the south-east of the country. Another was formed in 1912 at Baranavichy, this time in the west of Belarus.

Something that both cities do have in common, though, is that they are both big rail towns. Gomel contains one of the biggest rail junctions in the country, while Baranavichy was a village until the railway turned up in 1871, and the city grew around two major rail junctions. In many parts of the world, railways and rail workers were important in spreading the new sport, and it seems likely that rail played a key role in spreading it across Belarus, too.

After the First World War, Belarus ended up as part of the Soviet Union, so the list of local league champions has that rather proudly industrial feel of so much Soviet-era sport, with team names incorporating elements such as Dinamo, Traktor, Metallurg, and even Torpedo.

A number of the clubs formed in that era, for example, BATE Borisov (with the BATE standing for Borisov Automobile and Tractor Electronics) and Dinamo Minsk, have gone on to have big careers in the post-USSR era.

The nickname of the men's national team is the White Wings. Both men's and women's national teams have a fairly uneven track record.

Belgium

Ah, the land of Ypres, Poirot, *moules frites* and (sometimes very strong) beer. It's just across the Channel from here and, not surprisingly therefore, football got to Belgium directly, with an Irish connection as well.

Football in Belgium started early. It was being played in English schools in Brussels in the 1860s. A young Irishman, Cyril Bernard Morrogh, is said to have brought a ball and started playing with his friends at the Josephite College of Melle, outside Ghent, in 1863.

There is little doubt that the game was popular in schools and it may well have been encouraged by the Catholic Church, as it was in Latin America, as a way of combining healthy minds and healthy bodies. Football was also popular with British port workers in Antwerp and employees at the British Cockerill factory in Liège.

The first football club in Belgium was Royal Antwerp, known unsurprisingly as 'The Great Old'. The club began life as Antwerp Athletics Club and participated in many sports, including cricket, rugby, tennis and cycling, but started playing football in 1887. While Brits were involved in founding this club, it was by no means solely an expat enterprise.

Antwerp did take on teams from visiting British ships, but by 1890, it had also played against Breda in the Netherlands. Football spread rapidly, with Brugsche in Bruges, Racing FC in Brussels and FC Liègeois all playing by 1893.

At this early stage Belgium was also a favoured touring destination for English clubs. East London Clapton FC were the first visitors in 1890, thrashing Antwerp 8-1. Other visitors in the 1890s included Cambridge University, Old Westminster and Enfield. These early tours show both the enthusiasm for the game on both sides of the Channel and, of course, the ease of travel. Nice little ferry journey.

By 1895, there were ten clubs playing football in Belgium and they formed both the Belgian Union of Athletic Sports and a national championship. FC Liègeois won the initial championship. In the Paris Olympics of 1900 students from Brussels University played an exhibition match against a French side.

In 1901, Jorge Diaz, the president of Beerschot Athletic Club, organised a tournament between a Belgian side and a Dutch one. The Belgians won all their games. Interestingly, these games are not recognised as internationals because the Belgian side contained four English players, which shows the continuing influence of the Brits even as the Belgians were mapping their own future.

Given how football had spread through Belgium, it is no surprise to find that it was one of the founding members of FIFA in 1904. Its first international, against France, a 3-3 draw was played the same year.

Women's football in Belgium also got off to an early start. In the 1920s there was a women's league that was dominated by Atalante de Jette and sufficient interest to field a national side, which played a series of internationals against the French. The French were generally the stronger side and Belgium triumphed in only one of the seven games.

Antwerp hosted the Olympics in 1920 and football was part of it. The Belgians were coached by the Scot Willie Maxwell, who had worked with Leopold FC in Brussels before the First World War. Belgium were fortunate and got a bye to the quarter-final as Poland withdrew to fight Soviet Russia. When they made it to the final they were up against Czechoslovakia.

As it turned out, 65-year-old English referee John Lewis and his officials played a major role in the result. The Belgians were awarded two penalties and a Czech player was sent off. The Czech team was so incensed they all walked off in anger. The match was abandoned and Belgium got the gold medal.

British influence on football in Belgium did not end after the Olympic final. In 1955, Harry Game was appointed manager of Antwerp FC. Harry had been a physical training instructor during wartime and had completed an FA coaching course afterwards. Unable to find a suitable coaching job in Britain, he had gained experience with Panathinaikos in Athens before moving to Antwerp, to be closer to home. Harry led Antwerp to a Belgian Cup triumph in 1955 and their first League Championship in 1956–57, before leaving. In 1965, he returned for a second spell in charge but sadly was less successful. Rather than a triumph, Antwerp were relegated and Harry resigned.

Despite all their talent, the Belgian national side have somewhat struggled to match their early competition success. However, in their 'first golden age' during the 1980s Belgium did finish as runners-up to West Germany at the 1980 Euros. Their 'second golden generation' finished third in the 2018 World Cup in Russia.

The women's national team, too, have had some fairly mixed results, but they did qualify for the Women's Euros both in 2017 and 2022.

In recent years, Belgium has had more influence on the Premier League than Britain has had on the development of the game in Belgium. More than fifty Belgians have played in the top flight here and many of the stars of Belgium's current 'golden age' have exhibited their skills in the Premier League. Vincent Kompany won the Premiership four times as captain of Manchester City, and was joined at the club by Kevin De Bruyne, the great creator of goals. Chelsea have benefited from the skills of Eden Hazard and Thibaut Courtois. Spurs have had a trio of Belgians in Jan Vertonghen, Toby Alderweireld and Mousa Dembélé. Then there's Christian Benteke, who has played for Liverpool, Aston Villa and Crystal Palace, while Romelu Lukaku has played for Everton and Manchester United as well as Chelsea. This seems a handsome recompense for the time and effort spent encouraging the game in Belgium more than a century ago.

Belize

Belize is a small country on the Caribbean coast of Central America. In the old days, British troops roamed the jungles of Belize to deter neighbouring Guatemala from pursuing border disputes too enthusiastically.

The country has Mexico to the north, Guatemala to the west and Honduras to the south, and it began life as a British settlement set up on previously Spanish-controlled territory. The settlement lived through Spanish attempts to destroy it and became the crown colony of British Honduras in 1862. It became independent and changed its name to Belize in 1981. It will, therefore, come as no surprise that, yes, we brought football to Belize.

The first football seems to have been played in unofficial games between visiting sailors, either from merchant ships or the Royal Navy. They were opposed by British Hondurans, many of whom had learnt the game during their studies in Britain and Europe. H. Melhado OBE, who was born in Belize but had a British mother, Ana Carrington, played in one of these games in 1896.

A football league was established in 1919 with an H. W. Beaumont as president and a W.M. McField as secretary. The names of the early clubs also show a strong British influence. There was a Colonial Football Club, a St John's College Club, a Preston, a Rovers, an Oxford, a Surrey and a Wesley Old Boys.

Another feature of the football in British Honduras was, as in so many other places around the world, the British Army. The Royal Sussex Regiment fielded a team in the early days and was credited with improving standards of play. Later, teams from Belize City made regular trips to the Army camp for matches.

One colourful feature of football in Belize is the team names. The new capital, Belmopan, has the Belmopan Bandits, and the league also contains the Placencia Assassins; the Valley Pride Freedom Fighters, based in Dangriga; and the San Pedro Pirates. Among the women's teams are Jewel Fury.

The Belize national side is known as 'The Jaguars'. They have never qualified for the World Cup, but they did qualify for the 2013 CONCACAF Gold Cup.

Benin

This country is situated on the African coast to the west of Nigeria.

The French invaded and took over the area in 1892. It's possible that some early football influence reached here from then British-controlled Nigeria, but a lot of the early experience came from France or other French colonies. The first Black football team in Porto-Novo seems to have been created by Africans working for the French, moving to Benin and taking their footballs with them. The earliest proper football clubs were formed in the period between the world wars.

A lot of football teams around the world are associated with assorted fierce and/or strong animals. However, Benin's national team has traditionally been known as the Squirrels, although occasional attempts have been made to come up with a new name. Having the Squirrels up against the Super Eagles or Indomitable Lions, for instance, sounds a bit of a mismatch.

Benin have had a fairly mixed career internationally, but did make it to the quarter-finals of the Africa Cup of Nations in 2019. In 1966, the Royal Navy took to the pitch in Benin. Anti-aircraft frigate HMS *Puma* turned up in Benin's major port Cotonou and a team from the ship played a team from Benin's army.

Rather more significantly, a number of Beninese players have done their bit for British football. They include key international Stéphane Sessègnon, who has played here for Sunderland and West Bromwich Albion.

Bhutan

In 1910, Britain signed a deal with the Himalayan kingdom of Bhutan that gave Britain a lot of control over the country's foreign policy, but guaranteed Bhutan independence on domestic matters. Consequently, unlike a lot of other places where Britain had influence in the early twentieth century, Bhutan does not seem to have got football directly from Brits. Instead, the sport seems to have mainly arrived in the 1950s, and been brought there by foreign teachers, particularly those from India.

Even after football had finally been introduced, the sport did not grow quickly in Bhutan. The Bhutan Football Federation wasn't formed until 1983, and didn't join FIFA until 2000. The men's national team reached the semi-finals of the SAFF (South Asian Football Federation) Championship in 2008. In 2010 the women's national team was formed.

Bolivia

Yes, it's South American, no, it's not one of the first countries most people tend to think of when they think of the genius of the continent's football. Having said that, they have been to the World Cup three times, and they did win the Copa América in 1963, when they also hosted it.

Britain seems to have had somewhat less influence on the development of football in Bolivia than in neighbouring Chile, Paraguay and Brazil, but it was still definitely involved.

There is a story about a diplomatic incident in 1868 that, even if it's not true (which it may not be), is worth telling all the same. The President of Bolivia, General Mariano Melgarejo, invited a British diplomat to a reception in honour of Melgarejo's new mistress. The diplomat felt the invitation was unfitting to his status and refused the invite, only to end up being paraded around the central square in La Paz tied to a donkey and getting a good view of its backside. Queen Victoria was 'not amused' and crossed Bolivia off her map. While it seems difficult to verify the details of this story, it is clear that diplomatic links with Bolivia at the end of the nineteenth century were not close, although this may have had more to do with the British involvement during the War of the Pacific of 1879–84, which led to Bolivia losing access to the Pacific.

The first football played in Bolivia may have been by sailors on British ships visiting the Bolivian coast in ports that were to become part of Chile in 1884. Engineers working on the Antofagasta & La Paz Railway Company played informal games at La Paz, where the altitude of 3,640m gave the local Indians a significant advantage. While some workers came from Chile, Argentina and Uruguay, some also came from Britain. However, it was not until 1909 that Sir John Jackson became involved in building a railway across the Andes from Arica to La Paz.

The geographical isolation that followed defeat in the War of the Pacific may have delayed the development of football in Bolivia. The first football team in Bolivia was Oruro Royal, founded in 1896 by locals, and English feet were on the pitch in its first match. Possibly only two of them, but English feet nonetheless, as the Reds defeated the Blues 7-1.

The Bolivian national team that went to the first World Cup was largely recruited from the Royal Oruro Club and was defeated by Yugoslavia despite wearing the slogan 'Viva Uruguay' on their shirts to impress the Uruguayan referee.

Britain's most lasting influence on football in Bolivia may be in the names of some of the clubs in Bolivia's top league.

A La Paz club formed in 1908 was originally called just The Strong Football Club, but when strong wasn't strong enough, that became The Strongest, the name they still play under. And indeed over the years The Strongest have had at times a pretty formidable track record. In 1930, they lived up to their name by winning the Bolivian league without conceding a single goal. There is also an Always Ready founded in 1933. Always Ready versus The Strongest sounds like it ought to be a good match.

There is currently no women's football league in Bolivia but some existing men's clubs have begun to explore the possibilities of women's football. In 2018, at a trial run in La Paz, more than 100 women turned up, keen to make their future in the game.

Bosnia and Herzegovina

Like many places in the country, the Grbavica stadium suffered a lot of damage during the war there in the 1990s. However, in the years after the war ended in 1995, the ground was restored, and now once again hosts, among others, the Bosnia national football team.

Football came to Bosnia and Herzegovina in the early twentieth century, probably via other places in the region where it was already established.

Croatia, where Brits had established the game in the late nineteenth century, was probably one of the areas that was influential in this respect. In 1905, a group of young men from the Croat community in Mostar formed a sports club that would evolve into Zrinjski Mostar, one of the most famous and successful teams in Bosnia and Herzegovina. In 1908, a group of students from Mostar and Sarajevo travelled to Zagreb in Croatia, to play a match and get better acquainted with the rules of the game.

In the period after the First World War, Bosnia and Herzegovina was part of the new country of Yugoslavia, and became part of the Yugoslav football system. In 1992, as Yugoslavia fragmented, war came to Bosnia and Herzegovina. After the fighting, the country retained its external borders. However, internally it was split into two linked, but, in many senses, separate entities: the Federation of Bosnia and Herzegovina, which combines the mainly Bosniak and Croat areas, and Republika Srpska, which has the mainly Serb areas. Football reflects that division, with a top-tier nationwide Premier League, and lower-tier leagues in the two separate areas.

Internationally, players from Bosnia and Herzegovina played for the Yugoslav team until 1992. In 2014 Bosnia and Herzegovina qualified for the World Cup.

Slovakia beat the national women's team 11-0 in Bosnia and Herzegovina's first international but the team have improved considerably since then.

A number of players with Bosnian heritage have made a contribution to the game in Britain, including former Manchester City striker Edin Džeko and Everton goalkeeper Asmir Begović, both of whom were part of the national team in 2014.

Botswana

The world's greatest sport seems to have first become properly established in what is now Botswana in the 1930s. At the time it was part of the British Empire it was called Bechuanaland, and it was heavily under the influence of neighbouring South Africa. In 1949, the Bechuanaland Union African Soccer League was formed.

At about the same time, though, other events were happening that would have even more far-reaching consequences for the history of Botswana.

Seretse Khama had been born in 1921, the grandson of King Khama III, and in 1925, after his grandfather's death, he inherited his throne, with his uncle becoming regent. After the Second World War, Khama was in London training as a barrister, and there he fell in love with and married the white English woman Ruth Williams. Due to the racist attitudes of the period, the marriage was very controversial, particularly in South Africa. Khama was forced into temporary exile from his homeland and compelled to renounce his throne.

However, if those who objected to the marriage thought they had now heard the last of Khama, then they were in for a disappointment. Instead of disappearing, he formed the Bechuanaland Democratic Party, won elections, and led his country to independence. In 1966, he became the first president of Botswana.

And, among all his other passions, Khama took an interest in football. He is, for instance, said to have been involved with the interestingly named Miscellaneous Sporting Club, formed in 1962 in Serowe, the town of his birth.

The Botswana men's and women's national teams have had a few successes internationally, like when the (male) Zebras qualified for the 2012 Africa Cup of Nations after beating Tunisia, and over the years they have had some assistance from British coaches. There has also been plenty of passion in the domestic game, and the names of some of the clubs involved, like Morupule Wanderers FC, Phodisong Rovers and Mahalapye's Queens Park Rangers, reflect some of the British heritage of the game in the country.

Brazil

This is a country that, to some, is synonymous with football. If you asked people around the world to name the country they think of first when somebody mentions football, many would say Brazil. Yet there wouldn't have been any Brazilian football without Britain.

Brazil have won the World Cup five times and were allowed to keep the original Jules Rimet Trophy after their third victory in Mexico in 1970. This was the legendary team of Pelé, Tostão, Jairzinho and Rivellino. Scotland, by comparison, have a slightly more modest track record. However, having said all that, it is a fact that the foundations of Brazilian football were first laid by Scottish pioneers at the end of the nineteenth century.

Britain had closer links with Brazil than with most other South American countries. For instance, Thomas Cochrane from Scotland was put in charge of the Brazilian Navy in 1823 and helped Pedro I drive the Portuguese out of Brazil. As a reward, Cochrane was given the title Marquess of Maranhão in the Empire of Brazil.

By the middle of the nineteenth century, 50 per cent of Brazilian imports came from Britain, while Britain imported coffee and raw materials from Brazil. Britain also supplied railways, banking and shipping. And, of course, football.

Despite all the trade links, football seems a comparatively late arrival in Brazil, and it is difficult to be exactly sure who first played football in the country. It might have been British sailors knocking a ball around. There is also a story that would credit the Jesuits with introducing football in the 1880s at St Louis School in Itu near São Paolo.

However, a six-a-side match between British textile workers in Bangu, a small town outside Rio de Janeiro, is recorded as being organised by Thomas Donohoe in September 1894.

Donohoe was a textiles expert who was born in 1863 in Busby, Renfrewshire. In 1892, looking for work, he set off for Bangu, Brazil. When he arrived and found work, he was disappointed to find that there was no football club. His wife, Elizabeth, joined him in Brazil in 1894, bringing a football, which was put to good use in a game staged outside the textile factory. This is the story marked in Bangu by a large statue of Donohoe, which suggests it was a Scot who introduced football to Brazil.

In 1904, British managers went on to found Bangu Athletic Club and the town is very proud that this was the first team in Rio de Janeiro to allow non-white players to play.

The player usually regarded as the 'founding father' of Brazilian football, though, is Charles Miller, who organised, refereed and played in the first eleven-a-side match in São Paolo in April 1895. His father, John, was a Brazil-based merchant, shipping goods back to Scotland, and his mother, Charlotte, was a member of the Fox family who built the railway between São Paolo and Santos on the coast.

Charles was sent to school in England, where he seems to have played a lot of football. When he returned to Brazil in 1894, he brought with him a passion for football, a copy of the football rules and two footballs.

In São Paulo, Miller grew bored of playing cricket with São Paulo Athletic Club and persuaded them to try football. The first match was a British affair between the São Paulo Railway staff and staff from the gas company. But the locals soon picked up the new sport enthusiastically, and by 1901 Miller had helped to found a local league.

The expansion of the game was, to some extent, an international effort. For instance, Americans, Germans and, of course, Brazilians were also involved. Nevertheless, it was the British who won the first three league titles, with Miller at the heart of the SPAC team (São Paulo Athletic Club).

Donohoe was not the only Scot to help export football to Brazil. Jock Hamilton was born in Ayr, although he made his name playing for Wolverhampton Wanderers, Watford and Fulham. In 1907, he worked as a coach for Club Athletico Paulistano, where his guidance and knowledge of the Scottish short passing game helped them to claim the league title.

Another Scot to have a major role in early football in Brazil was Archie McLean. He had played football for Ayr and St Johnstone before taking up a job with J&P Coats in São Paulo. In 1912 he founded a local team, which he named Scottish Wanderers, as indeed many of them were.

We should also mention here the British connections of the São Paulo football team Corinthians. The club was founded in 1910 by workers of the São Paulo Railway. They took their name from the famous amateur English club of the same name that had toured Brazil in 1910, and showed their strength by beating Charles Miller's SPAC 8-2, and in Rio triumphing 10-1 against Fluminense.

Football soon spread to Rio de Janeiro. Oscar Cox was the son of George Emmanuel Cox, the English vice-consul in Ecuador, and in 1901 he arranged the first football game in the city. He had picked up the sport while studying in Switzerland. The following year he founded Fluminense, and in 1906 they were the first winners of the Rio State Championship. To try to raise standards, the club appointed an English coach, Charles Williams, who had worked with the Danish team at the Olympic Games in 1908 in London.

In 1914, on the eve of the First World War, Exeter City stopped in Brazil on their way home from Argentina to play a game in Rio de Janeiro. Exeter players were too tired to visit São Paulo as well, so the Brazilians created a team from players from both cities. The team were known as the Seleção (the selection), which is now the nickname of the Brazilian national team.

The game was nearly cancelled at the last minute, when Exeter players took their shirts off to go for a swim and found themselves arrested for 'gross indecency'. Some diplomatic charm resolved the issue and 3,000 spectators turned out at Laranjeiras Stadium to watch the spectacle. The match showed how far the Brazilian game had diverged from the British one. Playing fluent fast-moving football, the Seleção won 2-0. Meanwhile, Exeter's more physical approach left one Brazilian star covered in blood and missing a couple of teeth. Exeter were invited back to play a centenary tour in Brazil in 2014 – no hard feelings!

On the international stage, Brazil at first had tough competition from Uruguay and Argentina. It was Argentina that hosted the first Copa América and Uruguay who would host the first World Cup. However, in 1919 Brazil first lifted the Copa América.

The classic yellow, green and blue of Brazil is actually, strangely, a product of defeat. Up until 1950 Brazil wore a white strip. However, they were so upset after Uruguay beat them 2-1 in the final of the World Cup, which Brazil hosted and which they considered their own, that they changed their strip.

Once they started winning World Cups they were difficult to stop. They won consecutive competitions in Sweden in 1958 and in Chile in 1962. They missed out in 1966 but Pelé won his third World Cup in Mexico in 1970. Brazil went on to win the trophy that replaced the Jules Rimet original in the USA in 1994 and again in South Korea in 2002. In these victories they have played some stunning football. England are yet to win a World Cup game against Brazil, but John Barnes's wonderful solo goal in a friendly against Brazil in 1984 showed a shared love of the beautiful game.

On their shirts the Brazilian women's team have the same five stars for world championships as the men's team, but they are yet to win a World Cup. However, they have also faced more hurdles than the men. While there is some evidence of women playing football before 1914, attempts to recruit more players led to it being banned in 1941 and this was not lifted until 1979. A league was set up two years later and the first international was played in 1986.

While the women may not be quite able yet of matching the men's achievements, they have dominated the Women's Copa América, winning seven of eight titles.

The list of great Brazilian players who have played for British clubs is, of course, long, but should at least mention here names like Anderson, Philippe Coutinho, David Luiz, Fernandinho, Roberto Firmino, Rafael and Willian.

Brunei

Brunei, or Brunei Darussalam, is well-known for its oil industry, and it seems likely that, as in some other oil-producing countries, workers in that industry played a significant role in introducing football. British influence was strong in Brunei for much of the twentieth century, and its oil workers were already in the country before the Second World War.

In the period after 1945, the Brunei Shell Recreation Club became a location for club football in Brunei, and soon locals were forming their own teams, too. In the 1950s the Brunei State Football Amateur Association was created. Among club names that perhaps show something of a British influence on the Brunei game are Kota Ranger FC, a major force in Brunei football in the 1980s and '90s, and AM Gunners FC.

The national team has had quite a lot of English and Scottish coaches over the years. In 1999, a team from Brunei won the Malaysia Cup.

Bulgaria

Bulgaria's finest hour to date, in terms of international football success, has probably been the 1994 World Cup, when they reached the semi-finals after beating a range of teams, including Argentina and defending world champions Germany. But then that Bulgarian team did include Hristo Stoichkov.

We can't really say that we gave Bulgaria football directly. Instead, the great sport arrived in the country from us indirectly, via Switzerland.

As we will see in the Swiss chapter, Switzerland was one of the earliest countries to share our passion for the sport. The very first football club in Switzerland, the Lausanne Football and Cricket Club, was founded in 1860 by English students. And it was Lausanne that a certain Bulgarian, Georgi Zhivkov, visited in 1893.

Zhivkov, however, wasn't any old Bulgarian tourist on the lookout for Toblerone or something. (Just as well really, since Toblerone wasn't invented until 1908, so he'd have had a bit of a wait if that's what he was after.)

He was the Bulgarian Minister of Education, and he was in Lausanne to find out the latest advances in physical education and organised sport. As a result of Zhivkov's visit, a number of Swiss turned up in Bulgaria to assist in training the nation's youth.

Perhaps the most significant, in terms of introducing football to Bulgaria, was Georges de Regibus, who became a teacher at Varna High School for Boys in 1894. In Switzerland, he had played as goalkeeper and he had, fortunately, brought a football with him, so soon Bulgarian kids were kicking a ball on the Black Sea coast.

Georges de Regibus would eventually retire to Lausanne and die there, but Bulgarian football would play on. A number of Bulgarian football clubs were already in existence before the start of the First World War, although CSKA Sofia, perhaps Bulgaria's most famous team, wasn't founded until 1948. CSKA stands for Central Sports Club of the Army.

The women's game in Bulgaria has mostly been dominated in recent years by FC NSA Sofia, also based in the capital.

Among Bulgaria's twenty-first century best has been, of course, Dimitar Berbatov, of Tottenham Hotspur, Manchester United and Fulham, and the captain of Bulgaria.

Burkina Faso

This was probably not one of the first countries in Africa to get football, and, when it did get it, adopting the sport only had a little to do with us. However, since getting the sport, it has done pretty well with it.

The colonial power was France and, despite Burkina Faso having a long border with Ghana, a country where Britain introduced football very early, the sport doesn't seem really to have properly arrived north of the border until the period between the world wars.

In 1934, a French colonial rail project reached Bobo-Dioulasso, now Burkina Faso's second largest city and located in the southwest of the country. The director of a French company decided to add some foreign talent to help form a company football team, and in 1935 Union Sportive Bobolaise was formed from a combination of locals, players from other French colonies and those from the British colony of Gold Coast, or as it is now, Ghana.

Burkina Faso became independent as Upper Volta in 1960, and changed its name to its present one in 1984.

The national team reached the semi-finals of the Africa Cup of Nations in 1998, 2017 and 2022, and reached the final in 2013. Among the players who have represented Burkina Faso is Bertrand Traoré, who has also, of course, played for Chelsea and Aston Villa.

Women's football has made some progress, with, for instance, the U-20 national team having some success.

Burundi

It is a country with a complex history, but, going briefly through some major aspects, the African Kingdom of Burundi lasted for centuries until 1966, but was also part of German East Africa in the late nineteenth century and early twentieth century. After that, with its northern neighbour Rwanda, it was part of the Belgian colony of Ruanda-Urundi, until Burundi separated from Rwanda and Belgium and became independent in 1962.

Somewhere in all that lot, football arrived and flourished. Clubs were being formed by the 1920s. A Burundian club with a name that will sound a bit familiar to British readers is AS Rangers FC, who are known there as 'Les Lions', or simply as 'Les Gers'.

Internationally, Burundi haven't had a huge amount of success, but the men's national team did qualify for the Africa Cup of Nations for the first time in 2019. Saido Berahino is among the Burundian players who have contributed to football in Britain.

Lydia Nsekera was president of the Football Federation of Burundi from 2004 to 2013, and in 2013 she was also the first woman formally voted onto FIFA's executive committee.

Cambodia

At the time when football arrived there, Cambodia was under French control, so the sport probably came via France or other colonial territories, rather than directly from Britain.

Many of the locals took to football, and it became popular among the political and administrative classes. Norodom

Sihanouk, Cambodian politician, royal and leader of Cambodia for much of the twentieth century, played football at school and became a proponent of the game.

Cambodia got independence in 1953, and, in 1972, Cambodia reached the semi-finals of the AFC (Asian Football Confederation) Cup. Tragically, by that stage, Cambodia had been sucked into fighting linked to the war in Vietnam, and, in 1975, the Khmer Rouge took control of the country. Many hundreds of thousands died in the years they remained in power. The Phnom Penh Olympic Stadium, which had seen a number of important football matches, was used by the Khmer Rouge for executions instead.

Since that terrible time, Cambodia has struggled to regain the international form they showed in 1972. However, a number of its domestic teams have qualified for AFC Cup football.

Cameroon

It is 1 July 1990, and the England team of Lineker, Platt and Gascoigne are up against the Cameroon team, the Indomitable Lions, of the great Roger Milla and Ekéké, in the quarter-final of the World Cup. With eight minutes to play, Cameroon are 2-1 up, and, in the end, it's only two penalties coolly taken by Lineker that will save England and take them through to the semi-final. It was that close, that late, and, frankly, even many people in England thought that the better team on the day had lost.

Cameroon is situated on the west coast of Africa. The Germans were the first European colonial power to control it, followed after the First World War by the French (in most of the country) and the British (in a smaller part of it).

Obviously, in the small British-held territory in the south-west of the country, we were involved in the development of football. France, though, would become the dominant European influence on football in much of Cameroon in the 1920s.

However, even with that being true, there is an intriguing link to other sources of football in the French-controlled zone. Club Athlétique du Cameroun, based in the major port city of Douala, was founded in 1924, and seems to have been pretty much the first proper team formed in Cameroon. A key figure in its foundation is said to have been a commercial agent and pioneer photographer called George Goethe, who was from the then British-controlled territory of Sierra Leone.

The foundation of other clubs would soon follow, including, in 1927, Oryx Club de Douala, which would go on to be a dominant force in football in newly independent Cameroon in the 1960s, and would win the first African Cup of Champions Clubs in 1964.

Whatever the original source of football in Cameroon and the influences on it, football rapidly became a national passion and the country became an African football superpower.

The men's national team has qualified for the World Cup numerous times. They have also won the Africa Cup of Nations multiple times. In 2022, of course, Cameroon hosted the tournament and came third, after a spectacular recovery from being behind to Burkina Faso by three goals. In 2000, Cameroon took Olympic football gold. The women's national team has been very successful, too.

And the list of players from Cameroon, or with Cameroonian heritage who have contributed to British football with their talents is long, and, of course, includes names like Geremi, Benoît Assou-Ekotto, Joël Matip and Sébastien Bassong.

Canada

We gave Canada football, and we gave it early.

Canada was the first country outside Great Britain to set up a national football organisation, when the Dominion Football Association was founded in 1877. But even before that there were people kicking a ball in Canada.

Various types of football were taking place in the dominion; however, the first game using Football Association rules was played in Parliament Street, Toronto, in 1876. It featured Carlton Cricket Club and Toronto Lacrosse Club. While it is common to find cricket clubs playing football in the early days, this is a rare mention of a lacrosse club taking up the sport.

Canada was another country where the Scots played a key role. David Forsythe, who was born in Perthshire but moved to Canada as a child, is considered the 'father of Canadian soccer'. After graduating in Maths from the University of Toronto, he became a teacher and a founder member of the Dominion Football Association. In 1880, he also founded the Western Football Association.

In 1885, Forsythe was a member of the WFA team that defeated an American Football Association team 1-0 in New Jersey. Three years later, Forsyth took a Canadian team to Britain. It is a tribute to his success in spreading the game that he was the only British-born member of the squad. All the remainder were born in Canada. The Canadians did pretty well, winning and losing an equal number of games.

The highlight for Canadian soccer in the pre-First World War years was perhaps the gold medal won by the Ontario Club Galt at the 1904 Olympics in St Louis Missouri. Only three teams entered, Galt and two from St Louis. The Canadians thumped the Christian Brothers College 7-0 and St Rose 4-0.

By 1914, football had spread from Ontario across the country. The British links remained strong, with the famous amateur team Corinthians touring across Canada in 1911 and returning in 1924. The Duke of Connaught, Governor General of Canada, presented a cup named after himself to the national champions beginning from 1913. The first winners were Norwood Wanderers and in 1915 it was won by Winnipeg Scottish.

While soccer was growing in Canada, however, it had strong competition from rugby, Canadian football (like American football) and ice hockey. Football continued during the First World War but many players joined up, some receiving awards for bravery, like Hugh Cairns from Saskatoon, who won the Victoria Cross.

Between the wars, football continued its slow progress in Canada. In 1926, a National League was formed. Teams such as Toronto Ulster United, Toronto Scottish and Hamilton Thistles give us a clue about the heritage of those who were playing.

After the Second World War there was more immigration to Canada, but the influence of Britain was reduced. When the North American Soccer League began in 1968 it featured two Canadian teams, the Toronto Falcons and the Vancouver Royals. Other Canadian teams to feature in the NSL include Montreal Manic, Calgary Boomers, Vancouver Whitecaps and Toronto Blizzard. The names reflect the importance of commerce and marketing in the North American game as opposed to heritage links.

On an international level, the Canada men's national team has never reached the heights of Galt, the 1904 Olympic Champions, although they did qualify for the 1986 World Cup in Mexico and will be at Qatar 2022.

The women's game had a difficult beginning. In 1922, when the English women's team Dick, Kerr Ladies toured Canada, the Dominion Football Association threatened to ban any clubs that fielded a women's team to play them. Consequently, Dick, Kerr Ladies faced men's teams. However, by the 1950s opposition to women playing football in Canada had weakened. McGill University formed a team, which played against McDonald College, Bishop's University and some high schools. There are also reports of a Ladies Soccer Championship in Nova Scotia.

Now, football is highly popular among girls in Canadian schools and the national team has enjoyed great Olympic success. In 2012 and 2016 they won the bronze medal, and in 2021, in Tokyo, they topped this by defeating Sweden 3-2 in a penalty shoot-out to take gold. And in 2015 Canada hosted the Women's World Cup, in which England beat them in the quarter-finals.

Cape Verde

An island nation off the coast of West Africa, it's traditionally known as Cape Verde in Britain, but its own people call it Cabo Verde, which is Portuguese for Green Cape. This is a big clue that Cape Verde was Portuguese-controlled for centuries, before it became independent in 1975. Not surprisingly, therefore, the Portuguese played a major part in introducing football to the islands. More surprisingly, we seem to have had something of a role, too.

Football properly came to the islands in the early twentieth century. If you look at some of the oldest clubs in the islands, you find the sort of names and symbols you would expect in a country with strong sporting links to Portugal. There is, for instance, Sporting Clube de Praia, founded in 1923, which has a lion symbol like that of Sporting Clube de Portugal. Among the oldest clubs in the islands, however, you will also find the much less Portuguese-sounding FC Derby.

British ships have been sailing past, visiting and occasionally attacking Cape Verde for centuries. By the late nineteenth century (after we had stopped attacking it) there was a flourishing British expatriate community there, and, no doubt, it brought footballs with it, as so many other British expatriate communities around the world did.

The port of Mindelo, on São Vicente, one of the islands that make up Cape Verde, had become a coaling station for the British East India Company and the Royal Mail Steam Packet Company in the mid-nineteenth century, and in the late nineteenth century it also became an important telecommunications hub for the British Empire too, thanks to an undersea cable.

In 1929, at a time when Derby County was going through a particularly strong period in football in England, FC Derby was established in Mindelo. It can be difficult to get information on the early history of clubs in some countries, but one version, at least, says FC Derby of Mindelo was formed by Britons, and since Mindelo had a large and influential British community at the time, it seems likely that is true. Over the years, FC Derby has become one of the most successful clubs in Cape Verde.

Internationally, Cape Verde has qualified for three Africa Cup of Nations tournaments. In 2013, the 'Blue Sharks' reached the quarter-finals, and in 2022 they reached the round of sixteen, quite an achievement for such a small country. In a friendly in 2015, they also beat mighty Portugal 2-0.

Women's football in Cape Verde, however, only started getting properly organised in the last two decades.

Central African Republic

Yes, it's central, it's in Africa and, constitutionally, it's a republic. It is also a country that has seen some very difficult times.

Football almost certainly reached the area via France, rather than directly from here. Prior to independence in 1960, the country was a French colony. In the period between the First and Second World Wars, Ubangi-Shari, as the region was known to the French authorities, was the location of numerous abuses committed by the colonial authorities and by large private companies that had bought concessions. It was also the location for much of the Kongo-Wara rebellion against the colonial authorities.

For these reasons and others, organised football clubs for the locals don't really seem to have started much until the 1940s (although, presumably, French military personnel and administrators played the game there earlier than that). AS Tempête Mocaf and Olympic Real de Bangui, still two of the country's major clubs, were both initially formed in that decade.

The Central African Republic is not one of Africa's stronger national sides, but has had the occasional surprising success, like its 2-0 win over Algeria in the qualifying stages for the 2012 Africa Cup of Nations. The women's national team played its first international match only fairly recently.

Chad

The country is in central northern Africa with Sudan to the east, Niger to the west and Libya to the north.

For the most part the area has not seen much British involvement, although, during the Second World War, the Long Range Desert Group did use it as a base from which to attack Axis targets in southern Libya.

It seems fairly certain that football came to Chad, again, via France, rather than directly from Britain. France was the colonial power there for much of the twentieth century.

Renaissance FC, founded in 1954 and playing in the capital in N'Djamena, is one of the country's oldest and best clubs.

The national men's team hasn't had much luck qualifying for World Cup finals or Africa Cup of Nations, while the women's team hasn't been in existence for very long.

Chadian footballers have, however, produced some significant achievements playing for teams outside their own country, in France, for instance.

Chile

The origins of the name Chile are unclear; however, it doesn't seem to have anything to do with chilli or indeed 'chilly', although the southern tip of this amazingly long, thin country is genuinely very close to the Antarctic.

In football terms, Chile, for the average Brit, has been somewhat in the shadow of its neighbour, Argentina. However, Chile has a very rich history in the sport, having, for instance, hosted the World Cup in 1962 and won the Copa América in consecutive years in 2015 and 2016. It also has the second oldest football association in South America. And, yes, we took football to them.

The United Kingdom took football to Chile in the nineteenth century. By the time Chile became independent of Spanish control in 1818, British merchants had already begun to see Valparaíso on the Pacific coast as a useful trading base and a useful stop after getting round Cape Horn. Merchants keen to exploit Chile's natural resources of silver and copper were quickly followed by railway engineers and bankers to make sure that an infrastructure was created to get the valuable resources to the coast. By 1914, thousands of Britons had emigrated to Chile and many had settled in Valparaíso. It was some of these merchants and their schools who introduced football to Chile.

The first football in Chile was probably played at the Mackay and Sutherland School, which was run by two Scots, Peter Mackay and George Sutherland (they obviously thought long and hard about the school name). It was here that in 1882 a football club was formed, although it is not known exactly what type of football they played.

Then, in 1892, the Valparaíso Football Club was set up by David Scott. Its first game was a friendly against the employees of local merchants. The following year, Valparaíso played home and away games against a team from the capital, Santiago Cricket and Athletic Club. Both clubs fielded entirely British teams with a strong Scottish element. Encouraged by the success of this fixture, a Valparaíso XI took on an Argentine Buenos Aires XI and drew 1-1.

In 1894, Scott called a meeting to establish the Chilean Football Association. Representatives from Valparaíso FC and McKay and Sutherland Athletic were joined by Colegio San Luis and Victoria Rangers, and in 1895 the Football Association of Chile was formed with Scott as its first president. Football spread rapidly from Valparaíso to the capital Santiago and with it came a rivalry between teams based in Valparaíso, who were seen as largely British and European, and those in Santiago, who were more local.

In the unofficial Copa América of 1910, the Chilean team included names like Gibson, McWilliams, Joe Robson and Campbell. The team from Argentina had a somewhat similar make-up, so Britain was well represented in the early stages of the Copa América.

The standard of football played in Chile before 1918 is difficult to measure. On an international level it was not until 1926 – at the thirty-fourth attempt – that they achieved a victory, thumping Bolivia 7-1. It is, therefore, surprising that the Chilean player Ramón Unzaga, who played for Club Atlético y de Futbol Estrella de Mar in Talcahuano, claims to have invented the spectacular overhead bicycle kick in 1914.

By 1918, British influence had faded a bit. Valparaíso was in decline due to the opening of the Panama Canal, Valparaíso FC had folded and the Mackay and Sutherland School had closed.

Some British influence, though, has remained in Chilean team names. There is, for instance, an Everton de Viña del Mar football club founded in 1909 by Anglo-Chilean admirers of the Liverpool namesake, which plays in the Primera Division, and a Rangers from Talca, founded by a Scotsman.

Women's clubs have had some interesting names, too. In the 1950s, for example, there was one called Las Atómicas. The women's national team may not have won the Copa América but they were runners-up twice, in 1991 and 2018. Chile were the last team to qualify for the Tokyo Olympics and they also went to the 2019 World Cup.

Alexis Sánchez is among the Chilean stars who have played some of their football for teams in Britain, while manager Manuel Pellegrini won the Premier League with Manchester City.

China (plus Hong Kong and Macau)

China has given the world many major inventions but it didn't give us modern football, even though it did come up with a rather similar game.

Cuju or 'Kickball' began as military training in the third century BC. It was played for at least 1,000 years, but had died out before Brits arrived in the seventeenth century. There were rules, coaching manuals, marked out pitches, goals and team colours. The ball was leather, filled with perhaps fur or feathers, and kicking was the main method of moving the ball. There were even celebrity players. It had many of the features of modern football, but still there doesn't seem to be a direct link between this well-developed Chinese game and modern football, which Brits introduced to Shanghai and Hong Kong in the nineteenth century and the Portuguese introduced to Macau at roughly the same time.

As one of the results of two Opium Wars (a shameful chapter in British history) in the nineteenth century, Britain got Hong Kong and the ability to develop trade along the Chinese coast, including in the great port city of Shanghai.

The first football match in Shanghai took place in 1879 when John Prentice, a marine engineer from Glasgow, led the Prentice Engineers against Shanghai Athletic Club. By 1907, Shanghai had a football league with Prentice as its president and a trophy donated by Thomas Dewar from the Scottish whisky firm Dewar's. Brits, French and Portuguese teams competed for the trophy. British Christian missionaries also helped spread the game in the country.

The first club, Hong Kong Football Club, was founded by another Scot, Sir James Stewart Lockhart, in 1886, twenty-four years after Britain had gained the territory. The club's first match was against the Royal Engineers. Army and Navy sides including HMS *Centurion*, the Royal Welsh Fusiliers and the Royal West Kent Regiment were to feature prominently alongside Hong Kong Football Club in the early competitions established by the Brits. By 1908, Hong Kong had both a league and cup competition. The first Chinese club, South China Football Club, was started for students in 1910. Three years later, South China sent a team to a Far Eastern Championship Games in the Philippines.

From 1911 through to 1949, revolutions, civil war and foreign invasion had a devastating effect on China and also slowed the development of football there. However, the Chinese Football Association was formed in 1924, the country joined FIFA in 1931 and competed in the 1936 Olympics. In Hong Kong, South China challenged the British teams and won its first title in 1923.

In 1949, the communists took full control of almost all of China. A demonstration game was played for Chairman Mao in order to mark the creation of a new state.

Chinese communist football developed, to a great extent, as it did in post-war Eastern Europe. Internationally, China mainly played other communist countries. Domestically, football clubs were mainly attached to trade unions and the army.

One interesting variation to this approach would be provided by Guangzhou FC. When football restarted after Mao's Cultural Revolution of 1966–76, Guangzhou chose to start from the bottom up by hiring a foreign coach to work with the youth players rather than the first team. Improvements took some time but, finally, Guangzhou would win eight Super League titles between 2011 and 2019.

In the 1990s Chinese domestic football opened up to capitalism. Jia-A and now the Chinese Super League have employed foreign stars, including Paul Gascoigne at the Heavenly Horse club. Young Chinese players come to the UK for development. For example, Li Tie played for Everton and Sun Jihai for Crystal Palace, Manchester City and Sheffield United.

So far, however, advances in the domestic game have yet to bring the men's national team the success for which China hopes. The men qualified for the Tokyo World Cup but were eliminated in the group stage.

By contrast, the 'Steel Roses', China's women's national team, have shown what can be achieved. They have been runners-up to the USA at both Olympics and World Cup. China was beaten 2-1 in the 1996 Olympics and lost 5-4 in a World Cup penalty shoot-out in 1999. So near but yet so far.

Hong Kong ceased to be a British colony in 1997 but it still has its own football team today. Similarly, Macau ceased to be a Portuguese colony in 1999 and also still has its own team.

Colombia

The last few decades haven't exactly been easy for Colombia, what with civil conflict and drug wars. In sporting terms the country is perhaps more well known for its cyclists than footballers. However, they did win the Copa América in 2001 and they have played in six World Cups, including 2014 and 2018. And, yes, we have strong links to the first football games in Colombia.

The sport was comparatively slow to develop as it was hampered by wars and very difficult transport connections. An estimated 100,000 Colombians lost their lives in the Thousand Days' War between 1899 and 1903, and by 1912 the country had only 1,061km of railway line. Transport between the inland cities of Bogotá and Medellín and the ports on the Caribbean coast could take months and was only really with the development of air travel that the country became a little more united and connected.

Somewhat confusingly, there are four towns in Colombia that claim to be the home of football – Barranquilla and Santa Marta on the Caribbean coast, the capital Bogotá, and Pasto in the south of the country. All have a claim to have been developing football in the first two decades of the twentieth century.

Football was first played in Barranquilla in 1904 by Brits working for the Colombian Railway Company, constructing a railway between Barranquilla and Puerto Colombia. Subsequent development of the game in the city was taken on by Arturo de Castro, a wealthy Colombian. He had been introduced to the game at university in Britain and returned to Colombia with a copy of the rules and a ball, which he used to interest his friends. He went on to form Barranquilla FC, who played their first match in 1908. The Barranquilla team all had Colombian names, so British influence may have been short-lived.

In neighbouring Santa Marta there is also a British link. The earliest game in Santa Marta in 1909 allegedly featured British sailors and workers involved in the export of bananas.

In Pasto, British influence came (somewhat ironically in name terms) from a Leslie Spain. Mr Spain was sent to Panama to find out where Panama hats might be made. From Panama he was sent to Pasto, where he set up a factory to make the headwear and export it back to Britain. He also set up a football team for his workers. In 1909 a match was played in a square in Pasto, where players had to play around the central water fountain.

In Bogotá, football probably began in the National Military School in the 1880s, where it was one of several sports introduced by an American Colonel Henry Lemly to encourage strength and fitness. It is not clear where Lemly picked up his love of the game (although there was, as we shall see, plenty of football being played in the USA by the 1880s).

After the Thousand Days' War, however, football reappeared in Bogotá as one of the sports on offer at the Bogotá Polo Club. Once again, there is a British link as both Jose Maria and Carlos Obregon, who introduced football to the club, had been educated and started playing football in Britain.

The sport grew from these disparate beginnings, and by 1928 football was the most popular sport at the National Olympic Games in Cali.

By this time, Argentina was a more important influence on Colombian football than Britain. However, in 1939 Jack Greenwell (see Peru) was hired to take charge of the Colombian national side and to improve football in Barranquilla. After a rocky start, where only thirteen of the nineteen selected players attended his first training session, he was deemed to have been a success. He was invited to take charge of Independiente Santa Fe in Bogotá and led them to the state championship.

One of the interesting features of football history in Colombia is a sense of fair play. In the 1920s, when Deportivo Independiente Medellín were beaten 6-0 by Bogotá, the Deportivo manager described the result as a 6-0 draw. Even today there is an amateur side playing in Colombia named Fair Play.

Women's football is also popular in Colombia and there is a professional league. The national team, led by the remarkable Natalia Gaitán, has had some success in the last decade. They qualified for both the London and Rio Olympics and reached the 2011 and 2015 World Cups. Closer to home, they were runners-up in the Women's Copa América in 2010 and 2014.

A number of Colombians have played for British teams, including James Rodríguez, Luis Díaz, Radamel Falcao in England and Alfredo Morelos in Scotland.

The Comoros

This is an island nation in the Indian Ocean. For much of the twentieth century, until they declared independence in 1975, the islands were French-controlled and this influence remains strong, so it seems most likely that football arrived here via France rather than directly from Britain.

And it seems to have arrived comparatively late. Chirazienne FC, for instance, one of the oldest clubs in the country, wasn't founded until 1950. Coin Nord, one of the country's most successful clubs, wasn't founded until 1960.

The national side is nicknamed Les Coelacantes, after the coelacanth, a prehistoric fish once believed long extinct that turned up in a fisherman's catch in the 1930s. Looking at the coelacanth, it doesn't really look like a traditional football mascot.

Les Coelacantes do, however, seem to have been improving in recent years. In 2021 they qualified for the Africa Cup of

Nations, their first major tournament, and managed a surprise 3-2 defeat of Ghana. They got beyond the group stage, but then, sadly for Comoros fans, were up against giants Cameroon and were eliminated. A key element in their success has been Nadjim 'Jimmy' Abdou, formerly of Millwall.

The women's national team have had a bit of a tougher time, including being beaten 17-0 by South Africa in 2019.

Congo, Democratic Republic of the

This is the Congo country that used to be a Belgian colony. It suffered some of the most brutal colonial rule, and was later Zaire under the dictatorial Mobutu. Still later it suffered terrible, devastating wars that killed large numbers of people in the late 1990s and the early twenty-first century, and has seen some violence since then. The (rather long) official name of the country is often abbreviated as DRC or DR Congo.

A key figure in the beginnings of football in the DRC is one Raphaël de la Kethulle de Ryhove. It's another rather long name and this, in turn, is often abbreviated to De la Kethulle. He came from a Belgian noble family, but there is a British connection. He was born in 1890 and educated first in Bruges and then at the religious Scheut congregation in Anderlecht. He grew up at a time when the new British game of football was taking Belgium by storm. FC Bruges, or Club Brugge, was founded in 1891 as Brugsche FC, and RSC Anderlecht was founded, as Sporting Club Anderlechtois, in 1908.

In 1914, though, it was the German Army instead that took much of neutral Belgium by storm, and De la Kethulle, just after being ordained a priest, escaped the chaos of the German invasion, as many Belgians did in the early days of the war. Specifically, he escaped across the Channel and came to Britain. Here he experienced London life and tended to other Belgian refugees, and then in 1915 he returned to Belgium to serve as a stretcher-bearer on the front line. In 1916, he was on the move again and, this time, he was headed for what was then the Belgian Congo.

Once there, he became a major force in developing local education and sport. In 1919, the Association Royale Sportive Congolaise was formed, and, by the following year there were football leagues in what are now the cities of Kinshasa and Lubumbashi. Brits were among the European nations forming teams in the Congo at that time. De la Kethulle also introduced another British institution to the country, creating the first scout troop there.

The racist attitudes of many colonial administrators somewhat impeded the growth of football among the locals but it spread nonetheless.

Some of DR Congo's most famous clubs, such as TP (Tout Puissant or All Powerful) Mazembe, have become some of Africa's more successful. In 1974, the country (then called Zaire) made it to the World Cup, where Scotland beat them 2-0. The country has also twice won the Africa Cup of Nations, and, in 1998, the DRC women's team took third place in the equivalent women's tournament.

A number of talented players with DRC heritage have trod the pitches of the Premier League, including Arthur Masuaku and the LuaLua brothers.

Congo, Republic of the

This is the other Congo country. It has often been called Congo-Brazzaville, after its capital, Brazzaville.

Around 1910, when the country was still a French colony, French and other European expatriates, some of them perhaps

British, were already playing football in Brazzaville. In 1923, the Stanley Pool Championships saw white teams from French and Belgian Congo competing against each other.

Missionaries in Brazzaville thought football a moral leisure pursuit for the locals, and so it was added to the curriculum at schools.

Local enthusiasm for the new sport grew. In 1929, the Native Sports Federation was formed to organise football for the local Africans, and in 1931 Étoile from Brazzaville beat a team from the Belgian Congo 5-1. However, in 1936, in a move that hugely damaged the local game, the French authorities reacted to the growing skill and self-confidence of local teams by trying to ban Africans from wearing boots or shoes when playing football.

The Republic of the Congo became independent from France in 1960 and the Congolese Football Federation was formed in 1962. The men's national team has qualified for the Africa Cup of Nations a number of times and won it in 1972. The victorious team that year included the PSG legend François M'Pelé. The women's national team has been to the Africa Women Cup of Nations (or African Women's Championship as it was then known) on a couple of occasions.

A number of players with heritage from this Congo, including Christian Bassila, have made a contribution to football in Britain.

Costa Rica

The Costa Rica team announced themselves rather loudly and effectively to British football fans when they defeated Scotland 1-0 in the 1990 World Cup, giving Scots another dose of World Cup heartache.

Football came comparatively early to Costa Rica and there was a strong British link with its development in the country.

The first recorded match, in 1887, was organised by Oscar Pinto Fernández, who brought a ball back from England and organised a match with a friend. It is also possible that there was a game almost a decade earlier in 1876 in San José but it is not clear who was playing.

Football began among the Costa Rican elite, who had studied in England and football was part of their education. It was boosted by British businessmen keen both to develop the coffee trade and to play their favourite game.

As the coffee trade expanded, the need for a railway to take goods from the central area to the Atlantic coast for export to Europe was obvious. The railways brought British workers to Limón and with them came more football.

The game was supported by both the government and the church. Consequently, it spread rapidly across all social classes.

By 1921, a National Football League had been established with seven clubs: La Libertad, Limonense Gymnastic Society, Spanish Gymnastic Society of San José, Liga Deportiva Alajuelense, Club Sport Cartaginés, Club Sport Herediano and Club Sport La Unión de Tres Ríos. Herediano won the first league championship.

British influence reappeared in 1946 with the appointment of Randolph Galloway as manager of the Costa Rican national team. Galloway had played for Nottingham Forest and Tottenham Hotspur. He may have been part of a move by the FA to expand the influence of British football as the Empire faded. He also managed several Spanish clubs, so the language question can't have been a problem.

The Costa Rica national side have become a bit of a Central American powerhouse, winning the Central American Cup eight times. They have also qualified for the World Cup a number of times. In 2014 Costa Rica shocked England in Brazil by qualifying from Group D by defeating Italy and Uruguay and drawing with England. This eliminated England at the group stage.

The first women's football match was in the national stadium in 1950. Since then the game has grown in popularity and more than 35,000 fans turned up to watch an U-17 World Cup qualifier against Venezuela. Costa Rica was chosen to host the 2022 U-20 World Cup.

Croatia

It would be fair to say that Croatia weren't a hugely popular team with England fans on 11 July 2018. When Mario Mandžukić scored 109 minutes into the match to put Gareth Southgate's team out of the World Cup and prevent England reaching their first final since 1966, some may have been regretting that we ever gave Croatia football at all. But we did and, for a nation of little more than 4 million, they have done pretty well with it.

It all started in the port city of Rijeka with a naval engineer from Lancashire, Robert Whitehead. He started a business in the port and became the inventor of the modern torpedo (it is said that he naively hoped his invention would make war obsolete). He also brought over British workers with their footballs and encouraged them to play the sport. In 1873, they decided to celebrate the opening of the Rijeka to Karlovac rail line with a football match that included local technical staff from Rijeka and some from the state railways.

Seven years later, we were at it again, with English workers from the Oak Extract Company taking on locals in Županja in the east of Croatia.

The Croats did not need a lot of prompting and took fairly rapidly to this new sport. Franjo Bučar, who would later become founder and president of the Yugoslav Olympic Committee, helped promote football in the country, and by the early twentieth century local clubs were being formed. In 1911, Hajduk Split, which would become one of the most successful clubs in both Croatia and Yugoslavia, was formed.

Before the First World War, Croatia was part of the Austro-Hungarian Empire but after the Armistice it became part of a new country, Yugoslavia. Nationalist aspirations did not, however, disappear among all Croats. During the Second World War, Germany and Italy invaded Yugoslavia, and a short-lived Croatian state emerged, allied to Hitler.

In the period after the Second World War, Croatia was part of Tito's Yugoslavia, and nationalist ambitions were strenuously repressed. However, by 1990, Tito was long dead and Yugoslavia had started to crumble. On 13 May that year, Dinamo Zagreb were on the pitch in the Maksimir Stadium Zagreb to take on Red Star Belgrade. In what is now widely seen as a forerunner of the wars that would soon tear Yugoslavia apart, a riot erupted, in which Serb and Croat fans battled each other, and the Dinamo captain was filmed kicking a policeman.

Croatia became independent in 1991, and the war there ended in 1995. The years since then have seen great triumphs for Croatian football. There are far too many famous Croatian footballers to mention them all, or even most of them, but we certainly have to mention Luka Modrić and, of course, Davor Šuker for their contributions to football both here and in mainland Europe.

In the women's game, Iva Landeka has captained the national team and played for a number of clubs across Europe.

Cuba

For some reason, Cubans seem to have more passion for baseball than football. Well, there's no accounting for taste, and Cuba is quite close to the United States. Football is, however, still hugely popular and, yes, we did have a role in introducing Cubans to their second most-loved sport.

After Spain lost the Spanish–American War of 1898, Cuba eventually became an independent country.

Football came to Cuba as it came to lots of places, via a combination of locals who had studied in Britain and acquired a passion for the sport there, and Britons who were working and living in the country and had brought their passion and their footballs with them.

Sometime in the early twentieth century, Manolo Rodríguez, who had studied in Britain, helped found a football association in Cuba.

In 1907, the first football club, Sport Club Hatuey (Hatuey was a local chief who fought the Spanish invaders in the sixteenth century), was founded and soon after, in 1909, the Prado Football Club was also created. However, the name 'Prado' didn't really reflect the club's close links to the British community in Havana – team line-ups contained names such as Thompson, Tucker, Orr, Ogilvis, Houldsworth, Onfroy, Meyers, Evered, Lismore, Webber, Davis, Stone and Edwards – and soon the club was renamed as the much more British 'Rovers'. On 11 December, Rovers took on Sport Club Hatuey, in perhaps the first proper match in Cuba, and beat them 1-0, with Orr scoring. It was as Rovers that the team won the Cuban National Football Championship in 1912 and 1914 (they let Hatuey win in 1913). In 1916, the Cuban Football Federation was reorganised, with Scot William A. Campbell as president.

By 1938, Cuba were ready to go to their first World Cup, the first Caribbean country to do so (sadly for the country, it would also, as of 2022, be their last visit). They scraped past Romania to reach the quarter-finals, only to come up against Sweden, who beat them 8-0.

Cuba has, however, done better in the Caribbean Cup, and won it in 2012. In 2018 the women's national team qualified for their first CONCACAF Women's Championship.

Che Guevara apparently liked football, but then, of course, he was originally from Argentina. Although he actually seems to have preferred rugby, having played fly-half for a university team.

Cyprus

In 1864, Frank Darvall Newham was born in Barrow upon Soar, a village in northern Leicestershire. In 1900, by then an Anglican priest and Director of Education for the British colonial administration of Cyprus, he brought the world's greatest sport to the island.

That year he founded The English School in Nicosia to provide an English education, and on the curriculum, of course, was football. The first ever football match on the island was played at The English School, and, in 1912, as he saw enthusiasm for the game had spread both in schools and among the wider population, Canon Newham introduced a cup competition.

Among the earliest local football clubs was Anorthosis Famagusta FC, formed in 1911. By 1932, there was a national league, and in 1934 the Cyprus Football Association was created.

APOEL FC, one of the island's most famous clubs, and one with an international track record, was established in 1926. In 1948, a political split linked to the Greek Civil War saw APOEL players with left-wing sympathies form their own club, now another of the most famous clubs in Cyprus, and bitter rivals of APOEL, AC Omonia.

In 1960, Cyprus became independent from the United Kingdom. The national team have caused a few surprises in their time, including beating the Republic of Ireland 5-2 in 2006, and defeating Wales 3-1 in 2007. The women's national team have had a slightly tougher time, including Scotland beating them 10-0 in 2021.

Ray Wood, goalkeeper for, among other teams, Manchester United, Huddersfield Town and Bradford City, coached the Cyprus national team for a time in the early 1970s.

Czech Republic – Czechia

Yes, you can call the country Czechia, and in some senses it would appear that might be more correct, but in Britain, few people seem to use the name, and Czech Republic still seems acceptable, so we will go with that here.

The Czech Republic has, of course, produced some influential Premier League greats. Petr Čech (Čech by name, Czech by nationality!) won almost every trophy available with Chelsea, from the Champions League and Europa Cup to Premier League titles and FA and League Cups. Vladimír Šmicer, Milan Baroš and Patrik Berger have all starred for Liverpool.

And, yes, we did have something to do with the start of Czech football.

When football began in Prague towards the end of the nineteenth century, the city was in Bohemia, which was, in turn, in the Austro-Hungarian Empire. The sports side of life was dominated by gymnastics, but young people were looking for a new sport to help develop a Czech identity and make them part of modern Europe. The chosen sport was football, spread from Britain via Vienna.

Slavia Prague was founded as a sports club by Prague students in 1892. Football soon became one of its key sports, but it also functioned as a Czech language society and literary club. It was a meeting point for liberal nationalists and future political leaders.

Sparta Prague, Slavia's great rivals, were founded in 1893 in a then working-class area of the city, Vinohrady. The first derby between the sides was a 1-0 victory to Sparta in 1896.

Another early club was Deutsche Football Club, formed by the German Jewish community in 1896 from a rowing club.

Regular contact between Prague clubs and Britain helped develop both the culture and technical standard of Czech football. In 1906, Dr Petrik was so impressed by the red with white sleeves strip of Woolwich Arsenal, that it was adopted by Sparta Prague – but, for some reason, with black socks.

Both Oxford and Cambridge Universities toured between 1899 and 1901. Professionals toured too, with Celtic arriving in 1904 and Arsenal, Manchester United and Crystal Palace in 1908. The Corinthians made three tours before the First World War.

The Czechs emerged from the war as part of a new country, an independent Czechoslovakia that also included Slovaks. Some British influence on football, though, remained. For example, both Slavia Prague and Sparta Prague had Scottish managers.

John Madden, an ex-Celtic player known as 'the Codger', became manager of Slavia Prague in 1905. He had previously been a successful player who played for Celtic. As a manager he was a strict disciplinarian, encouraging his players to train hard and avoid alcohol and tobacco. In his twenty-five years in charge, Slavia won 134 of 169 matches. He remained in Prague during the Nazi occupation, as he was afraid of losing his pension, and now has a stand named in his honour at the club's ground.

The other Scottish manager was John Dick. John had captained Arsenal and played more than 250 games for the club before becoming coach of Deutsche in Prague in 1912. During the war he remained with the club, even playing for them in 1917. In 1919, he joined Sparta Prague, where he won five consecutive titles between 1919 and 1923. His team had the nickname 'Iron Sparta' and lost only one competitive match out of forty-nine. By this stage Sparta had a claim to be one of the best club sides in Europe.

The Czechoslovakian team at the Amsterdam Olympics in 1920 was dominated by Sparta players. They were an exciting team to watch, scoring fifteen goals en route to the final and beating Yugoslavia, Norway and France on the way.

Against Belgium in the final, though, they didn't even get a silver medal. Two down and reduced to ten men, they walked off in anger at the English referee, John Lewis.

However, they did collect silver medals at the 1934 World Cup in Italy. Sparta player Oldřich Nejedlý won the 'golden boot' as the Czechoslovakian team defeated Romania, Switzerland and Germany. In the final they lost 2-1 to Italy after extra time.

Czechoslovakia, however, went one better at the Euros in 1976. In the final they faced the 1974 World Cup winners West Germany. The Czechs squandered a two-goal lead and for the first time the competition came down to penalties. Antonín Panenka stepped up to take the final Czech penalty. In converting it he made history. Czechoslovakia were European Champions and a new penalty technique of sending the goalkeeper the wrong way, then chipping the ball into the space he had vacated, was born. Neither West Germany nor Czechoslovakia still exist, but the Panenka lives on.

In 1993, the Czech Republic separated peacefully from Slovakia. Since then the Czechs have been to all the Euros and, so far, one World Cup. They reached the final of the Euros at Wembley in 1996 but were beaten 2-1 by Germany, the winner a 'golden goal'.

There is a Czech women's team but they are yet to qualify for any major championship. However, there is a domestic league with eight teams, which has been dominated by Prague sides.

Denmark (plus the Faroe Islands)

England faced Denmark at Wembley in the semi-finals of the Euros in 2021. And for the Danes, on that day, it was, of course, pretty much all about playing for Christian Eriksen, their colleague who had suffered a heart attack in their opening match and was still recovering. For England, of course, it was about whether the dream that 'football was coming home' could go a little further. The Danes did Eriksen proud, but it was England in the final.

The match revived a long-standing rivalry that stretches back more than a century, but that was all to come after we gave the Danes the world's greatest sport.

The first football in Denmark appears to have been played by British sailors in Copenhagen and by the 1870s there was a football club of English immigrants in the city. However, it was Britain-loving Danes who really set about developing the game in the country. Many of these had come into contact with football while being educated at top British private schools or at Oxford and Cambridge.

Kjobenvans Boldklub (Copenhagen Ball Club) or KB played some form of football with handwritten rules in 1879. Young lawyer Frederik Markmann became chairman of KB and helped promote the game in Denmark and KB developed a very popular youth school. A variety of ball games, including cricket, were played while Markmann used his legal training to standardise football rules.

In 1886, he helped translate the Football Association rules into Danish. The following year the first game using these rules was staged and KB defeated the Non-Commissioned Officer School's students 8-0.

To start with, as had happened in England, cricket and football were associated with each other and played by the same clubs. Usually, the clubs were mainly about cricket with football as something to keep men fit in the winter. By 1889, there were thousands playing football and cricket in Denmark, and Markmann organised the Dansk Boldspil-Union (Danish Ballgame Union).

In 1896, football was included in the school curriculum for both primary schools and lower secondary schools. By 1904, the game was sufficiently established that the DBU (Danish Ballgame Union) applied to be affiliated to the Football Association in England. Their application was rejected and instead the Danes joined France, Belgium, the Netherlands, Spain, Sweden and Switzerland in founding FIFA in Paris to promote football.

On the pitch, the Danes hosted tours from British clubs. Queen's Park from Scotland visited in 1888, 1889 and 1908. The Corinthians also toured in 1904, as did Newcastle United and Southampton. While all the British sides won comfortably, the Danes were to show what they had learned at the London Olympics in 1908.

The international rivalry between England and Denmark can be traced to that tournament, when football was officially included in the Olympics for the first time. Great Britain reached the final as expected, fielding an entirely English side. The Danes had an English coach, Charles Williams, and had the Danish triple jump and 800m record holder Nils Middelboe and a professor, Harald Bohr, whose brother Niels Bohr won the Nobel Prize for physics. Britain won the gold medal, defeating the Danes 2-0. Four years later in Sweden the final would be repeated, with the Brits coming out 4-2 winners.

In 1992, at the Euros in Sweden, Denmark and England would meet once again. This time it was the opening group game rather than the final. It ended 0-0 but, while England went home after the group stage, the Danes went on to defeat Germany 2-0 in the final. Champions of a tournament for which they failed to qualify, and only got a place in when civil war forced Yugoslavia to withdraw. The Danish side contained one very familiar face – Peter Schmeichel, the Manchester United goalie.

Danes are, of course, now a familiar sight in the Premier League. Schmeichel's son Kasper won the Premiership title with Leicester City and Andreas Christensen has won both the Champions League and the Europa League with Chelsea as well as the FA Cup. Tottenham have Pierre-Emile Højbjerg; Southampton, Jannik Vestergaard; and Brentford have both Mathias Jensen and Christian Nørgaard. Danes have been playing in Britain since at least 1912, when 'The Great Dane' Nils Middelboe signed for Chelsea. Interestingly, Nils decided to remain an amateur at Chelsea and earn a salary as a banker on the grounds that he wasn't that passionate about football.

The Danish national men's team has a decent record at the Euros and the World Cup. The Danish women have not quite been able to match their record but they have come close. They were runners-up in the Women's Euros in 2017 and came third in 1991 and 1993. They also reached the quarter-finals of the 1991 and 1995 Women's World Cup, but were unable to progress beyond the group stage at the 2022 Euro in Britain, even with UEFA Women's Player of the Year, Chelsea star Pernille Harder.

And we couldn't finish our look at football within the boundaries of the Kingdom of Denmark without a quick mention of, yes, the Faroe Islands. These are a self-governing community within Denmark located in the North Atlantic even further north than Shetland. From 1940 to 1945 we occupied the islands and no doubt our soldiers and sailors played a bit of football with the locals. The Faroes did not play an international game away from home until 1962, when they played Iceland, and did not join FIFA until 1988. However, in 1992 they won their first competitive international, defeating

Austria 1-0 in a Euro qualifying game and in 1999 they managed a 1-1 draw with Scotland in the same competition.

Djibouti

It's a small country on the east coast of Africa, with Ethiopia to its west, and, across the sea, Yemen to its east. It is situated on some key sea routes, so it may well be that sailors from assorted countries, including Britain, were playing football there from early on. However, France was the colonial power, and probably, therefore, football came to the country via that route, rather than directly from Britain.

French Somaliland (as the country was then called) was seized from Vichy authorities by British and Free French Forces in 1942, so, no doubt, some British feet were kicking footballs around at that time.

The French Somaliland Football Federation was formed in 1947, and, after independence from France, the Djibouti Football Federation was formed in 1979.

It's probably fair to say that, being such a small country, they have struggled a bit at international level, but they did recently draw against Gambia. The women's team played its first official international in 2006.

Dominica

In the nineteenth century and much of the twentieth century, the island of Dominica was controlled by Britain.

Many from Dominica volunteered to serve in the First World War, and it may be that, as happened in the Bahamas and elsewhere in the region, some of those returning to this little

Caribbean island brought with them a passion for football they gained during their service overseas.

Equally, as is true elsewhere in the Caribbean, football in Dominica has had to try to compete against cricket, so popular in the region, for the enthusiasm of the locals. The national football team's home ground has been Windsor Park, which looks, in reality, more like a cricket ground.

There is a rather British feel to some of the team names in Dominica, like Middleham United.

Being a small country, Dominica is no football superpower, but the men's team did crush the British Virgin Islands 6-1 in 1997.

However, some players with family connections to the island have played with distinction elsewhere, including in Britain. Karina LeBlanc, for instance, whose father came from Dominica, was a distinguished goalkeeper for a number of North American women's sides, as well as the Canadian national team. And both of the parents of Vince Hilaire, who played for Crystal Palace, Portsmouth and Leeds in the difficult days of the 1970s and '80s when racism was extremely widespread, came from Dominica.

Dominican Republic

The Dominican Republic shares the island of Hispaniola (yes, it is an actual island, with a name meaning Little Spain, and is not just the ship in *Treasure Island*) with Haiti. It lies just east of Cuba and a few hundred miles north of Colombia.

The country was a Spanish colony and it had a turbulent nine-teenth century. The Spanish finally withdrew in 1864 after a popular revolt. A Dominican Republic was established and the USA became the most influential power in the area.

The first football was probably played by visiting sailors in the late nineteenth or early twentieth century. The majority of these seem to have been from Spain, France and Holland, but it is possible that some Brits were also involved.

In the 1930s many Spaniards decided to settle in the republic. Some were driven out by the effects of the Great Depression and others moved because of the Spanish Civil War. These migrants brought football with them and set up clubs across the country. The most successful clubs were Pindu, in Santo Domingo, and Cóndor, in La Vega. There were also Duarte, in San Francisco de Macoris, and Santiago, in Santiago de los Caballeros. The players in these clubs were mostly from Spain and other European countries, although there do also seem to have been some Brazilians involved.

Under President Trujillo in the 1950s, there was an expansion of football and the Dominican Soccer Federation was established. New clubs were founded with strong Spanish links. The French, Portuguese and the English also seem to have had a role in this expansion, although the details are hard to establish. Only one team in the Federation, Club Refor de San Cristóbal, featured Dominican players at this stage.

It was the Bolivian teacher Quispe Mendoza who set about encouraging Dominicans to play football. He made the game popular in schools and working-class areas. Mendoza also began promoting the game to women and taking on those who deemed football a male preserve. By 1967, the republic was ready to play its first international against neighbouring Haiti. The resulting 8-0 defeat showed that there was still some ground to make up if football was to match baseball in the country.

The country joined FIFA in 1959, but has yet to qualify for a World Cup. However, in 2012 they did qualify for the Caribbean Cup and in January 2021 they drew in a friendly with Serbia. There is now a professional league and enthusiasts are hopeful that this will turn out stars for the future.

Ecuador

It may seem obvious, but the name Ecuador is the Spanish for Equator. Bearing this in mind, it is not surprising that the capital, Quito, is only about 40km from the line.

Football was slow to arrive and develop in Ecuador compared with elsewhere in South America. This may have been because Britain had much less influence in the country than it did further south in Chile and Peru.

Britain did leave its mark, with William Cowley giving the Galápagos Islands names such as James, Charles and Albemarle, and there was, of course, Darwin's work there. However, the Galápagos were not to become the birthplace of Ecuadorian football. There was also some early Albion shooting on Ecuador's soil, but this was a unit of British and Irish volunteers, who helped Ecuador fight for independence from Spain, not a football team.

However, Guayaquil Sports Club, Ecuador's first football club, was established in 1899 in the busy port city of Guayaquil. It was set up by Juan Alfredo Wright and his brother Roberto, who had been introduced to the game while at school in Britain. They had tried it again when they stopped in Lima on their journey home to Ecuador and played with Union Cricket Club.

The game proved popular in Guayaquil, where trade provided links with Europe and America. By 1903, there were four more clubs in Guayaquil: Club Sport Ecuador, Asociación de Empleados de Guayaquil, Libertador Bolivar and Unión. By 1906, there were also clubs being founded in the capital Quito, like Olmedo and the interestingly named Gladiator.

By 1912, football was sufficiently established for both Wright brothers to start for Guayaquil in their first match against rivals Quito. It was a triumph for Guayaquil. The local newspaper that reported the match may have put the players' positions in English

– back (left) and forward (right) – but there was little other evidence of British influence.

One fascinating aspect of British involvement in football in the country is the career of Pedro Alberto Spencer, who played for both Ecuador and Uruguay. He was born in Ecuador but his father was a British Jamaican. He began his career playing in Ecuador for Everest but also turned out for Peñarol in Uruguay. He won eleven caps with Ecuador and five caps for Uruguay. While he became the first Ecuadorian footballer to score at Wembley, at the time he was playing for Uruguay. He scored the consolation goal in a 2-1 defeat.

Antonio Valencia of Wigan Athletic and Manchester United is one of the talents from Ecuador who has played in Britain.

Ecuador have yet to win the Copa América and although they have qualified for three World Cups, 2002, 2006 and 2014, they only got beyond the group stage in 2006. The Ecuador women's team has also struggled somewhat to make a huge impact at international level. This is unsurprising as there is still no professional women's league in Ecuador and the league itself was only established in 2013. They did, though, manage to reach the 2015 World Cup final in Canada, guided by a very young coach, Vanessa Arauz León.

Egypt

For many Brits, Egypt suggests visions of pyramids and pharaohs. And the national team is actually known as the Pharaohs and there is also a Saudi-backed Pyramids FC in Egypt's Premier League.

Britain occupied Egypt in 1882 to safeguard its commercial interests in the Suez Canal. And with the Brits came football.

In the 1890s the Army organised both a Regimental Challenge Shield and a Cairo Football Challenge. Some of the games played in this period were restricted to Brits, some were played in front of Egyptians, and in some Egyptians actually participated. The upper echelons of Ottoman Egypt shared many of the same interests as the Brits.

In 1903 British and Italian railway engineers working in Cairo teamed up to organise Cairo's first football team, El Sekka El Hadid SC. It still exists today. By 1911 both of Cairo's great rivals had started: Al-Ahly Sporting Club, founded by student Omar Lotfy with financial assistance from Alfred Mitchell-Innes, and Kasr El-Nile Club, which went on to become Zamalek, begun by Belgian George Merzbach. From the start Al-Ahly fielded an all-Egyptian line-up, while the future Zamalek was also open to foreign players.

Egypt soon even had its own football hero, Hussein Hegazi, who debuted for an English professional club, over a century before Mo Salah. Like Salah, Hegazi was very fast and a goal scorer. Son of an Egyptian cotton farmer, he learned to play football at school. In 1911 he moved to England to study engineering at University College London. In London he played for Dulwich Hamlet. He also played a game for Fulham and scored for them before deciding his loyalties lay with Dulwich. In 1913 he moved on to Cambridge University. He must have been some athlete, as at times he appears to have played for the university in the morning and Dulwich the same afternoon.

Hegazi returned to Egypt in 1914. He played for Al-Ahly, and the club that would become Zamalek. He also played for Egypt at both the 1920 and 1924 Olympics, becoming the oldest Olympic goal scorer (before being replaced in that status by Ryan Giggs in 2012). His name lives on in Hegazi Street, Cairo.

In the First World War, the strategic importance of Suez led the United Kingdom to declare a protectorate and impose martial law. This was, not surprisingly, unpopular and support for a more independent Egypt grew.

Egyptian football emerged from the First World War with a national competition. The Sultan Hussein Cup began in 1916 for both British and Egyptian teams. Between 1916–17 and 1919–20, the winners were British Army teams. From 1920 all winners were Egyptian and the clubs that would become Zamalek and Al-Ahly triumphed.

Between the wars, Egyptian football set records. In 1920, Egypt became the first African nation to enter the Olympic football competition. In 1924, they defeated both Hungary (3-0) and Sweden (5-0). In 1928, they reached the semi-finals before being eliminated by Argentina.

In 1934, Egypt became the first African side to play in a World Cup finals. British influence continued with a Scottish manager James McCrae. Sadly for Egyptians, their team was eliminated in the first round, but at least they were there.

The Pharaohs have a proud record in the Africa Cup of Nations. They have been champions seven times and runners-up three, including in 2022. They have been to the World Cup three times so far. At club level, Al-Ahly and Zamalek both still have formidable records.

Egyptian women's football has made somewhat slower progress. In their first international game in 1993, Russia defeated them 17-0, but there is now a domestic league and the Cleopatras have qualified twice for the Africa Women Cup of Nations.

El Salvador

Its name means The Saviour in Spanish, and El Salvador is the smallest and most densely populated of the Central American countries.

The first recorded game in the country did actually feature what seem to have been British players. On 26 July 1899, on the

Campo de Marte in Santa Ana, there was a game between teams from Santa Ana and San Salvador. The local team won 2-0 and had a Roscoe in defence and an H. Butter in the forward line, while San Salvador featured H. Downie, F. Drew and Pilkington in attack. The Brits may have been merchants as the British controlled the shipping trade on the west coast of Central America after the Spanish withdrew in 1821. They could also have been sailors either from merchant ships or the Royal Navy, as both were frequent visitors to the area.

Just over twenty years later, football had developed in the country to the extent that it was ready to take on the world, or at least Costa Rica.

There is no agreement about the score in El Salvador's first international match, in 1921. It wasn't recorded in the local press and historians are divided between those favouring a heavy 7-0 Costa Rica win or those arguing for a more modest 3-0. Among those playing for El Salvador was civil engineer José Alcaine, who went on to build the Olimpico Stadium. Other players went on to set up the Hércules Sports Club, El Salvador national champions in the 1930s. By this stage most British involvement seems to have ended, but the professions of the players and their ambitions suggest they were part of a wealthy class, who probably dominated the sport at this stage.

It was not until 1928, in their fourth international match, that El Salvador scored a goal. Gustavo Marroquín made up for lost time by putting five past Honduras in a friendly. The following year, El Salvador appointed a manager. They chose an American, which shows how American influence had largely replaced that of the United Kingdom in this area by then.

However, like neighbouring Honduras, El Salvador is perhaps best known in terms of international football for its involvement in the 1969 Football War. (There is a narrative of events leading up to the war in the chapter on Honduras.) Both teams were competing to be the first Central American team to qualify for a World Cup. After games in both countries there was a decider in Mexico, won by El Salvador. This was followed by a Salvadoran invasion of Honduras.

The war was perhaps not really about football. Some historians have tried to rename it as the 'War of the Dispossessed' in reference to the large numbers of Salvadoran poor who had settled in Honduras but then found themselves being forcibly evicted from their land and the country. It was the Salvadoran National Assembly that started the idea of the Football War when they passed a resolution condemning the Honduran government for retaliating against Salvadorans due to the results in recent football games.

This announcement predated the final match and the actual match in Mexico was comparatively peaceful. There were no cards shown on the field, and chants of 'Murderers' aimed at Honduran players by Salvadorans was the closest it got to violence.

In the end, El Salvador would be, thanks to their victory over Honduras, the first Central American team to play in a World Cup finals, but it was a chastening affair. They were defeated in all three group games, by Mexico, Belgium and the Soviet Union.

El Salvador would next qualify for a World Cup in 1982. Qualification itself was a major triumph for a small country emerging from another conflict, this time a terrible civil war. In Spain, Luis Zapata scored El Salvador's first World Cup goal and celebrated accordingly. Unfortunately, it was only a consolation in a record-breaking 10-1 defeat by Hungary. The agony and the ecstasy of World Cup football. Further defeats against Argentina and Belgium saw El Salvador fall at the group stage once again.

El Salvador has had some success in regional competitions.

Success for the women's national team has often been hard to find.

Equatorial Guinea

At the time when football was spreading across Africa, Spain was the colonial power here, and it is probable that the Spanish were involved with the introduction of football to the area.

Some of the major club names today like Real Rebola and Atlético Malabo reflect this Spanish heritage. However, football seems to have come comparatively late to the country, and racist attitudes among officials and administrators during the colonial period may have impeded the sport's development.

The country became independent in 1968, the Equatoguinean national team played its first international in 1975 and Equatorial Guinea joined FIFA in 1986.

Considering how a small a population the country has, it has achieved quite a lot of football success. Equatorial Guinea have been to the Africa Cup of Nations on three occasions, and reached the quarter-finals in 2022. The women's national team qualified for the 2011 Women's World Cup, and have won the Africa Women Cup of Nations twice.

On the domestic side, one of the more successful clubs recently has been the interestingly named Leones Vegetarianos (Vegetarian Lions).

The father of Arsenal legend Lauren came from Equatorial Guinea.

Eritrea

In 1890, the Italians proclaimed the establishment of a colony in a coastal region of Africa to the north of Ethiopia. They called it Eritrea, a name derived from the Greek word for 'red' because it is on the coast of the Red Sea. Football, therefore, got from here to the country not directly, but indirectly via Italy. There were clubs being formed there in the 1930s, with the first football championship taking place in 1937–38.

The Italians also built the Cicero Stadium in the capital Asmara, which is still used for football today. It is not named after the famous orator of the first century BC, but instead in honour of Francesco Cicero, an Italian entrepreneur who was more famous for selling furniture and running a lido with a restaurant and piano bar.

By the time of the first football championship there, though, Italian Eritrea did not have long left. In 1941, a decisive victory by British and Allied forces over the Italians at the Battle of Keren saw Eritrea come under British administration, where it remained until 1951. No doubt, as elsewhere, the British soldiers and administrators brought their footballs with them. Red Sea FC, one of Eritrea's most successful clubs, was founded in 1945 during this period.

In 1952, a federation was formed between Ethiopia and Eritrea, but in 1962 Ethiopia extended its control over the country. A long guerrilla war followed, with the Eritrean Liberation Front demanding independence from Ethiopia. Eventually, in 1993, after a referendum, independence was internationally recognised.

During the period under Ethiopian control, some Eritrean players, like Italo Vassallo and his half-brother Luciano, played for Ethiopian sides and the Ethiopian national team.

Eritrea were runners-up in the 2019 CECAFA (Council for East and Central Africa Football Associations) Cup. The women's team played their first international in 2002.

However, recent years have seen a number of instances of Eritrean international footballers fleeing the oppressive situation that now exists in the country.

Estonia

The most northern of the trio of Baltic states, it would be fair to say that Estonia is not one of the world's leading football nations. Even in the Baltic Cup, which is just for Lithuania, Latvia and Estonia, Estonia hasn't done that well. Well, the weather can be pretty cold and there is competition from other sports. The cup is perhaps the world's oldest international tournament, having started in 1928, and is still (after a break between 1940 and 1991 when the three countries were under Soviet control) running today.

There are, of course, despite all that, still plenty of people in Estonia enthusiastically playing men's and women's football today, and it seems to have been us Brits who took the sport there.

In the late nineteenth century the area was part of the Russian Empire, but the Baltic was also a major trading area for British ships seeking, among other merchandise, timber. It seems that some of the British sailors involved brought footballs with them in the late nineteenth century and introduced the locals to their game. The locals liked it, or at least enough of them did to start forming clubs.

By 1912, a number of teams, including SK Tallinna Sport and Viljandi JK Tulevik, had taken to the field. The First World War would follow, then a period of independence, then a period as part of the Soviet Union, and finally independence again, but the Estonians would never lose their love of football.

Among Estonians particularly in love with the game, we should mention goalkeeper Mart Poom, capped many times, many times the country's footballer of the year, and also a man who, in his career, has guarded the goal for a few English sides.

Eswatini

This is the country that used to be called Swaziland, and is probably still better known by that name to a lot of people in Britain. It is a small country, mostly surrounded by South Africa, but with a border with Mozambique in the east.

The country was a British protectorate when football arrived there. The first clubs seem to have been formed in the 1950s, and some of the best-known teams have names that reflect the British heritage of football in the country. There are, for example, the Mbabane Highlanders, the Manzini Wanderers and Milling Hotspurs. One of the major sports venues in the country is the Prince of Wales Stadium in Mbabane.

There are some other great club names in Eswatini, too, but football can be a cruel sport, and it's a bit sad and brutal to read of clubs with names like Gege Happy Stars and Eleven Men in Flight being actually relegated.

Internationally, the men's team came third in the 2021 COSAFA (Council of Southern Africa Football Associations) Cup and the women's national team has had some recent good results, including beating Angola and the Comoros.

Ethiopia

So who, in 1944, were the first winners of the first Ethiopian football league? Yes, it was a British team.

In 1935, Mussolini, in a hurry to build an Italian overseas empire to match those of the ancient Caesars, invaded Ethiopia. The Ethiopians fought bravely, but there was a limit to what they could do militarily against modern weaponry, and a few months after the Italians invaded they entered the capital, Addis Ababa.

Something the Ethiopians could do against the Italian invasion, however, was play football.

The Italians had brought footballs as well as weapons with them. Saint George happens to be the patron saint of Ethiopia as well as England and a few other places. The Saint George Sports Club of Addis Ababa and its football club became something of a symbol of nationalist resistance to the Italians during their occupation, something the Italians attempted to counter by organising opposition both on and off the pitch.

The Italian occupation was not, however, to last long. In 1941, British and Ethiopian forces swept the Italians aside and liberated Addis Ababa. Emperor Haile Selassie returned to his people.

By 1944, Addis Ababa was ready for a proper football competition. Five teams took part, representing some of the capital's key communities at the time, with Ethiopian, Italian, Greek, Armenian and British teams involved. Saint George represented Ethiopians, but the British team from BMME, the British Military Mission in Ethiopia, took the title.

Since then, Saint George has gone on to be one of Ethiopia's most successful teams. And Ethiopia went on to compete in the first Africa Cup of Nations, in 1957, and to host it and win the tournament in 1962. The women's national team has also had some success in the equivalent tournament, taking fourth place in 2004.

Fiji

Fijians tend to be better known for their love of the oval ball, having quite a reputation in the world of rugby. However, yes, football did also arrive in Fiji while Britain was the colonial power there.

Not all the outside influences on early football, though, were British; some say it was French missionaries who introduced the game to Levuka in the late nineteenth century. And the Reverend Brother Mark, a Marist missionary from New Zealand, may have been the first to introduce football to Suva.

However, Britons were certainly in the mix somewhere. In the early twentieth century, for example, both HMS *Powerful* and HMS *Torch* landed football parties to take on local teams. Having said all that, both Navy teams allegedly lost.

Soon local teams were competing to win the Ricarnie Cup.

Despite Fiji's success on the rugby pitch, there is still plenty of passion there today for football. In 2018 the women's national team, after beating Papua New Guinea 5-1 in the semi-finals, made it to the final of the OFC (Oceania Football Confederation) Women's Nations Cup. Sadly for Fiji, New Zealand were their opponents in the final and New Zealand won 8-0.

Finland

Yes, it's cold there in winter, yes, ice hockey is big there, yes, they were at the Euros in 2021, and, yes, we gave them football.

One account has British sailors arriving at the coastal city of Turku in the 1890s bringing football. Another version specifies English sailors, merchants and businessmen as starting football in Finland at the same time. So there at least seems to be pretty much agreement on the timing and the involvement of sailors from the UK.

In Finland there are clubs that seem to have been founded in the 1880s, like OLS Oulu and Helsingin Ponnistus, which went on to have football clubs, but these are multi-sports clubs, and the football element seems to have arrived later. Helsingin Ponnistus, for instance, was mainly a gymnastics and athletics club in its early days. The club has also played bandy, which, it turns out, is sort of hockey on ice with a ball, rather than actual ice hockey.

By 1906, there was a national football competition, and in 1907 the Football Association of Finland was formed. In 1912, Finland went to play football at the Olympics in Sweden. There, Great Britain won the gold medal, and Finland fought it out with the Netherlands for the bronze. Well, when we say 'fought it out', it wasn't really that close; the Netherlands beat them 9-0 with Jan Vos scoring five times. Still at least they didn't do as badly as Germany. Austria beat them 5-1 in the first round.

After a promising early start in Finland, though, football seems somewhat to have lost out to ice hockey. One of the major football stadiums in Finland, where both the country's major club and the national side have played, only has about 10,000 seats.

However, the Finland men's national team did finally make it to the Euros, in 2021, and the women's national team reached the semi-finals of the Women's Euros in 2005.

Among Finns who have done their bit for football in Britain we should mention Sami Hyypiä and now Teemu Pukki.

France (plus Overseas Departments and Regions)

Yes, we gave the beautiful game to La Belle France.

Football first arrived, at the Normandy port of Le Havre, in 1872. Rev. George Washington (interesting name) and a group of Oxbridge-educated expats set up Havre Football Club. At first the game they played was a mixture of football and rugby. The club's light and dark blue strip combined the colours of Oxford and Cambridge.

In 1873, Havre FC crossed the Channel to play an international game against Portswood Park Football Club in Portsmouth. Both clubs were also cricket clubs, but Havre opted for a football match. This may have been a mistake as they were heavily defeated.

Brits spread football by founding sports clubs in Paris. In 1890, Standard Athletic Club was formed, with a crest featuring the British Royal Standard. The following year, White Rovers began, with William Sleator as treasurer. Sleator imported corner flags and goalposts from England, but had to sweet talk customs officials to allow their entry to France. The first game, against a YMCA XI, attracted a crowd of just ten.

By 1894, six Parisian clubs were competing for a trophy donated by James Bennett Jr, publisher of the *New York Herald*. Standard AC defeated White Rovers 2-0 in a replayed final. The majority of players were Brits, but the following year a French outfit, Club Français (they thought long and hard about that name), became champions. Football was very small-scale in France at this stage. And it had serious competition.

The penny-farthing was invented in France in the 1860s and by the 1870s there were semi-professional races. Chain-driven, geared bikes encouraged the popularity of cycling, and the Tour de France began in 1903. Cycling was the sport for working-class spectators, but the wealthy French preferred rugby. In 1882, students in Paris set up Racing Club and in 1883 Stade Français emerged. Rugby also spread in Toulouse and south-west France.

However, some in France had big ideas about football, and in 1904, FIFA, the Fédération Internationale de Football Association, was formed in Paris. The driving forces were Robert Guérin, a journalist for *Le Matin*, and Wilhelm Hirschman from the Netherlands. This was something of an achievement as by 1914 France did not yet have a national football association or national league.

The First World War boosted the popularity of football in France. It spread across the country and thrived, as the country organised and modernised, to win the war. Cup competitions were staged to improve morale. The British Army, the Catholic Church and cycling authorities all held competitions. The most significant and long-lasting of these was the Coupe De France. Started in 1917 by Henri Delaunay with forty-eight clubs, it was based on the FA Cup.

Women's gymnastics club Fémina Sport began playing football against schoolboy teams and women played an exhibition match in front of a large crowd before a France–Belgium international in 1918.

Football emerged from the war as France's most popular spectator sport. In 1919, the various French sporting authorities united to form a single body, the French Football Federation (FFF). It even included two women's clubs, Fémina and En Avant. In the 1920s women played a series of matches against celebrated English side Dick, Kerr XI. The games were staged in both England and France in front of sizable crowds.

Perhaps France's biggest contribution to world football was the World Cup. Until 1928, the Olympics was also a football world championship. There was tension between the amateur ideals of Pierre de Coubertin and the Olympic movement and FIFA, which favoured an open competition. Jules Rimet, president of FIFA, and FIFA secretary Henri Delaunay proposed a World Cup competition in 1930 with Uruguay as hosts. The honour was Uruguay's because they had been the victors at both the 1924 and 1928 Olympics. The famous small gold trophy was named after Rimet. France was eliminated at the group stage in Uruguay and in the end never got its hands on the trophy. In 1970, it was given to Brazil for their three victories.

French football turned professional in 1933. In the 1970s the French government put money into improving training and sports facilities and the fan base began to expand. By the 1980s Canal Plus had brought TV money into the game and club sponsorship increased. In 1984, France also had a talented manager, Michel Hidalgo, and a squad including Michel Platini. On home soil Les Bleus defeated Spain to become European Champions. Then in 1998, Aimé Jacquet led his squad to World

Cup victory in Paris. Les Bleus have now won two World Cups and two Euros, and France has become one of the world's great football nations, even though the French Club game has yet to achieve much European success.

A bunch of talented players have crossed the Channel from France to play some amazing football here. They include Thierry Henry, Nicolas Anelka, Patrice Evra, Marcel Desailly, David Ginola, Patrick Vieira, Paul Pogba and, of course, the one and only Eric Cantona.

The women's game was banned by Vichy France during the Second World War, but it re-emerged in the 1960s with occasional games in Reims and Alsace. FIFA marks an unofficial World Cup in Mexico in 1971 as the first international for French women. What about games against Dick, Kerr Ladies though?

Today, France has a professional women's league, has hosted the 2019 Women's World Cup and been a regular quarter-finalist at both the World Cup and Euros. We look forward to seeing them in action in England in 2022.

The French overseas territories have contributed to the success of Les Bleus by providing some star players. In the Caribbean, Lilian Thuram, one of France's most capped French players, came from Guadeloupe, and Florent Malouda came from French Guiana.

In Martinique football began after the First World War, and tiny Saint Martin only got its first proper clubs in 1970. Neither has, so far, produced any French stars.

French Guiana, situated between Brazil and Suriname in South America has, in some senses, a bit of an identity crisis. It's a French territory but some locals support Brazil and others France. So there's a good chance somebody is going to win.

Réunion is an island situated off Madagascar, and gave France and West Ham Dimitri Payet. In 2020, their team

Saint-Pierroise enlivened the Coupe de France by reaching the final thirty-two.

Tahiti and New Caledonia are both FIFA members and compete in the Oceania group. Tahiti has 146 clubs with over 11,000 players. In New Caledonia club football started in 1933. New Caledonian Christian Karembeu found fame with Les Bleus in both the 1998 World Cup and 2000 Euros.

Gabon

Football came to Gabon via France, rather than directly from Britain.

France was the colonial power in Gabon in 1897 when a certain Owandault Berre allegedly turned up with a football in his bag and brought the sport to the country. By the 1920s, matches were taking place and clubs were being formed.

Gabon became independent in 1960 and the national men's team has qualified numerous times for the Africa Cup of Nations. The women's team, however, has yet to match the success of the men's.

There doesn't seem to be much (or, perhaps, any) evidence of British involvement in the introduction of football to Gabon. However, Gabonese contributions to the game in Britain have included, of course, those of a certain Pierre-Emerick Aubameyang.

The Gambia

The Gambia played its first international match in 1953 as British Gambia, and that gives a pretty clear indication of how football in the country began.

The part of the African coast in which The Gambia is situated was valuable to European merchants for slaves, gold and ivory. The Swedish, Portuguese, Dutch, French and British all competed for power there and the British won. No doubt British military personnel and colonial officials brought their footballs with them to the region in the late nineteenth and early twentieth century.

Among the early teams in The Gambia were military outfits including Royal Navy and RAF teams. There was also a Hotspur FC. It's unclear exactly when some of these teams were formed, but they do seem to have been in existence by 1940.

When Brits talk of 1940 they tend to talk of Dunkirk and the Battle of Britain. However, it was quite a significant year in The Gambia, too.

The fall of France in that year, and the subsequent agreements signed between the Vichy regime and the Nazis, meant that much of the northern part of the Atlantic coast of Africa was now controlled by a government sympathetic to Britain's enemies. The Gambia found itself surrounded by unfriendly Vichy French territory.

In September 1940 a British naval task force attempted to install General de Gaulle and a Free French administration in Vichy-controlled Dakar, to the north of The Gambia. The initial peaceful attempt to persuade the French authorities to switch to de Gaulle failed, and fighting ensued in which both British and French ships were damaged and personnel from both countries killed. The task force eventually withdrew and the French bombed Gibraltar in retaliation.

The Gambia was for some time, therefore, a somewhat lonely Allied outpost on the coast. However, at least they had football and football clubs to help keep them going.

The country became independent in 1965 but kept the passion for football. In 2021, The Gambia qualified for the Africa Cup of

Nations finals for the first time ever and, in January 2022, they reached the quarter-finals.

Modou Barrow has played for both the Gambian national team and a number of sides over here.

In 2016 Fatim Jawara, who had played for the Gambia national women's team as goalkeeper, tragically drowned in the Mediterranean while trying to reach an Italian island from Libya by boat.

Georgia

Georgia has a rather similar flag to England. It's white with a red cross on it – the main difference between the two being that the Georgian one has four little red crosses between the arms of the big red cross. This similarity is not perhaps surprising since England and Georgia have a patron saint even more similar than their flags. Both share St George.

However, somewhat confusingly, while the US state of Georgia is definitely named after a George (our King George II, as it happens) the origins of the country's name are controversial – particularly since the Georgians have another name for their country, Sakartvelo.

Fortunately, there does seem to be some agreement where Georgia (the country) got its football from, and, yes, that is the Brits.

Poti is a port on the Georgian coast, associated by some with the story of Jason and the Argonauts. Sometime in the first years of the twentieth century, ships turned up bearing, not ancient Greek warriors, but English sailors who brought with them, instead of helmets, and shields, footballs. The locals liked what they saw and Georgian football was born. It soon spread to the capital, Tbilisi, and British soldiers are reported to have played against the locals in the period after the First World War, during the British military intervention in the Caucasus.

At the time of football's arrival, Georgia was part of the Russian Empire, and it then, after a brief period of independence from 1918, became part of the Soviet Union. Joseph Stalin was not, in fact, Russian. He was Georgian.

The country regained its independence in 1991. Georgians love football and there is fierce competition in the domestic league, but internationally they haven't had vast amounts of success.

Georgia play their home matches in a stadium that used to be named after Lenin (who wasn't Georgian) and was then named after Boris Paichadze. He grew up in Poti only a couple of decades after the English sailors had arrived with their footballs, became a leading star of Soviet football, and has been voted best Georgian player of the twentieth century.

Germany

Let's be honest, any victory for England over Germany at football is, for an England fan, sweet. The success of Gareth Southgate's team at the 2021 Euros ended fifty-five years without a win against the Germans in international competitions. In those fifty-five years Germany picked up three World Cups and three European Championships.

Germany's history with the beautiful game is, however, much more complex than this list of successes might suggest and, yes, it all started with the Brits.

Britain had strong German links in the nineteenth century. Queen Victoria married a German prince, middle-class Germans sent their children to British public schools, and British sailors and merchants were regulars in German ports. Consequently, British ball games began to appear there in the 1870s.

In 1872, Edward Ullrich helped students at Heidelberg College Rowing Club play some form of football in the winter. Two years later Rev. Bowden started Dresden English Football Club and by 1875 there was enough football taking place there for Oxford University to go on a football tour of Germany.

In the late 1880s clubs began to appear in Hamburg and Berlin. Sports Club Germania in Hamburg, which went on to become Hamburger FC, was founded in 1887. In Berlin, teenager Paul Jestram and his three brothers formed BFC Germania 1888. BFC Germania is the oldest German club still playing under its original name.

Two other Berlin clubs soon appeared and in 1890, the German Footballers' Union played a championship in Berlin, which BFC Germania won.

The Franco-Prussian War had led to German unification in 1871. The proud (and big) new nation of Germany wanted to compete with Britain in Africa and in building dreadnoughts, but, to begin with, it was not so sure about football. Some German clubs chose specifically German names to emphasise their nationalist credentials.

The German Footballers' Union (BDF), taking an aggressively nationalist stance, decided it did not want to accept foreign players, so a rival Deutscher Fussball und Cricket Bund began in 1891 with eight clubs. Viktoria Berlin 89 won the first two championships. Some clubs fielded all-British sides but others featured a mix. In 1892 English FC Berlin, despite its name, had German, Dutch, Danish and Australian players.

The year 1900 saw the start of the Deutscher Fussball Bund (DFB), a nationwide football association, and the German Army and Navy both took up the game. Football spread down to the lower middle class, who had time to play. The working class did not yet have sufficient free time to take an interest in the game. By 1914, football was becoming a respectable German sport.

The standard of football in Germany before the First World War was comparatively low. A German team that toured England in 1896 played four games and conceded forty-six goals without reply. By contrast, ten years later, the strictly amateur Corinthians toured Germany, scoring twenty-three goals in two games against BFC Germania and FC Victoria Hamburg.

To improve the standard of football, some Germans opted to import British coaches, and William Townley led FC Karlsruhe to the championship. England striker Steve Bloomer took charge of Berlin Britannia in 1914, while Fred Pentland had control of the German Olympic team. The First World War saw both Pentland and Bloomer interned at Ruhleben alongside many other British footballers. Football became a method of maintaining their mental health for many Brits detained there and thousands of games were played. Unsurprisingly, Pentland declined the offer of continuing to work with the German team after 1918.

Mass support for football emerged in the 1920s, but it remained an amateur game.

The Nazis saw the propaganda potential for football but the reality was, of course, unpredictable. Hitler turned up to watch Norway eliminate Germany from the 1936 Olympics. In Vienna, a game against Austria to celebrate the Anschluss ended in a 2-0 defeat. Between 1939 and 1942 Germany played thirty international games to maintain morale. However, in 1942 when Sweden defeated Germany 1-0 and against Slovakia the crowd marked a period of silence for the war dead by muttering, the game was pretty much up.

In 1954, West Germany won the World Cup. A country that had been defeated, partitioned and whose infrastructure had been destroyed, came out of international isolation to become world champions. The team, managed by Sepp Herberger and captained by Fritz Walter, embodied the spirit of the new nation: hard-working, modest and anxious to escape Nazi shadows.

Hungary started firm favourites that year and did indeed beat West Germany 8-3 in the group stage. However, victories against South Korea and Turkey took the Germans through. Wins against Yugoslavia and Austria led to a final rematch against Hungary. Down by two goals in the first half, West Germany eventually won 3-2. A German legend, 'the Miracle of Berne', emerged. Some claim Hungarian star Puskás was injured. Others point to the revolutionary new German boots with screw-in studs. Adi Dassler, founder of Adidas, had made his first fortune.

Germany's post-war economic miracle was accompanied by a football miracle. German wealth powered football triumphs. Professional football finally arrived in 1963 with the creation of the Bundesliga. While Germany doesn't have as many European club champions as England, Spain or Italy, Bayern Munich are six-time Champions League winners and have also held all four European cups. The Premier League has German talent like Jürgen Klopp and Thomas Tuchel managing top clubs. Skilful players have starred at leading clubs with, for instance, Jürgen Klinsmann at Spurs, Michael Ballack and Antonio Rüdiger at Chelsea, Mesut Özil and Jens Lehmann at Arsenal and Leroy Sané at Manchester City.

In 1927, Lotte Specht began a women's football club in Frankfurt, only to be forced to play against men's teams as there were no other options. There are reports of women's games at German universities in Munich and in Berlin during the 1920s. The Nazi regime ended these experiments with its message that women were mainly for 'Kinder, Kirche, Küche' ('Children, Church, Kitchen'). Some conservative social attitudes outlived the Nazis and in 1955 the DFB threatened to ban any club that allowed women to play. It was not until 1970 that the organisation recognised the women's game.

Progress has been rapid. German women won the World Cup in 2003 and 2007 and were runners-up in 1995. They have won the European Championships eight times (but not in 2022). The club game is thriving, too. Wolfsburg have won the Champions League twice and appeared in five finals in the last decade.

Ghana

On the flag of Ghana is a prominent Black star. The Ghana men's national football team is nicknamed the Black Stars, and that seems fair enough, since they have one of the most distinguished track records in football in Africa, including winning the Africa Cup of Nations four times and losing five other times in the final. In 2010 they made it to the quarter-finals of the World Cup. Ghana has also hosted the Africa Women Cup of Nations in 2018 and has regularly done well in it.

As in so many other countries, it seems to have been British sailors who first kicked a football around in this region, and introduced the locals to the fun of the world's greatest sport. That happened in the late nineteenth century, in what was then the British colony of the Gold Coast.

However, by the time the sport was getting organised in the country of his birth, a Black star from there was already delighting crowds over here with his talents on the football pitch. Arthur Wharton had come to Britain in 1882 to train as a missionary, developed a talent for football, and found himself playing professionally, as a goalkeeper, for Preston North End, Rotherham Town and Sheffield United. Wharton left football in 1902, and by that time the inhabitants of the Gold Coast had already fallen in love with the sport.

By 1903, encouraged by their Jamaican-born headmaster, a group of twenty-two pupils of the Cape Coast Government Boys' School had formed the basis of Excelsior, the first football club in the region.

On Boxing Day that year, one half of Excelsior took on the other half in a match at Victoria Park, and other demonstration matches across the region followed. In 1911, the oldest team still playing in Ghana, Accra Hearts of Oak Sporting Club, was founded by Moffat, Nettey Okrau and Bruce Tagoe, and by 1920 there were enough teams in existence to form the Gold Coast Football Association, which would later become the Ghana Football Association.

The governor of the Gold Coast at the time was Sir Frederick Gordon Guggisberg. Born in Canada, he had been commissioned as an officer in the Royal Engineers, and had finished the First World War as commander of the British Army's 100th Brigade. He was also a keen sportsman, and in 1922, he inaugurated a football league, with the winner, which that season was Accra Hearts of Oak, taking the Guggisberg Shield.

In the 1950s, Stanley Matthews himself would play a number of exhibition games for Hearts of Oak.

Connections between football in Ghana and football in Britain are still strong. Plenty of Ghanaian stars, including, for instance, the mighty Michael Essien, have followed in Arthur Wharton's footsteps to play their sport here, while English football has plenty of fans over there. Berekum Chelsea are one of Ghana's leading teams, and pretty much the entire town of Juaben are Aston Villa fans.

Greece

How could we not start this section with the glory that was Greece at the 2004 Euros?

England went out in the quarter-finals against host nation Portugal, after yet another tragic (for us England fans) penalty shoot-out. Greece, having qualified second to Portugal in their group, beat France 1-0 in their quarter-final, the Czech Republic

1-0 in the semis and then took on Portugal in the final. Despite Greece having already spoiled the host's tournament by beating them 2-1 in the group stage, you could still somehow never believe that, on the big stage of the final, the Greeks would pull it off against the Portugal of Scolari and Ronaldo. But they did! Such is the delight of football and the delight of Greece in 2004.

The Greeks, of course, have given us a lot culturally, like democracy, philosophy, and Homer (the poet, not Simpson). They even had an ancient ball game called *episkyros*, and an ancient carving shows a naked Greek bloke apparently bouncing a ball on his thigh. However, in reality the game seems to have been more like rugby. Modern football, it certainly wasn't. That came to Greece from, yes, us.

Actually, Britain had quite a lot of significant contact with Greece in the nineteenth century. We had given assorted assistance in the fight for Greek independence from the Ottomans, including sending them Byron and helping destroy an Ottoman and Egyptian fleet at the Battle of Navarino. And we had been running Corfu and a few other Greek islands under the name of the United States of the Ionian Islands.

In 1863, HMS *Marlborough*, flagship of our Mediterranean Fleet, and HMS *Trafalgar* happened to be at Piraeus, the port of Athens, and teams from the two ships are said to have played a game of football according to Eton rules. However, it was on 29 January 1866 that the first game of anything like proper football seems to have been played in Greece. Again, the Royal Navy were involved, this time against a scratch team of locals in Corfu, shortly after we had handed the island over to the Greek government. We had given up the island, and we apparently lost the football match as well.

By the early 1890s, Brits in Athens were regularly playing football with assorted others, and Greeks in Turkey were taking to the football pitch, too. Soon the inhabitants of the mainland of Greece developed their characteristic passion for the game.

In 1906, the Intercalated Olympics were held between the 1904 and 1908 full games. A semi-final between a team from Athens and a team from Thessaloniki ended in a brawl, and the Athenians were then beaten by a Danish team 9-0 in the final.

Some of the great Greek clubs were established well before the First World War. In 1908, for instance, Panathinaikos was founded. They had a British coach, John Cyril Campbell, and a goalkeeper, Konstantinos Tsiklitiras, who won medals in the then Olympic sports, standing long jump and standing high jump – useful skills for a goalie.

Since then, Greece has never quite acquired sustained super-power status in the world of football (and the women's national team has often struggled) but Greek football has certainly had its moments.

In 1971, Panathinaikos, for instance, would tread Wembley's turf in the European Cup final against the mighty Ajax. Ajax won 2-1. Greek players have contributed to British football. And that win in 2004 is still one of football's epic underdog success stories.

Grenada

It's a country that has mainly kept out of the world news head-lines, except, of course, over the US invasion of the island in 1983. And it has mainly kept out of the world football headlines as well but plenty of people still love the sport there.

Football came to the Caribbean island early in the twenti-eth century when Grenada was part of the British Empire. As elsewhere in the Empire, educational establishments proved key in the early development of the sport. St George's Grammar

School opened on the island in 1885. In 1910–11 the school was given a new name and a new home and soon the Grenada Boys' Secondary School football team was taking to the pitch.

Shortly after that, other clubs came into existence and in 1924 the Grenada Football Association was created and a league was formed. One of the most successful Grenadian clubs in recent years has been Queens Park Rangers. That's Queens Park Rangers Sports Club of Gouyave, not the one here.

The men's national team, the Spice Boyz, have been runners-up in the Caribbean Cup several times, and have qualified for the CONCACAF Gold Cup three times. The women's national team are, of course, the 'Spice Girlz'. No, not those ones.

Arthur Wharton, perhaps the first Black professional footballer anywhere, came to England from Africa (see Ghana), but his father was from Grenada. And Grenada international Jason Roberts had a long career in English football with various clubs.

Guatemala

Guatemala may have got its name from Guhatezmalha, which means 'Mountain of Vomiting Water', referencing the large number of volcanoes in the area. It lies at the northern end of Central America, with Mexico to the north and west, Belize and Honduras to the east and El Salvador to the south. It is perhaps better known over here for its fruit, sugar and coffee than the quality of its football but there is still plenty of passion there for the world's greatest sport.

The first ball game played in the area was the Mayan Pok-Ta-Pok, where it is suggested human sacrifice was sometimes connected with the ritual. You can make many criticisms of football today, but human sacrifice at the end of the match isn't one of them.

Football was imported to Guatemala from Britain by Guatemalan boys returning from an education in Britain. One of the popular institutions seems to have been St George's College, Weybridge, where the Aguirre Matheu brothers, Carlos and Jorge, studied. It was this family that went on to help start the Hércules Club in 1910. Another popular venue for Guatemalan students was Crystal Palace Engineers School. Other Guatemalans attended Brighton College and the English Naval Cadets Academy.

The first football match was played in Guatemala City, in 1904, at Villa Linda field. Guatemala FC took on Olympic FC, which was based in the same city. Olympic FC won the initial game. The same year the two teams competed for the Copa Centroamericana (now the CONCACAF Nations League), where they played each other ten times. Guatemala ended up as the first champions, winning six matches and drawing one.

The following year the pair were joined by Gay SC and by 1911 there were more clubs competing, like Corinto, Gay SC, Guatemala FC, Hércules, Michigan, Ohio, Olympic FC, Sport, Standard and United. Some of the team names clearly indicate the strength of American influence in the area.

League football in Guatemala is a bit of a duopoly. Since the game went professional in 1942, the two Guatemala City-based clubs, CSD Comunicaciones and CSD Municipal, are almost neck and neck in championship wins.

Guatemala got its first taste of international football when it hosted the Centenary Games in 1921. This was an Olympic-type sports festival to celebrate the centenary of the independence of Central America from Spain. It also suited Guatemalan political ambitions as the country attempted to unite the countries of the region. Guatemala defeated Honduras 9-0 but Costa Rica beat them 6-0 in the final.

At an international level, Guatemala has somewhat struggled to establish itself in the world of football. While it has qualified for three Olympics, 1968, 1976 and 1988, it has yet to qualify for the World Cup. Now, however, that Guatemala has a chance to rebuild after the civil wars that it suffered in the late twentieth century, perhaps it will experience more international success in the future.

Guinea

In 1898, French military forces captured local leader Samory Touré. His defeat was a key stage in the French establishing control of what is now Guinea, a country on Africa's Atlantic coast.

By the 1920s, under French rule and influence, football clubs were being established in the area. In 1951, what would become one of Africa's great clubs, and the three-time winner of the African Cup of Champions Clubs, Hafia FC was formed. And seven years later, in 1958, Guinea declared itself independent from France under Ahmed Sékou Touré, who traced his descent from Samory Touré.

Guinea were runners-up in the 1976 Africa Cup of Nations and have reached the quarter-finals a number of times. Naby Keïta of Liverpool has also played for the Guinea team.

The women's team started their proper international career with matches against Nigeria in the 1991 African Women's Championship (now the Africa Women Cup of Nations). They lost twice, but due to the early stage of development of the competition, that was in the semi-final.

Guinea-Bissau

This country is next door to Guinea on Africa's west coast. Before independence it was called Portuguese Guinea and it is now named Guinea-Bissau because its capital is Bissau. As you can guess from the name Portuguese Guinea, Portugal was the colonial power here and it seems likely that football came to this country via that route rather than directly from Britain or any Brits.

The names and history of some of its oldest and best-established clubs clearly show that Portuguese heritage. For instance, Sporting Clube de Bissau was founded in 1936, as a local version of Sporting Clube de Portugal, Sporting Lisbon. Similarly, Sport Bissau e Benfica was founded in 1944, as a local version of, yes, you guessed it, Benfica.

The national team has qualified a few times for the Africa Cup of Nations.

Women's football has made rather slower progress.

Guyana

Guyana is situated to the east of Venezuela, and when you know that Guyana used to be British Guiana, it won't come as a huge surprise that, yes, we brought football there.

It was already being played in the nineteenth century and by 1902 the Guyana Football Federation had been formed, as had the first club. Founded in the capital Georgetown, it was, unsurprisingly, called Georgetown FC.

By 1905, British Guiana were playing internationals, or at least *an* international. Trinidad and Tobago beat them 4-1. However, it would be fair to say that, after making such an early start at football, much earlier than many countries, Guyana's progress on the international stage has been slow and at times controversial.

At least there has been plenty of passion (plus some controversies) in the domestic league over the years, where some of the teams have names that show that British heritage, like, for example, Buxton United. In addition, many players with Guyanese heritage have found success abroad.

It's important to mention here two of the earliest Black footballers in British football.

Andrew Watson was the son of a Scottish planter, Peter Miller Watson, and Hannah Rose, a local woman in British Guiana. In his distinguished football career he scored a string of firsts, including being the first Black player to win the Scottish Cup, and the first Black captain of an international team, when he captained Scotland.

Willie Clarke, whose father came from British Guiana, was the first Black professional player to score in the English football league.

And Guyanese heritage is still producing talented footballers. Today there are players such as Otesha Charles, who has played for a number of English clubs as well as the Guyana national women's team.

Haiti

Footballers in Haiti have had a lot to put up with that their counterparts in most other countries haven't. For instance, there was the horrific 2010 earthquake, during which many stadiums became temporary homes for those who had seen their own houses destroyed.

And in the early twentieth century, when so many other countries were taking to the football pitch for the first time, Haiti was going through a period of huge political instability. Between 1911 and 1915 the country had six presidents, each of whom ended up dead or in exile.

Then, in 1915, US President Woodrow Wilson, worried about Haiti's debts to American banks, sent in the marines. Any footballs the American troops brought with them were presumably of the oval, American kind, and the US then occupied the country until 1934.

In fact, all in all, it's fairly impressive, in some senses, that anybody in Haiti managed to organise national football development at all. But they did.

A football federation was formed in 1904, although it's not clear how many matches were actually played in the years after that. In 1905 or 1908 (sources vary) Union Sportive Haïtienne of the capital, Port-au-Prince, took on Athlétique de Port-de-Paix, and won 1-0.

By 1925, though, Haiti was ready to tackle the world of international football. Sort of. It played three matches against Jamaica and lost all of them.

France was the colonial power in Haiti in the eighteenth century and it's probably fair to say that British influence on the development of football probably came mostly via that route rather than directly.

But we can't talk about Haitian football, of course, without mentioning that 1974 goal. Haiti had qualified for the World Cup in Germany, and they were up against mighty Italy with the Italians' star goalkeeper, Dino Zoff, unbeaten in twelve matches. After all that, Haiti's Emmanuel Sanon dodged past Zoff and scored. OK, Italy won in the end, but still, what a goal!

The women's national team has had some success at regional level, too.

Honduras

In 2014, just before heading to the Brazil World Cup, England played Honduras. They were held to a disappointing 0-0 draw by a side that finished with ten men. Frankly, it wasn't a good sign for the tournament.

The Mayans were playing ball games at Copán as early as the

eleventh century, but perhaps the first version of association football played in Honduras featured, yes, the British.

The earliest recorded game was in 1896 in Port Cortes. British sailors made up the teams and crewed the ship that brought the football, but the influence of French immigrants in Port Cortes was also significant.

Football was already being played in neighbouring British Honduras at this stage. It is likely that British sailors working either in the banana trade or shipping hardwoods would have played the game in harbours along the Caribbean coast of Honduras.

The game was popular first with the Honduran wealthy, some of whom were educated in Europe or Britain. However, it was also encouraged by the Honduran government. In 1906 a Guatemalan professor, Miguel Saravia, was hired to teach football at a school in Tegucigalpa, the capital city. Interest in football continued to grow and by 1920 the sport was more popular than baseball.

The first professional team, Club Deportivo Olimpia, started in 1912 as a baseball club, which makes a change from the more usual combination of cricket clubs taking up football.

By 1935, there were sufficient teams to form a national association, and in 1946 Honduras joined FIFA. They qualified for the World Cups of 1982, 2010 and 2014.

However, the most extraordinary event linked with Honduran football is, of course, the Football War of 1969.

In the 1960s there were disagreements between Honduras and its smaller neighbour, El Salvador. Large numbers of poor immigrants had crossed from El Salvador to Honduras looking for a more prosperous life. While the El Salvador government supported this migration as it eased competition for land, it increased the same problem in Honduras and the government set about a programme of forced repatriation. The borderlands between the two countries became lawless, with gangs dispensing summary justice. It was against this backdrop that the two countries found themselves playing for the big prize of qualifying for the Mexico World Cup.

The first game was in Honduras, where the visitors had to endure a noisy and disturbed night before the match and Honduras emerged with a 1-0 victory. By the time of the second game in El Salvador the anger had increased. Inside the stadium, Honduran supporters were pelted with water bombs filled with urine and the Honduran national flag was burned and replaced with a rag. El Salvador eventually ran out 3-0 winners. Unfortunately the aggregate score was not used and a decider was required.

The game was hosted in Mexico City and was a very close affair. El Salvador were leading 2-1 but Honduras scored a late equaliser to send the game into extra time. El Salvador then scored and qualified for the World Cup.

On the day of the game, El Salvador broke off diplomatic links with Honduras because of attacks on its citizens. On 14 July it launched airstrikes on Honduras and invaded the country. The war only lasted seventy-two hours before supplies ran low and a ceasefire was negotiated. Although football was not the real cause of the war, it was the spark that started it and it was a real war that killed many, not a metaphorical one.

On a more positive note in 2014, when Honduras qualified for the World Cup, the BBC decided that La Ceiba, just along the Honduran coast from Port Cortes where the sport was first played in the country, might, in some sense, be the football capital of the world.

The idea was that enthusiasm for the game in this small town of 100,000 inhabitants was such that it had provided 30 per cent of the Honduran squad. This included some playing for British clubs like Maynor Figueroa from Hull City, Wilson and Jerry Palacios from Stoke City, and Arnold Peralta from Rangers in Scotland.

Women's football has progressed somewhat more slowly but the national team did beat Belize 8-0 in 2014.

Hungary

It's definitely a country with an intriguing football history.

Loads of people, for example, know that Hungary was the first national side that was not from Britain or Ireland, to defeat England at home, when they slaughtered them 6-3 in 1953. Less well known is that Hungary also played a key role in developing modern football in Latin America and in Italy. And, fascinatingly, at the centre of Hungarian footballing influence was the English coach Jimmy Hogan.

When it comes to the question of who first brought a football into Hungary, various names are suggested. Whoever really did bring that first football, there was initial confusion about the rules of *Angol labda* (English Ball). László Kostovic, for instance, allowed his pupils to hit the ball with their hands due to a mistranslation of the rules.

In 1897, the well-established Budapest Gymnastic Club took up football, staging an exhibition match between Reds and Blues. They also played a game against the Englishmen of Vienna Cricket Club in front of a large crowd. Other gymnastics clubs and educational institutions soon adopted the new sport.

In Budapest, Ferencváros, which became one of Budapest's major clubs, was founded in 1899, and their big rivals MTK Budapest came into being in 1901.

That same year twelve clubs established the Hungarian Football Association and a championship, and in 1907 Hungary joined FIFA, which was possible because the country had been granted some independence within the Austro-Hungarian Empire in 1867.

The new clubs, eager to learn about the 'beautiful game', invited English clubs to tour. In 1902, Oxford University played four games against Budapest sides. The dark blues scored loads of goals, without conceding a match to their hosts. The Corinthians toured in 1904, leaving behind a Corinthian Cup to encourage the spread of the game. Manchester United visited in 1908, winning convincingly but being attacked by spectators who were angered by their physical play. In the world of Budapest football, it seemed clear to many that what they needed was British coaches.

By 1914, Ferencváros had won eight of fourteen championships playing a kick and chase, English-type game. Their rivals MTK decided that, in order to compete, they would adopt a 'Scottish' passing game.

In 1904, Edward Shires, a typewriter salesman and skilled footballer, joined MTK when he moved from Vienna. Through Shires, MTK acquired a new manager, John Robertson, who had played for Rangers and been player manager at Chelsea. MTK won the championship in 1913–14.

It was also Shires who helped MTK pick up William Hogan during the First World War. Hogan had been coaching in Vienna in 1914 (see Austria) but was interned when war broke out. During the war Hogan was transferred to Budapest, where he became manager of MTK and led them to three championships. Hogan believed possession and mastery of the ball was the key to successful football and he saw these as skills that he could teach. At MTK he had the facilities to develop his ideas and as the senior players were often on active service, he had access to young players.

The immediate impact of Hogan's arrival was that, in newly independent Hungary, MTK remained champions until 1925 and Hungarian football changed from kick and rush to a short passing game. However, it would not be until after the Second World War, with the 'golden team' of the 1950s that the long-term impact became clear.

Between the wars, the greatest football achievement for Hungary was reaching the World Cup final in Paris in 1938, defeating Dutch East Indies, Switzerland and Sweden before losing to defending champions Italy. Elsewhere, players like Dori Kürschner and Béla Guttmann in Brazil and Emérico Hirschl in Argentina spread the Hogan message to Latin America. In Europe, Hungarian coaches spread it to Serie A in Italy.

After the Second World War, Hungary became a communist state in 1949, and the Hungarian Socialist Workers Party could see the propaganda value of a successful football team. Their coach, Gusztáv Sebes, understood this role. The Hungarians were blessed with spectacularly talented players. Ferenc Puskás was the star, but there was a strong supporting cast. Sebes provided a safe environment for his stars where they could experiment with their football and enjoy a celebrity life without fear of criticism.

At the Helsinki Olympics in 1952 they won the gold medal. They also wowed the crowds, scoring twenty goals in five games. In 1953, they humiliated England at Wembley with that 6-3 win, and to emphasize their superiority they won a return game in Budapest 7-1. Sebes explained the victories by crediting the football introduced by Hogan. Poor Hogan was a hero in Hungary but a lot less popular with some in England.

Hungary started the 1954 World Cup as favourites. In Budapest the victory celebrations were already organised. In the final in Berne, though, they lost 3-2 to West Germany after squandering a two-goal lead. The parties were abandoned. The golden team were sent for retraining but there were to be no second chances. The 1956 Hungarian Revolution led stars like Puskás to escape Hungary and find a career with Real Madrid.

In many senses, Hungarian football is still trying to recreate the glories of the early 1950s.

The women's team has yet to qualify for a major championship but the game is growing. In 2019 Budapest played host to the Women's Champions League final. Hungarian Zsanett Jakabfi has an impressive haul of trophies from her time with Wolfsburg in Germany, winning six Bundesliga titles and two Champions Leagues.

Iceland

The year 2016 was the first time that most of us here really became aware of football in Iceland. Before that, the country had been a place vaguely connected with glaciers, locations for car ads, very long surnames, the Cod War, and the occasionally amusing confusion with the shop of the same name.

However, on 27 June 2016, Iceland gained a whole lot of new associations, particularly for us England fans. It was England in the last sixteen of the Euros against a team then ranked thirty-fourth in the world, representing a nation of just 330,000 people. To most England fans it seemed like it should be easy.

When Wayne Rooney scored a fourth-minute penalty, we thought it might be. But two Iceland goals destroyed that illusion, and when desperate England efforts on the pitch and desperate England fans' willing off the pitch failed to produce an equaliser, we had to acknowledge there was a new force in European football. Admittedly they haven't quite lived up to the promise of 2016 in recent years but few England fans would underestimate them again.

In the hours after the match, as the full, sad reality sank in, some of us may even have regretted exporting the world's greatest sport to Iceland in the first place, but football is such a positive force, it's hard to remain bitter about the past for too long. Plus there is that traditional British admiration for the underdog. Not, obviously, when your team is actually playing an underdog (unless we are at least three goals ahead of them), but at some stage before the match and at some stage after it.

Brits do seem to have played a significant role in introducing football to Iceland. The earliest club was founded there in 1899. It is Knattspyrnufélag Reykjavíkur ('the Ball-kickers of Reykjavik'), often abbreviated to KR Reykjavik or even just KR. It is both the oldest and the most successful club in Iceland. It won the first Icelandic championship, in 1912, and it is still winning them in the twenty-first century. Somewhere in the origins of KR seem to have been some Scots. A Scottish engineer called Frank McGregor is said to have been instrumental in the founding of the club.

Another Scot mentioned is a printer called James Ferguson. In 1895, he seems to have moved from Glasgow to Reykjavik to work for the publisher of a newspaper. Ferguson was an enthusiastic athlete, and formed and led a group called the Reykjavik Gymnastics Club. Part of the club's remit was ball games, and Ferguson taught a number of boys, including the publisher's sons, how to play football. When the team that would become KR Reykjavik was founded in 1899, it included a number of Ferguson's pupils.

In addition to their success in the Euros in 2016, Iceland also qualified for the 2018 World Cup, and since 2009, the women's national team have qualified for four Women's Euros in succession. Plenty of Icelandic players have also displayed their talents with British teams, Gylfi Sigurðsson being one of the best known.

India

It's a big country with a big love of sport. True, it's another sport from Britain, cricket, where India has really excelled so far, but Indian football still has a long and distinguished history.

Perhaps the first football game was played in 1854 in Calcutta, where a Calcutta Club of Civilians took on the Gentlemen of Barrackpore. This predates the formation of the FA in 1863, and it is unclear precisely what rules were being followed, but there definitely was football of some description being played by Brits before 1858.

A rugby game between English and Scottish regiments was played at Christmas 1872. The trophy, the Calcutta Cup, is now awarded here to the winners of international matches between the two countries. However, more importantly for this book, the match also sparked the formation of Calcutta Football Club, one of the oldest clubs in India, which switched from rugby to football in 1894.

By 1900, football in India was thriving, and there were several clubs in Calcutta. The Indian Civil Service formed Dalhousie AC, workers in the jute mills made up a Trades Club and they were joined by sides representing Naval Volunteers, Police and Customs.

The Army saw football as a good method of keeping soldiers active and motivated. Sepoys, Indian soldiers serving in the British Army, were also encouraged to play. British regiments played in Madras (now Chennai), Delhi, Bangalore and major cities across the country.

In 1888, Sir Mortimer Durand, Foreign Secretary of British India, started a football competition, the Durand Cup, for Army units. It is the longest-running club competition outside the UK. Scottish units were particularly successful, winning all bar one of the tournaments pre-1900.

Brits started the Indian Football Association and the IFA Shield competition in 1893. By 1898, there was even a Calcutta Football League. Although there was the Rovers Cup in Bombay and the Portuguese had spread football in Goa, at this stage the sport remained mainly confined to Brits, mostly in Calcutta. However, that was already changing.

The All-India Football Association traces football among Indians to Nagendra Prasad Sarbadhikari. In 1877, Sarbadhikari was walking past the grounds of Calcutta FC (then still a rugby club) with his mother, when he was asked to kick a ball back that had gone astray. He returned the ball, but then bought his own. However, his English schoolmaster, a fan of proper football, was having none of that, got him a round ball instead and taught him to play with his friends. More widely, schools modelled on English public schools helped spread the new sport among the children of the Indian wealthy.

It is part of the genius of football that, even though it came from here, soon it becomes a part of the cultures that adopt it and it adapts to their needs. Some clubs were happy to model themselves on British clubs as mainly social and sporting institutions. However, others in India were keen to use football for political purposes as well.

Bhupendra Nath Bose, a lawyer, had formed Mohun Bagan, one of the oldest clubs in Asia, in 1889. It became a symbol of local identity. In 1911, Bagan defeated a British military team to win the prestigious IFA Shield. It was a major event in the progress of Indian football.

Another major advance came in 1940 when Mohammedan Sporting Club won the Durand Cup, the first Indian civilian club to do so.

One distinctive feature of Indian football at this time was that it was played barefoot, even when opponents wore boots. The

Indian football team at the 1948 London Olympics still mainly played barefoot.

In the period after independence, often thought of as the golden era of Indian football, India became a huge force in the Asian game. And in the football at the 1956 Olympics they came fourth.

Since then both men's and women's national teams have had significant successes in regional tournaments.

India now has a Super League, where Scot Owen Coyle has worked with Chennaiyin and Jamshedpur. The national team has recently had some help from English coach Stephen Constantine.

Indonesia

During the colonial period, Indonesia was occupied by the Netherlands, so a lot of early football influence in the area came not directly from us, but second-hand via the Dutch. However, we did play some part.

In 1896, for example, a Dutch team took on an English team in what was then Batavia and is now Jakarta, and we won 1-0 after one of the Dutch players had to retire hurt.

As elsewhere in the world, early football and early cricket were often linked. So, a Dutch club might play a visiting one at cricket in the morning and football in the afternoon.

Soon, however, the passion for football spread to the local population and as elsewhere the sport became a source of national pride, countering the influence of the colonial authorities. In 1930, PSSI, the Football Association of Indonesia was formed.

A team from the Dutch East Indies took part in the 1938 World Cup and contained both players of Dutch and local heritage. Hungary did beat them 6-0 in the only match they played, but at least they were there.

British boots were on the football pitch again in the country in the period following the Second World War and following the Japanese occupation. Photos and film show a team from the RAF taking on local civilians.

Today Indonesia has some long-established domestic clubs, with large and passionate fan bases. It has also had its moments in international football. Indonesia was due to host the 2021 FIFA U-20 World Cup, but that didn't happen because of the Covid situation.

In 2021, the Indonesia national women's team qualified for the AFC Women's Asian Cup for the first time in many years.

Iran

Iran versus USA in the 1998 World Cup was one of the great geopolitical grudge matches of world sports history. On that occasion Iran won. And, of course, the British and Iranian governments have not exactly been the best of friends in recent years.

From the Iranian point of view, a significant element in this has been resentment of past British political and military involvement in Iran in the middle decades of the twentieth century. Generally, however, few Iranians resent the fact that we did give them football.

British and Portuguese sailors may have played the game in Iran in the late nineteenth century, but details are rather scarce. However, as with some other countries, the development of the oil industry in the period before the First World War and the formation of Anglo-Persian Petroleum (now BP) gave a huge boost to the development of football, as oil workers arrived, bringing their footballs and football skills with them.

Some of the locals objected to men running around wearing shorts, but plenty of other locals were fascinated by the new sport.

In Tehran, a competition was started between British teams from the Embassy, Imperial Bank of Persia and the Indo-European Telegraph Company. Locals sometimes had to be recruited to make up numbers.

And the military played a part, too. For example, during the First World War British officers introduced the game to locals as part of their training for the South Persia Rifles.

Some schools also helped spread football. For instance, American Samuel Jordan made it part of the curriculum at the American College.

In the 1920s more locals took up the game. In the 1920s and '30s Iranian teams like Iran FC, Tehran FC and Tofan all won the Tehran League. When Reza Kahn became Shah in 1925, football became part of a programme of westernisation.

By 1948, Iran had a football association and was a member of FIFA. Iran qualified for the 1978 World Cup in Argentina. A 1-1 draw with Scotland earned them a point before elimination at the group stage.

Helping the development of Iranian football was Irish manager Frank O'Farrell, who led them to gold at the Asian Games and helped them qualify for the 1976 Olympics. Another Iranian hero was Alan Rogers, who managed the Tehran club Persepolis and led them to two league titles. Rogers was never a professional player but served in the Arctic convoys as a teenager in the Second World War, before running football competitions for Butlin's. This was enough to get him on an FA training course with Sir Walter Winterbottom, but not enough to find him a managerial post in England. After spells in South Africa and the USA, he ended up in Iran. His greatest achievements for Persepolis were in games against foreign opponents. A visiting Chelsea side were held to a draw, as were Manchester United and Stoke, while Newcastle were defeated.

The Iranian revolution of 1979 had a significant effect on football. Football clubs were nationalised, women were banned from attending matches, and attempts were made to censor TV coverage.

However, football did not die out, Iranians continued to play on the streets and in 1989 a semi-professional league restarted. When Iran qualified for the 1998 World Cup, crowds celebrated wildly on the streets.

Over the years, Iran has had some major success at international level, including winning the AFC Asian Cup three times, and qualifying for the World Cup six times.

Football is still a source of some dispute in Iran. Some conservatives fear the excitement and uncontrolled emotion of football, while some reformers see the game as an opportunity to gather and express their opinions.

Many Iranian women are keen football fans and there is now a women's national team and league. The women's kit includes head and full leg coverings.

Iraq

If you thought British troops have only been to Iraq in recent times you'd be very wrong. During the First World War, British troops fought bitter battles against the Turkish Army in what is now Iraq, and in March 1917, entered Baghdad.

The period following the British capture of the area and the end of the war saw the establishment of a Hashemite monarchy in the country but also a British administration over it that existed until 1932, and it was during this period that the foundations of Iraqi football were built.

British military personnel played football at their bases between themselves and also with local employees. Director of education Humphrey Ernest Bowman also encouraged football in schools. A match between two school teams was played in March 1918 and by 1921 there was a competition for school teams.

The exploitation of Iraq's oil fields would also bring in foreign workers with their own passion for the game. By 1923, the

Baghdad Football Association was arranging a wider football competition, with British club Baghdad Casuals playing a key role.

However, the passion for football soon became deeply rooted among the Iraqis themselves and, in 1931, a group of British-trained Iraqi air force personnel formed the oldest existing club, Al-Quwa Al-Jawiya, the Air Force Athletic Club. To great local excitement, soon after it was formed, the team played a match against a team from RAF Habbaniya – and won.

Despite this, British influence over Iraqi football remained a significant feature for a while. For instance, one of the most famous Iraqi footballers of all time, Emmanuel Baba Dawud, generally known as Ammo Baba, was born on the RAF base at Hinaidi, Baghdad. He learned to play the game at RAF Habbaniya, and by 1951 was playing for the RAF Employees (Assyrian) Club.

Ammo went on to become one of the best players in the Middle East, and then had a distinguished career as coach to the national team. Iraqi football saw its most tragic years when Saddam Hussein's vicious son Uday was in charge of it and tortured and abused players who displeased him. Despite all this, Ammo had the bravery on one occasion to refuse publicly to accept a medal from Uday.

Even with its tumultuous history, Iraq has had quite a lot of success at international level over the years. For instance, in 1986 they qualified for the World Cup, and in 2007 they won the AFC Asian Cup. The domestic game has seen plenty of fierce competition, too.

Ireland

In some senses there is an argument for not having an Ireland chapter in this book, because this is a book about how football got from the United Kingdom to the rest of the world, and when football took root in Ireland, all of Ireland was part of the UK. And still today, our links to Ireland are so strong that it feels to a great extent 'part of the family'. However, it is also very much an independent country with its own history and football culture, so this is the Ireland chapter.

Ireland had a long history of folk football. For instance, in 1518 the Archbishop of Dublin suggested fining assorted clerks for playing football. And the heritage of 'traditional Irish football' would be an element in the creation of modern Gaelic football.

Association Football in Ireland predates the partition of Ireland. John McAlery is usually recognised as the 'father of Irish football'. He organised an exhibition match between two Scottish teams, Queen's Park and Caledonian, at the Ulster Cricket Grounds in Belfast in 1878.

Ulster Cricket Club had already played a game in 1875 as part of a trial to decide whether the club should play football or rugby in the winter season. They chose rugby, which may have debarred this game.

A game was played in County Cork in 1877 between Lismore College and Penn's school. The game was fifteen-a-side and it is not clear whether it was football, rugby or Gaelic football.

A lot of early football was in Belfast, the industrial heartland of the north with strong links to Scotland. By 1880, a Belfast-based Irish Football Association was established.

In Dublin, the administrative centre of British Ireland, football was less popular. Rugby was already well established in Irish private schools before football arrived. Football also now faced competition from the Gaelic Athletics Association and Gaelic football. A set of rules for Gaelic football was created in 1885 and soon there were hundreds of clubs affiliated to the GAA. The game was popular with nationalists and attracted large crowds in rural communities. By 1905, the GAA imposed a ban on any of its members who played association football.

While Gaelic football and rugby slowed the development of football, they did not prevent it. In 1883, a Dublin Association Football Club was started with twelve men and a bearded, pipe-smoking goalkeeper. By 1884, there were five teams in Dublin, including one Scottish British Army team.

The British Army helped spread the game, but in doing so it turned some nationalists against it. Many national schools had neither a playing field nor even a playground. St Vincent College Castleknock was a notable exception. It not only played football but encouraged it by hiring a coach from the Army and even employed a former English international, Bob Holmes, to supervise the game. In 1892, Dublin University, Bohemians, Leinster Nomads, Montpelier and St Helens School founded the Leinster Football Association, affiliated to the Irish Football association. Soon after, Shelbourne and Shamrock Rovers, which still exist, were founded.

By 1914, Ireland was strong enough to win the British Home Championship, defeating Wales 2-1, England 2-0 and drawing 1-1 with Scotland. The team was led by Dublin-born Patrick O'Connell. Already, players from poorer parts of Ireland were heading to the professional game in England. O'Connell had joined Sheffield Wednesday before he played for Ireland.

As the First World War ended and the Irish War of Independence was fought, football in Ireland also split. A 1921 Irish Cup semi-final match in Belfast between Glenavon from Lurgan in the north and Shelbourne of Dublin ended in a draw. The replay should have been in Dublin, but Glenavon refused to travel south and the IFA rescheduled the match for Belfast again on the grounds that playing in Dublin was too dangerous. Shelbourne refused to travel again to Belfast and was thrown out of the competition.

Soon after that, football in Ireland was split between north and south. The Football Association of Ireland was formed in 1921 and was recognised by FIFA in 1923.

Ireland had its 'golden age' under the leadership of Jack Charlton. In 1988, Charlton led them to their first Euros, where they beat England 1-0 but failed to go beyond the group stage. In 1990, Ireland qualified for the World Cup finals for the first time and reached the quarter-finals. They were to qualify again in 1994 for the tournament held in the USA.

Many of Ireland's best footballers have left Ireland to find fame and fortune in England. A lot of great British sides have contained Irish players. There was, for instance, Johnny Giles at Leeds (1963–75). Liverpool had Steve Heighway in the 1970s and Ronnie Whelan in the 1980s, and Manchester United relied on Roy Keane in the 1990s and John O'Shea in the 2000s.

Irish footballers have also had an impact on the wider world, both as managers and players. James Donnelly led Turkey at the 1936 Olympics. Patrick O'Connell (already mentioned) won the Liga in Spain with Real Betis in 1935 and went on to manage Barcelona. After starring for Arsenal, Liam Brady won two Scudetti in Italy with Juventus. Anne O'Brien, who joined Stade de Reims as a teenager, was an outstanding player. In France she won three league titles, while in Italy she played for Lazio, Reggiana and Milan Salvarani and won six Scudetti.

Israel

This chapter looks at the development of Jewish football within the territory that would be British controlled under the Palestine Mandate and then, after 1948, looks at the game in the territory that became the independent state of Israel. The chapter on Palestine will consider Palestinian football within the territory that would become British controlled under the Palestine Mandate and then, after 1948, looks at the areas now recognised by some countries as the state of Palestine. In both stories, Brits played a central role.

Many sports associations were started at the start of the twentieth century in what is now the state of Israel, while it was still under Ottoman control. Many of these associations played some football, like the one founded in 1906 that became Maccabi Tel Aviv. The first newspaper report of a match was in April 1912 and it took place as part of the Rehovot Games. In 1913, gymnastics teacher Zvi Nishri published a book in Hebrew explaining how to play football. He was not a football fan, preferring individual sports, so the game must already have been popular. How these Jewish developments linked with the football spreading among Palestinians from missionary schools is not clear. Jews and Arabs were playing football, sometimes on the same pitch, before 1914.

Early in the First World War, Maccabi football club found themselves playing the Ottoman Army but from 1917, after British and Commonwealth troops seized control of the area, they played against the British Army.

The British recruited a Jewish Brigade in 1917 and many of its recruits were already footballers. The brigade had four squadrons, each with its own team. There were games between squadrons and a combined XI.

In the 1920s, after the League of Nations had assigned the territory to British control under the Palestine Mandate, more Jewish football clubs appeared. Some came from the Maccabi Sports Association, which became an umbrella organisation for many football teams. Maccabi, a Zionist movement named after Jewish rebel warriors, the Maccabees, who had fought to free Judea, also hoped to create a Jewish nation. Other clubs, founded by Maccabi's rival Sporting Association Hapoel (Workers), had a different message. They were a socialist club for the working class. Youth groups also formed teams.

The British tried to start local league and cup competitions. Unsurprisingly, British referees were accused of bias in their officiating.

Russian emigrant Yosef Yekutieli served as a PE instructor with the Ottoman Army during the First World War and took up a post with Maccabi afterwards. He was the driving force behind the formation of a Palestine Football Association in 1928 and joining FIFA in 1929.

British Police were the first league champions in 1932. Maccabi Tel-Aviv and Hapoel Tel Aviv won all the leagues thereafter.

Arab clubs formed a rival association.

Jewish football thrived and Austrian champions Hakoah Vienna visited in 1924 and 1925 to encourage Jewish football development. Maccabi Haifa toured the USA, winning five and drawing one of eleven games.

Since independence, Israeli football has inevitably been affected by the country's disputes with its Arab neighbours and the internal divisions in Israeli society.

Domestically, Maccabi and Hapoel teams have dominated. Maccabi Tel-Aviv have twenty-three league titles and Maccabi Haifa a further thirteen, while Hapoel Tel Aviv have eleven.

Israel now competes in UEFA groups, which makes World Cup qualification highly competitive. Nevertheless, Israel did qualify for the Mexico World Cup in 1970 and reached the quarter-finals of the 1968 and 1976 Olympics.

Unusually, Israel formed a women's national team in 1997 before it set up a national league. A women's league began in 1998 and has been dominated by ASA Tel Aviv, with eight titles, and Maccabi Holon, with six. The national team plays regularly but is yet to qualify for a World Cup or European Championship.

Israeli star Yossi Benayoun played some of his football in Britain.

Italy

Aah Italy, if there is a country in Europe you associate with sheer undiluted passion for the beautiful game, it's this one. And with passion has come experience and skill.

In Italy football is called *calcio*, which means 'kick'. Like many countries around the world, Italy had kicking games of various sorts long before association football. Calcio Fiorentino, for instance, was a ball game played in Renaissance Italy, somewhat similar to the folk football played in England. It's messy and quite violent. It's got few links to modern football, but in the 1920s nationalist dictator Mussolini made a big deal of it because it was Italian in origin, not British like the football that Italians love.

Football may have been first played in Italy by British sailors headed for India. The Suez Canal opened in 1869 and ships stopped, en route, in Genoa, Naples and Palermo.

The first proper clubs were started between 1887 and 1900 by a small, closely connected group of Swiss, British and Italian enthusiasts based in Turin, Milan and Genoa. These cities have been major forces in Italian football ever since.

Edoardo Bosio started Torino Football and Cricket Club in 1887, the earliest football club in Italy. Edoardo's family were Swiss but he was born in Turin and trained as an accountant. He was sent to Nottingham on business to work with Thomas Adams textiles, and here Nottingham Forest and Notts County had been playing since the 1860s. Bosio's main sport was rowing, but he found football a useful way of keeping fit in winter. He returned to Italy with footballs and his club used them to play in the winter, while in the summer they played cricket and rowed.

Football in Turin expanded slowly. In 1891, Bosio's club merged with Nobili Torino, a side that included the Duke of Abruzzi, to form Internazionale di Torino. Internazionale itself was then later taken over by FC Torinese. Bosio was still playing in 1900, when his goals helped Torinese to victory over Milan Football and Cricket Club, the future AC Milan.

Juventus, taking its name from the Latin word for youth, was formed by teenagers at the Liceo D'Azeglio in 1897. Its black-and-white-striped shirts came from Notts County, courtesy of John Savage, who played for Juventus in 1903. It was a breakaway group of Juventus players, financed by Swiss brewer Alfred Dick, who founded FC Torino in 1906, causing FC Torinese to collapse.

On the coast, Genoa Cricket and Athletics Club was started in 1893 by the British Consulate for the benefit of expats. In 1897, Dr James Richardson Spensley introduced football at the club. Its name consequently changed to Genoa Cricket and Football Club and they opened the club to Italians. In 1898, the club took on FC Torinese and lost 1-0. Soon afterwards the Italian Football Federation came to life and competitions began.

Milan Cricket and Football club was founded in 1899 by Herbert Kilpin and Alfred Edwards. Kilpin worked for Thomas Adams in Nottingham and came to Italy with Edoardo Bosio in 1891. An Italian fan from childhood, he formed a youth side named Garibaldi and became known as 'Il Lord' for his dynamism in midfield. He continued playing into his forties and led Milan to three championships. He liked whisky and he used to keep a bottle behind the goalposts. Until recently, Kilpin was a largely ignored figure and British Consul General Alfred Edwards got more recognition. Now it is Kilpin's face that features on the flags of AC Milan's 'Ultras'. Milan eventually dropped 'Cricket' from the name and Mussolini forced a change to AC (C for Calcio not Club).

In 1908, a dispute about whether Milan should focus on Italian players or field more Europeans led a breakaway group, 'brothers of the world', to establish Football Club Internazionale. In 1910, Inter Milan won its first Scudetto.

In southern Italy and Rome, football lagged behind developments in the more industrialised north. In Palermo, Ignazio Pagano established the Anglo-Palermitan Athletic and Football club in 1900. Pagano had been introduced to the game when his parents sent him to London and his club used to play against visiting sailors. In Naples, it was Cunard's William Poths who started Naples FC in 1905, with help from local Ernesto Bruschini.

Between 1890 and 1914, football spread rapidly through Italy. The first national championship in 1898 was a one-day knockout competition featuring four clubs from Genoa and Turin. Genoa won the first four titles with Spensley in goal.

The game spread beyond the big cities. Pro Vercelli fielded an all-Italian side to win five of six championships in 1908–13. Their secret: a young squad, possession football and practising set pieces.

International competitions appeared. In 1909 and 1911, Sir Thomas Lipton sponsored club tournaments in Turin. Both competitions were won by West Auckland, an amateur side from northern England with a team full of miners.

Although popular, the standard of football was quite low. Politically, Italians wanted control of their own game. In 1909, the IFF renamed itself Federazione Italiana Giuoco Calcio (Italian Federation of Football Players).

The First World War inevitably, as elsewhere, caused the death of some of the great figures of the local game. Spensley died during the war, allegedly shot by a German sniper while tending German wounded.

Between the wars, football thrived, despite some dubious refereeing decisions. There was at least one example of Mussolini's paramilitary black shirts stopping a game to intimidate the referee. In line with Il Duce's Italian nationalism, clubs dropped English names. Genoa became Genova and Internazionale became Ambrosiana. Serie A was formed as a national, openly professional league. Teams were allowed two foreigners but only one could play at a time. AS Roma was formed so the capital had its own team.

William Garbutt had played for Woolwich Arsenal and Blackburn Rovers before moving to Italy in 1912. He led CFC Genoa to the championship in 1915 before enlisting in the British Army. He rose through the ranks to become an officer and lived through both the battles of the Somme and Passchendaele. After the war he returned to Genoa to win two further titles and continued to work despite the Fascist restrictions on employing foreign coaches. With Roma he won a Coppa D'Italia and he led Napoli to third place in Serie A twice; a record for the club until Maradona arrived. He was interned in the Second World War. Italians still refer to managers as 'Il Mister' and Garbutt was the original 'Mister'. Over here, of course, in recent decades, since Gianluca Vialli, we have seen huge successes (with, of course, some failures) for a string of talented Italian managers.

In the 1930s, the Azzurri would win an Olympic gold and two World Cups. Italy also hosted the 1934 World Cup. Like Hitler, Mussolini saw the propaganda value of football and he made extensive efforts to publicise his version of Italy, from building new facilities to printing top-quality tickets. Transport to the stadium was free for Italians. The Austrian 'Wonder Team' began as favourites but lost out to the Italians in the semi-final. Vittorio Pozzo led the Italians to glory, and his secret weapon was using Argentinian players with Italian grandparents. He repeated the triumph in Paris four years later.

Women played football in Milan in the 1930s but there was opposition from social conservatives. In 1968, however, the Italian Women's Football Federation was founded. In 1970, the federation organised an unofficial world cup in Naples and Italy were the defeated finalists. Italy made a promising start to the European Championship in 1984 by reaching the semi-final and they were runners-up twice in the 1990s. Maintaining this standard has been problematic, but a fully professional league will help their prospects.

In many ways modern Italian football hasn't changed much from the early days. Juventus, AC Milan and Inter have dominated Serie A. Juventus have thirty-six Scudetti, with both Inter and Milan on nineteen. All have won the European Cup/Champions League. The Azzurri, current European Champions, won the World Cup in 1982 and 2006.

Graeme Souness and Trevor Francis played in Italy in the 1980s, David Platt and Des Walker in the 1990s, maintaining the UK connection. There are still passionate supporters and political intrigue. The main change is that British football now benefits from the skills and artistry of Italian footballers as well. There are far too many great Italian stars who have played here to name them all, but a few examples we have to include are Mario Balotelli, Roberto Di Matteo, Jorginho and Gianfranco Zola.

Ivory Coast

Ivory Coast, or Côte d'Ivoire, is, of course, one of Africa's great football nations. The national men's team has qualified multiple times for the World Cup and has won the Africa Cup of Nations twice. The national women's team qualified for the Women's World Cup in 2015 and came third in the Africa Women Cup of Nations in 2014.

The list of talented Ivorian players who have contributed so much to football in Britain is long, and includes names such as Didier Drogba, Emmanuel Eboué and the brothers Kolo and Yaya Touré.

The country was a French colony at one stage, but actually football enthusiasts from the British Gold Coast colony, now

Ghana, seem to have played a big part in introducing football in the 1920s.

Major clubs were being formed there in the 1930s and '40s – for instance, ASEC Mimosas, one of Ivory Coast's most famous teams, which then created one of the world's most well-known football academies, was founded in the capital, Abidjan, in 1948.

Ivory Coast became independent from France in 1960 and the Ivorian Football Federation was formed the same year.

Jamaica

Bob Marley was a huge football fan and loved a kick-about when he got a chance. Not only that, but his daughter, Cedella Marley, with her financial support, helped the Jamaican women's national team qualify in 2018 for their first World Cup, in France.

Football had an early start in Jamaica compared with some other parts of the Caribbean.

Already by 1883 the York Castle School XI was taking to the pitch, put there by one Rev. G.C. Hendricks. In 1893, the Kingston Cricket Club organised a football section, which became the first proper football club in Jamaica. By 1906, various teams were organising to compete for the Martinez Football Association Cup.

Sir Sydney Olivier (uncle of the rather better-known Laurence Olivier), who was a leading Fabian and governor of Jamaica from 1907 to 1913, joined in by supplying football trophies.

In 1910, the Jamaica Football Association (now Jamaica Football Federation) was founded, incorporating teams like YMCA, Railway, Lucas and St George's Old Boys. There were military teams as well.

By 1925, Jamaica was already playing international football, taking on a team from Haiti and beating them in three successive games.

Today Jamaica has thriving domestic football. And how can we discuss Jamaican international football without mentioning their win over Japan in the 1998 World Cup in France? That was a tournament that, frankly, wasn't much fun for either English or Scottish fans, but at least it gave the Jamaicans cause to celebrate. They had qualified for it after beating El Salvador, Canada and Costa Rica, all thanks to goals by Deon Burton. In Lyon, Theodore Whitmore put two goals in against Japan to secure victory.

And, of course, in addition to Burton's and Whitmore's performances over here, plenty of other Jamaican players and players with Jamaican connections have played a huge role in British football. John Barnes and Raheem Sterling are two obvious examples.

Japan

It's not all Sumo wrestling and martial arts in Japan. Having said that, it's not all football either. Baseball is actually the most popular sport, but football does have a lengthy history in the country.

Like China, Japan had its own ball game, *kemari*, which developed from the Chinese game *cujo*. It started in the seventh century and remained popular until the end of the sixteenth century. It was like hacky-sack, the aim being to keep the ball in the air, and it is still demonstrated in some spring festivals.

At the end of the nineteenth century, Japan was keen to develop links with Britain as it tried to strengthen its navy and modernise its economy. Football was recorded in 1871, less than a decade after the FA was founded. English teachers played the game with their pupils in Tokyo. In Kobe, European sailors including Brits played kick-arounds. A game in 1873 at the Imperial Japanese Naval Academy, organised by Canadian-born Lieutenant Commander Archibald Lucius Douglas, head of the second British naval mission to Japan, is recognised as the earliest modern football in Japan.

As trade developed, Brits established small communities in Japan and developed sports clubs. Scottish cricket enthusiast James Mollison founded Yokohoma Country and Athletic Club in 1868. Another Scottish fitness fanatic, Alexander Sim, founded Kobe Regatta and Athletic Club in 1870. In 1888, the clubs staged their first football fixture and Kobe won. Both teams still exist, the fixture is still played and there is a monument to Sim in Kobe.

Gendō Tsuboi spread football through schools by translating and publicising the rules. The 1902 Anglo-Japanese Alliance and Japanese assistance during the First World War improved links between the two countries even further. In 1918, the British ambassador, Sir William Conyngham Greene, and the embassy secretary, William Haigh, decided that helping Japan give its football a structure was one method of developing the friendship. The FA provided a silver cup to be used for a football competition based on the FA Cup. Haigh helped the Japanese form their own Football Association and in 1921 Emperor's Cup Tokyo FC won the first competition.

International football began in 1921, not with much initial success it has to be said. However, by 1930 Japan had joined FIFA and won a Far Eastern Competition, defeating the Philippines and drawing with China. Japan travelled to the 1936 Olympics, beating Sweden before being eliminated by Italy. Perhaps surprisingly, considering how socially conservative the country was at the time, some girls were being taught football at school prior to 1941.

The Second World War saw FIFA expel Japan and the Emperor's Cup was melted down for the war effort. After the war, football remained essentially an amateur sport. The best teams were sponsored by big firms like Nissan and Panasonic.

However, in 1993 the professional J-League began and has attracted some major foreign stars. Gary Lineker played for

Grampus Eight (Toyota) and Brazilian star Zico played for Kashima Antlers. The Antlers have now won six J-Leagues. In 2016, Antlers became FIFA Club World Champions, which shows how far standards have risen.

The Japanese Football Association symbol is a three-legged crow called a Yatagarasu holding a ball. This mythic creature guided Emperor Jimmu on his expeditions.

So far, Japan's football expeditions have not, however, led to a men's World Cup or Olympic title. Perhaps the biggest success was a bronze medal in the 1968 Olympics. However, Japan qualified for the last six World Cups and will be at the latest tournament in Qatar in 2022.

The Japanese women's team has, by contrast, had some major international successes, far outperforming the men. Japan became World Champions in 2011, defeating the USA in a penalty shoot-out. They were also runners-up to the USA in 2015. Now, there is a professional women's league, the WE (Women's Empowerment) League with eleven teams. Success breeds further opportunities.

Jordan

At the time when football first came to this territory, there was extensive British influence there and a significant British presence.

T.E. Lawrence, Lawrence of Arabia, had operated in the area during the First World War, assisting Arab rebels fighting the Turks. He probably didn't play football himself since he had something of a disliking for organised team sports, which he expressed in two articles he wrote before the war for his school magazine, attacking football and cricket. However, other Brits, including military personnel, businessmen and sailors, did bring their footballs to the entity then called Transjordan and formed clubs.

Amman was the main location of this early footballing development. For instance, the local British military command had its own team, which played in competitions, and in 1929 another British football club based in Amman, the Flyers, crossed the Jordan to take on players in the territory then controlled by Britain under the Palestine Mandate.

The locals began to notice and participate, and by the early 1930s, Jordanians were forming their own clubs. The Jordan Club began in 1928, followed by a Prince Talal club and others. Some were short-lived as they were reliant on Jordanian students, who were studying abroad, sometimes in Britain. In 1932, the club that would become one of the most successful in the country and, indeed, the region, Al-Faisaly FC – named in honour of Prince Feisal and known as the Blue Eagles – was formed.

In 1948, the creation of Israel and the accompanying fighting saw large numbers of Palestinians flee into Jordanian territory. From the refugee camps came Palestinian teams including Al-Wehdat and Al-Jalil. The Jordan Football Association itself was formed in 1949, but Jordanian football in the 1950s was a mixture of communities struggling to assert their identity.

Al-Faisaly FC dominated in the 1960s and '70s, adding to the prestige of the Hashemite rulers. However, by the 1980s Al-Faisaly's supremacy was under attack from Al-Wehdat.

Jordan have appeared in the Asian Cup four times, and have a good track record in football at the Pan Arab Games. Over the years, various Brits, including George Skinner in the 1960s and Danny McLennan in the 1970s, have coached Jordan's national team. Harry Redknapp had a brief time in charge more recently.

The national women's team have won the WAFF (West Asian Football Federation) Women's Championship on a number of occasions.

Kazakhstan

Not one of the more familiar countries to many British readers, but it is huge. In fact, it is the ninth largest country in the world. It is also said to be the largest landlocked country in the world, though that sort of depends on how you define landlocked since it has a long coast along the eastern shores of the Caspian Sea.

Even in the jet age, it is a long way from here, so in the era when we were exporting football to the world and travelling mainly by train, it was a *long* way from here and quite a long way from any part of the British Empire.

Nonetheless, it would seem that we did play a vital role in giving this big country the world's greatest sport.

There seem to be a number of versions of how it happened. In one, British merchants brought the game to Semey prior to the First World War. Another version is that local merchants who had seen the game in England brought it home to the region around the same time. There at least seems to be agreement on both merchants and Britain being involved somehow, and the time period.

The first clubs were already being formed there by 1913. One of the best-known Kazakh writers, Mukhtar Auezov, also turned out for Yarysh FC in the early twentieth century. During the First World War football became established in the area. Teams such as Olimp, Neptune and Yarysh were founded. The war also brought prisoners of war from the German and Austrian armies to Semey. These included skilled footballers, and games were played between locals and prisoners.

Semey is a city in eastern Kazakhstan that was known as Semipalatinsk during the period of Russian and Soviet control of the area. We gave Semey football, while the Soviets gave the area something a lot less appealing, a massive nuclear bomb test site, not a million miles from Semipalatinsk. During the Soviet period, Kazakh football was tied in with the USSR's football system.

It would be fair to say that Kazakhstan is not reckoned by most Britons as one of the major footballing nations; however, there has long been plenty of passion for the game there. And in 2002, the country took the geographically and politically interesting step of joining UEFA.

Women's football in Kazakhstan dates back to the Soviet era. Since independence, BIIK Kazygurt have dominated domestic football and have taken the opportunity to appear regularly in the UEFA Women's Champions League.

Kenya

When football came to Kenya, the country was still called British East Africa. And, in 1906, it is recorded that Mombasa FC took on The Boys FC, in a match arranged in honour of King Edward VII's birthday.

As in many places elsewhere in Africa, British missionaries played a major role in spreading this new sport among the locals. Scottish missionary Marion Stevenson was one of those who saw football as morally improving and regarded it as her duty to promote it. In 1909, in the first inter-school cup, a team from the Church Missionary Society in Kabete took on a team from the Church of Scotland mission in Thogoto. However, equally, as elsewhere in Africa, the locals would soon make the game their own.

Between the wars, local leagues, like the Mombasa League, were formed, and the Remington Cup tournament was introduced in which teams from different towns took part. In 1926, Kenya hosted (and won) the first Gossage Cup competition. This was donated and named for a soap manufacturer, and was later renamed as the CECAFA (Council for East and Central Africa Football Associations) Cup.

After the Mau rebellion of the 1950s, Kenya became independent in 1963. The same year saw the first season of the Kenya National Football League. That was won by the Nakuru All-Stars with the help of English football coach Ray Bachelor, who also went on to be the first coach of the national team.

One of the most notable and successful Kenyan clubs since then has been Tusker FC, named after a well-known beer.

The Kenyan men's national team has qualified for the Africa Cup of Nations a number of times and in 2016 the women's team made their debut at the Africa Women Cup of Nations. Kenyan football stars include Victor Wanyama, who has played for Celtic, Southampton and Tottenham Hotspur, as well as captaining his nation's team.

Kiribati

Kiribati is an island nation in the Pacific. It used to be called the Gilbert Islands until independence from Britain in 1979, and Kiribati, as it happens, is the local version of the name Gilberts. It also used to have territory on both sides of the international date line, which, obviously, used to cause a few problems.

Kiribati has, in some senses, despite Britain's links with the islands, not been particularly fertile territory for football. But then a lot of the football pitches there aren't fertile land either: they are coral sand. And it didn't help when Britain and the US used one of its islands (Kiritimati, or Christmas Island), as a location for experimentally exploding nuclear bombs, including hydrogen bombs, in the 1950s and early '60s. It's also possible that a lot of Kiribati won't exist too much longer since the islands are on average only a little above sea level, which, considering the situation with the world's oceans and climate change today, isn't good.

In reality, when you take all that into consideration, actually it's impressive how much football is played in Kiribati and with how much passion.

The locals first started playing organised football in the early 1950s and by the end of the decade village teams were competing with each other, even if the laws of football were sometimes only adhered to loosely.

Today there is a football league in which teams from various islands compete. And they have international men's and women's teams. Let's not dwell on the seventeen goals Papua New Guinea scored against Kiribati in one match, but let's instead pay tribute to the one Kiribati scored.

Korea, Democratic People's Republic of

This is the country usually known in Britain as North Korea. Of course, when you mention North Korea and football over here, you tend to end up discussing 1966, when North Korea made it to the quarter-finals of the World Cup, after beating Italy 1-0 at Middlesbrough's Ayresome Park.

Brits had already brought football to what is now South Korea by the end of the nineteenth century. Football seems to have been being played by assorted teams in Pyongyang, the capital of what is now North Korea, sometime in the first years of the twentieth century.

Certainly by 1921 there were a number of clubs in Pyongyang, and that year the All Joseon Football Tournament would see both northern and southern teams compete. In 1922, Muo FC from Pyongyang took the title.

After the Japanese administration was thrown out of Korea in 1945, the Democratic People's Republic was created in 1948.

North Korea has a domestic league, with one of its best-known teams being April 25 SC (named after the date of the creation of the original Korean communist guerrilla army). And, in addition to their success in 1966, the men's national team also qualified for the 2010 World Cup, and has reached the AFC (Asian Football Confederation) Cup a number of times.

The North Korea women's national team has also qualified for the Women's World Cup three times and has won the AFC Women's Asian Cup three times.

Korea, Republic of

This is the country usually known in Britain as South Korea. Of course, it has been one of Asian football's major forces, and, yes, we seem to have had a hand in introducing the South Koreans to the world's greatest sport.

The story goes that in 1882 HMS *Flying Fish* turned up in the port now known as Incheon. The ship was not the most war-like of the Navy's ships; it was a sloop that spent much of its career surveying. However, in 1882 it did manage to rescue some Japanese diplomats in trouble in Korea, and thereby earned the gratitude of the Emperor of Japan. At some point during its 1882 mission to Korea, the crew allegedly started playing football in the port. Whatever happened with *Flying Fish*, people do seem to have been kicking footballs in Seoul, now the capital of South Korea, at the Royal English School there, by 1896.

In the following years, the locals took an interest in this new sport, and by the 1920s were forming their own football clubs. In 1921, the All Joseon Football Tournament was started for all of Korea.

South Korea would see some rough times during the twentieth century, including Japanese occupation, during which football helped preserve Korean identity. And there was, of course, the bitter Korean War that would see British servicemen fighting, as well as sometimes kicking footballs around, on South Korean soil.

A passion for football remained strong among the South Koreans throughout it all. British sides including Manchester City, Dundee United and Coventry City played tour games in South Korea in the 1960s and '70s, and these helped keep the country in touch with the modern game.

South Korea has been to the World Cup many times and in 2002 they co-hosted it with Japan. They beat Portugal, Italy and Spain on their path to the semi-finals, only, when they got there, to see a seventy-fifth-minute Michael Ballack goal crush their hopes, as Germany defeated them 1-0.

The women's national team has been to three World Cups and in 2015 also made it to the round of sixteen.

Korean players, including, of course, the mighty Son Heung-min at Spurs, have also made a considerable contribution to football in Britain. Park Ji-sung, playing for Alex Ferguson's Manchester United, collected four Premier League titles and a Champions League medal.

Kosovo

If you were looking at the news at all in the late 1990s, you will already be aware that Kosovo had, to put it mildly, a somewhat complex history in the twentieth century (even today not all countries in the world have recognised it as a sovereign state) and the history of football there has its own complexities, too.

Austro-Hungarian troops probably played football in the parts of it where they were stationed in the First World War, and there is also a story that the first football in Kosovo arrived with a student who had come from Grenoble, in France, in 1919. However, football was well established in areas around Kosovo before 1914, so the real story may be even more complicated than that.

Certainly, in the period after the First World War, when Kosovo was part of the new kingdom of Yugoslavia, a number of major football clubs were founded. For instance, clubs were created in Gjakova and Pristina in 1922.

The Second World War followed, and then the Socialist Federal Republic of Yugoslavia was created, which broke up in the 1990s. When the Kosovo War ended in 1999, NATO forces, including British units, advanced into Kosovo. Inevitably this involved a certain amount of football. For instance, in August 2002, a BRITFOR team attempted to get revenge for a previous defeat by Pristina FC, but instead lost again.

Kosovo was accepted into UEFA and into FIFA in 2016, and the new member gave England some scary moments in September 2019 when the two sides met during the qualifying games for Euro 2020. Kosovo took the lead in the first minute and even though England then responded with five goals, Kosovo still managed another two before the final whistle. In November the same year, the women's team beat Luxembourg 5-0.

Arsenal player Granit Xhaka has family links to Kosovo.

Kuwait

Football came to Kuwait during an era of strong British influence there.

Sheikh Mubarak Al-Sabah looked to Britain to protect Kuwait from the Ottoman Empire and, eventually, it would became a British protectorate in 1918. It was officers and crew from the cruiser HMS *Fox* who played the first football game in Kuwait in 1902. Sheikh Mubārak also seems to have taken a liking to cricket.

There are further references to football in Kuwait in the 1930s. School students there were being taught the game by Palestinian teachers and formed a club. There are also reports of a game between an RAF armoured car unit and students in Kuwait in 1936. Football was being played both by Brits and Kuwaiti citizens but it wasn't yet organised.

By the 1950s, while still under the British protectorate, sports clubs like Al-Ahly Club, Al-Arabi SC, Al-Uruba and Al-Jazeera were formed with government funding. Full independence led to a major reorganisation of football, with the Kuwaiti league starting in 1961.

Many modern sides list their starting date from the formation of the league, even if they had played under a different name previously. Al-Jazeera, now called Quadsia Sporting club, Al-Arabi and Al Kuwait are the most successful clubs, each having won the league more than fifteen times.

Internationally, Kuwait has had a slightly mixed time. However, they did win the Asian Cup in 1980, and in 1982 they made it to the World Cup. On 25 June they were on the pitch against England in Bilbao. A Trevor Francis goal gave England a 1-0 victory.

Malcolm Allison, 'Big Mal', coached the national team in 1985–86. Maybe there is something about Kuwait and coaches who have 'big' nicknames, because 'Big Phil' Scolari was the coach in 1990. On 2 August 1990, Iraqi tanks thundered into Kuwait, starting the process that would lead to the Gulf War.

Women's football had a slow start in Kuwait but has made some progress.

Kyrgyzstan

The country is located between Kazakhstan and China. It seems to have been out of reach of any British merchants with a football in their luggage who may have made it as far as Kazakhstan or the far west of China in the late nineteenth and early twentieth centuries.

Imperial Russia had military control of much of the area at the time and, despite a revolt in 1916, Moscow's control continued in the Soviet era. Although there must have been games or kick-arounds before this, which presumably involved Russian merchants and soldiers, the Kyrgyz date their football from a match between a Bishkek team and a Kazakh team from Almaty (called Vemy at the time) played on 21 March 1921, making Kyrgyz football more than a century old. The Kazakhs won 3-1.

Development in the 1920s and '30s was slow, with little infrastructure. The Second World War, however, kick-started Kyrgyz football, as factories in the USSR were moved out of the way of the advancing Germans, and many football-loving Ukrainians and Russians suddenly arrived in Kyrgyzstan. After the war, Kyrgyz teams played in the Soviet leagues until Kyrgyzstan became independent in 1991 and established its own.

Frunze appears a lot in the list of names of Soviet-era football champions in Kyrgyzstan, since he was an early Soviet commander, born in the Kyrgyz capital Bishkek, and the Soviets thought it would be inspiring to rename Bishkek after him as Frunze. Not surprisingly, after the end of the Soviet Union, the locals decided they were not sufficiently inspired by Frunze (if they ever had been) to like their capital being named after him, and the city is now Bishkek again.

Football is now Kyrgyzstan's most popular sport. Dordoi Bishkek dominate the independent league, having been champions for the last four years and taking thirteen of thirty titles. In

2019, Kyrgyzstan defeated the Philippines 3-1 in the group stage of the Asian Cup and were regarded as heroes at home.

Women's football dates from the Soviet era, and a small league has operated in independent Kyrgyzstan.

Laos

It's probably fair to say that Laos is one of the countries in south-east Asia that the average Brit knows least about, and it's not exactly one of the better-known global football nations either. Nevertheless, there is still a great passion for the sport here and Britain has had a part to play.

Like Cambodia and Vietnam, Laos had a complex and tumultuous history in the twentieth century. It saw French colonialism, Japanese occupation during the Second World War, a guerrilla war against French rule, independence from France in 1953, then fighting between a royal government linked to the west and communist forces, resulting eventually in a communist victory in 1975. Laos is still a communist country today.

Somewhere in all that lot was football. It seems reasonable to assume that the French had a significant role in first introducing the sport to the country. The Lao Football Federation was formed in 1951 and Laos became a member of FIFA in 1952.

Laos played its first international in 1961, in which South Vietnam beat them 7-0. It wasn't a great start and Lao football wasn't going to get that much better any time soon – hardly surprising considering the wars in the country in the 1960s and '70s. Football got better established in the country in the 1990s, with the organisation of a new Lao domestic league, and in 1995 the Laos national team went to the Southeast Asian Games.

Since then, the Laos national side has had periods under two English coaches, Dave Booth and Steve Darby, and the women's team has also had a little success in regional competitions.

And, as in so many other countries in the world, even those very remote from Britain, the English Premier League continues to be a source of inspiration to ordinary Lao fans. In recent years they have organised their own fan football competition in which teams including Newcastle United, Queens Park Rangers and Swansea Lao fan clubs have all competed.

Latvia

Latvia is geographically the middle one of the three Baltic states.

In 2004, the year that underdog Greece won the Euros, underdog Latvia also made it to the tournament. Sadly for supporters of Latvia, there the comparison with Greece pretty much ends. To be fair, they were in quite a tough group. They lost to the Netherlands and the Czech Republic, but did manage to hold on for a goalless draw against Germany.

Football first came to Latvia in the early twentieth century and there are records of a match taking place in the capital Riga in 1906. It seems to have been expatriate Britons and Germans who brought the world's greatest sport to Latvia. Certainly it was people of those nationalities who founded some of the earliest football teams in the country, and that's pretty obvious from some of the team names. The Riga Football League was, for instance, won in 1911, 1914 and 1915 by, yes, Britannia FC.

Latvia won independence from Russia after the First World War and the Latvian Football Union was started in 1921. In 1922, Latvia took on Estonia for a 1-1 draw. Some of the early British influence on Latvian football continued. For instance, in 1927 Arthur William MacFerson, at one stage British Consul General in Latvia, helped found a new club in Riga. It was called Riga Wanderer, or Riga Vanderer.

The Soviet Union occupied Latvia in 1940, and then the Germans did. Latvia finally escaped Soviet control in 1991 and was free to resume its career in international football.

Latvia have a good record in the Baltic Cup. On the other hand, in November 2021, England women beat the Latvian women's team 20-0.

At one stage, Latvian striker, Marians Pahars, who made plenty of appearances for Southampton, managed the Latvian U-21 side.

Lebanon

The first football played in Lebanon was when it was still part of the Ottoman Empire, before the First World War. Teachers and students at the Syrian Protestant College in Beirut played against St George's School Jerusalem. While the Syrian Protestant College in Beirut was founded by American missionaries, it was a centre for the international community in the city, including Brits.

After the First World War, Lebanon, alongside Syria, was put under French control, and the arrival of more Armenians from Turkey, with its heavily British-influenced football in that period, helped organised football in Lebanon expand beyond expatriates and the wealthy.

For instance, Lebanese–Armenian Homenmen AA and Homenetmenen were already playing football in Beirut in the early 1920s, and soon other communities were taking up the sport as well. Al-Nahda Sporting Club, drawn from the local Lebanese Christian community, was founded in 1926.

A national team from Lebanon, still under French control, played its first official game in April 1940 against a team from neighbouring Mandatory Palestine, which was then under British control. The Mandatory Palestine team beat Lebanon 5-1. Just over a year later, with Lebanon then run by the Vichy French government, British and Allied forces advanced into the country from Palestine, and other directions, and achieved an even more devastating victory.

Lebanon has had a pretty mixed time since then, including, of course, the hugely destructive Lebanese Civil War of the 1970s and '80s. However, the men's national team has qualified three times for the AFC Asian Cup. Terry Yorath coached the Lebanese team for two years in the 1990s.

The women's national team has managed third place in the WAFF (West Asian Football Federation) Women's Championship on two occasions.

Lesotho

It's a small country totally surrounded by South Africa, and at the time when football came to it, it was the British Crown Colony of Basutoland.

Lerotholi Polytechnic, founded in 1905, played an important role in the early history of football in the country. In 1932, the Basutoland Sports Association was founded and the Basutoland Football Cup introduced. The same year, Matlama Football Club, one of Lesotho's best-known clubs, was formed.

The Kingdom of Lesotho became independent in 1966 and shortly after that the Lesotho National League was formed. We should probably also mention here Arsenal Maseru, based in the capital.

In 2000, the men's national team made it to the final of the COSAFA Cup but Zimbabwe beat them 3-0 in both legs.

Liberia

Liberia is unusual in Africa, since, in the nineteenth century, its main overseas link was not to a European colonial power, but to the USA.

Liberia's distinctive society started in 1822 when African-Americans were sent across the Atlantic to found a settlement in Africa. It was not any kind of smooth, painless process, but involved much suffering both for settlers and the locals who were already there. However, in 1847 the settlers declared their independence as the Republic of Liberia, the name coming from the Latin word for 'free', as in 'liberty'. Joseph Jenkins Roberts, born in Norfolk, Virginia, became the new country's first president.

American links to Liberia remained strong even after independence. US Navy ships, for instance, regularly assisted the Liberian government against rebellious locals throughout the nineteenth century and into the twentieth. That American influence may be one reason football seems to have come later to Liberia than to some other countries in Africa.

However, Liberian rubber production expanded in the 1920s and '30s and became vital to the Allied effort in the Second World War, and it was these decades that saw the proper establishment of Liberian football. One story claims the sport was introduced from the then British colony of Sierra Leone, which is on Liberia's north-western border.

Certainly some of the country's great clubs came into being in the 1940s, like Invincible Eleven, founded in 1943. It's a great name, but Invincible Eleven, sadly for their supporters, haven't proved invincible every time they have taken to the pitch. However, they did help create one of the world's great footballers, and probably the most famous Liberian ever. Yes, it's George Weah. He played for Invincible Eleven early in his career, and then went on to play for European clubs including AS Monaco,

Paris St Germain, AC Milan and, yes, for a short while, Chelsea and Manchester City. In 1995, he was voted FIFA World Player of the Year. After football he went into politics and was elected president of Liberia in 2017.

One of Liberia's leading women's football teams is called Earth Angels FC.

Libya

Sadly this country has been in the news in recent years a lot more for war and chaos than it has been for football, but the passion of Libyans for the sport is real.

Football seems to have come to Libya first via Italy rather than directly from Britain. In 1911, Italy invaded and occupied Libya, creating the colonies of Italian Cyrenaica in the east and Italian Tripolitania in the west. The invasion and subsequent occupation would cause huge suffering. However, the Italian troops did at least bring footballs with them.

There were still Libyan rebels fighting the Italians into the 1930s. However, in the coastal cities where the Italians held control more firmly, they were already forming football clubs. The six times champions of Libya in the 1920s and early '30s, for instance, were the Italian players of the 1st Libyan Legion of the Milizia. However, some of the locals were starting to pick up the game, too.

The Italian occupation of Libya was not to last. In the autumn of 1942 Montgomery defeated Rommel's German and Italian Army at El-Alamein, and in January 1943 the 8th Army, advancing westwards through Libya, entered the capital, Tripoli. From 1943 until Libyan independence in 1951, Britain controlled most of Libya and this period was vital in the creation of modern football in the country.

Some of the great clubs of Libyan football were founded in this period. Al-Ittihad of Tripoli was, for instance, formed in 1944. Al-Ahly, in Benghazi, turned professional in 1947. And in 1950, Al-Ahli in Tripoli came into being. The founders of the club had allegedly wanted to call it Independence but that wasn't to the liking of the British authorities.

After actual Libyan independence, there were still some British links to the local game. The Libyan national team, for instance, had a number of English coaches during the 1960s.

The Gaddafi era saw a lot of political interference in Libyan football. In 1982, Libya hosted the Africa Cup of Nations and Gaddafi marked the event by delivering a two-and-a-half-hour speech.

The civil war and chaos of the post-Gaddafi years has created its own problems for the sport. In 2014, though, Libya did beat Ghana on penalties to win the African Nations Championship.

Liechtenstein

Another of those small European countries that most of us probably only ever think about when it comes to football. It's also big in the financial world and there are a lot of wealthy people there, but how many of us ever discuss Liechtenstein's banks over a pint?

Liechtenstein has close links to both Switzerland and Austria (perhaps not surprisingly since it's sandwiched between them) and it seems most likely that football reached the little principality second-hand through one of its neighbours rather than directly from Britain.

It seems to have been after the First World War that Liechtenstein started establishing its own proper football clubs. For instance, in 1928 FC Kickers was founded. That seems a reasonable name for a football club and sort of like a tribute to the game's British heritage, as well as to the other Kickers clubs founded in the early period of football, in places like Switzerland and Germany.

FC Kickers did not have a long and glorious future ahead of them. In the final of the unofficial 1934 Liechtenstein championships, another team beat them 3-1 and the club was dissolved the following year.

Other clubs in Liechtenstein, however, soon came along that have lasted somewhat longer. For instance, FC Vaduz, founded in 1932, is still going strong and playing in the Swiss League. As is FC Balzers, founded the same year.

With a population of only a little over 35,000, Liechtenstein is inevitably going to struggle somewhat in international football. They started their international career in 1982 with Switzerland beating them 1-0, and they entered their first competition in 1994, the Euro '96 qualifying round, with Northern Ireland beating them 4-1 on their debut. Liechtenstein did, however, qualify for the UEFA European U-16 Championship in Scotland in 1998.

Liechtenstein has been surprisingly slow in developing women's football but in April 2021 the national women's team finally played its first official international match, which they lost to Luxembourg.

Lithuania

We have already seen that in the other two Baltic states, Estonia and Latvia, Britons played a key part in the introduction of football. It would seem logical that the same should be true of Lithuania, the most southern of the three, but so far it's been hard to find clear evidence.

Football certainly started at about the same time here as in Estonia and Latvia, or perhaps a few years later. According to one version, the first recorded match in Lithuania took place in 1911 in Kaunas between a home side and a team from Vilnius. It was allegedly a goal fest, with Vilnius winning 10-5.

However, there is also a suggestion that football was being played in some form in what is now Lithuania as early as 1892, and that by 1909 there was a football club in Memel. At that time, the port was German and in East Prussia. Border changes after the First World War, though, left it as the Lithuanian port of Klaipėda. It may, therefore, be that Lithuanian football came second-hand via other countries such as Germany, rather than directly from Britons.

Certainly football seems to have expanded significantly in 1919, and after, in the newly independent country. In 1919, Sveikata FC, Lithuania's oldest still existing club, was formed in Kybartai. The players came from various communities but there don't seem to have been any Brits among them. In 1922, a national championship was instituted, and in 1923 Lithuania played its first international, in which Estonia beat them 5-0. Nevertheless, the team went to the Paris Olympics the following year, and by 1931, a national championship had been instituted.

Occupation by the Soviets, then the Nazis, then the Soviets again, was to follow, with independence finally achieved again in 1991.

Football has, to some extent, suffered from the popularity in the country of basketball, but Lithuania has won a number of Baltic Cup titles and caused the occasional international upset elsewhere. And women's team Gintra Universitetas did reach the round of sixteen in the 2014–15 UEFA Women's Champions League.

In Britain, Heart of Midlothian, at one stage, had a lot of players from Lithuania.

Luxembourg

Aah Luxembourg, one of the very few European teams you usually feel almost 100 per cent confident your own team can beat. Though that ain't necessarily always so, as fans of the Republic of Ireland found out to their horror in March 2021, when they watched Luxembourg win 1-0 in a World Cup qualifier.

The man who was to bring football from Britain to Luxembourg and bring Luxembourg's football to the world was born in 1873 in the town of Roodt. He was called Jean Roeder and wanted to be an English teacher. So in 1890 he travelled from Luxembourg across the Channel to pursue his studies. Eleven years later he returned to Luxembourg fluent (presumably very fluent after eleven years) in English, but also fluent in the great new sport here, football. He then set about spreading his enthusiasm for the game with a passion.

This passion was not always shared by local farmers, landowners and land wardens, many of whom were unenthusiastic about allowing Roeder's students to trample their land. Many of his middle-class and academic friends also weren't that enthusiastic about this rough new sport.

Nonetheless, Roeder persisted and, on 9 December 1906, the Football and Lawn Tennis Club – CS Fola or Fola Esch (from its location) – was born. The rest, as they say, is football history.

It has not always been smooth football history. Luxembourg has a flourishing domestic league with fierce competition, but for a small nation of a little over 600,000, it would be fair to say that international competition has often not been that easy and successful.

In something of a sign of the future, in the Luxembourg men's team's first international, France beat them 4-1 in 1911, and in the Luxembourg women's team's first international, Slovakia beat them 4-0 in 2006. Nonetheless, as they say, everybody loves a trier (unless, obviously, the triers are actually beating your own team) and Luxembourg's teams keep on trying.

Madagascar

It's the fourth-largest island in the world, but not quite such a force in world football so far. France was the colonial power there during the early twentieth century, so the introduction of the beautiful game there was probably via France, rather directly from Britain.

Stade Olympique de l'Emyrne are one of the best-known teams in Madagascar and have a long history. Part of this was the occasion in 2002 when the team deliberately scored 149 own goals after a dispute over a refereeing decision.

French control of the island was interrupted in 1942, when British and Allied troops landed and seized it from the Vichy authorities. No doubt some of the British military personnel brought their footballs and skills with them, as well as their guns, obviously. After the Second World War, the French ruthlessly crushed the 1947 Malagasy Uprising, but eventually withdrew and Madagascar became fully independent in 1960.

In 2019, Madagascar qualified for the Africa Cup of Nations for the first time ever and reached the quarter-finals.

Malawi

Malawi is situated in eastern Africa, sort of west of Tanzania and Lake Nyasa. And before it was known as Malawi, the territory was called Nyasaland by Britain.

David Livingstone reached the area in the mid-nineteenth century, and by 1876 the Church of Scotland had founded a small mission and trading post south of Lake Nyasa, which was called Blantyre, after Livingstone's birthplace in Scotland. Livingstone himself was keen on sport and may have had a role in introducing football to Zambia. Certainly by 1880, people seem to have been kicking a ball around at the Blantyre Mission. Not only that, but by 1896 they had got themselves a proper club, the Blantyre Sports Club.

And it wasn't just at Blantyre that missionaries were helping spread the new sport. The Anglican missionaries at Likoma were also keen on what they saw as football's moral virtues, and in 1910 they brought a proper set of rules to the area. Enthusiasm for football started to spread, and by the 1930s, companies and welfare organisations were setting up their own teams.

Racist attitudes were, sadly, reflected in the colonial authorities' attitude to football administration. In 1935, the Nyasaland Football Association was formed for white players, while the Nyasaland African Football Association was created for Black African players.

However, as elsewhere on the continent, Africans in Nyasaland found that they could express both their enthusiasm for sport and their enthusiasm for self-determination through football.

In 1938, James Frederick Sangala, who had gone to school at Blantyre, helped set up the Shire Highlands African League. He would go on in 1943 to become a founder and acting secretary of the Nyasaland African Congress, which would press for greater rights for Africans. Finally, in 1964 Malawi gained independence from Britain.

As an independent nation, Malawi has won the CECAFA (Council for East and Central Africa Football Associations) Cup three times and they have qualified for the Africa Cup of Nations three times. In 2022, they made it to the round of sixteen.

Some of the names of clubs in the domestic league still reflect the British heritage of the game. In Blantyre, for instance, there is a Wanderers FC. The club has had various different prefixes to the name over the years, but has always kept the Wanderers element.

Malaysia

Yes, Brits brought football to Malaysia.

By the late nineteenth century, Britain controlled a variety of territories in Malaya and Brits brought their footballs with them. The locals soon adopted the new sport and by 1905 the Selangor Amateur Football League was thrilling spectators.

In 1920, HMS *Malaya* arrived to visit the land after which it was named. It seems fair enough that it did that, since the ship, costing almost £3 million, had actually been paid for by the Federated Malay States. HMS *Malaya* had an interesting history, including service in the Battle of Jutland, being torpedoed (but not sunk) in the Second World War, and shelling Genoa in February in 1941 alongside HMS *Renown* and HMS *Sheffield*. On that occasion, one of her shells hit Genoa Cathedral by mistake. However, perhaps her most lasting contribution has been to football.

During the 1920 visits, teams from HMS *Malaya* took on local teams at football and rugby, and to mark this, the captain and crew donated football and rugby trophies to be used for annual competitions in Malaya.

The first Malaya Cup football competition took place in 1921. After the state of Malaysia came into being in 1963, the cup was renamed, as the Malaysia Cup, and the competition is still going today. One of the great clubs of Malaysian football, Selangor FC, founded in 1936, has won the cup, as well as other honours, on numerous occasions.

In 2010, the Malaysia men's national team won the AFF (ASEAN Football Federation) Championship. In 1983, the women's national team came third in the AFC (Asian Football Confederation) Women's Asian Cup.

Maldives

Admittedly the average Brit tends to associate the country with sensationally beautiful islands and beaches rather than with football, but yes, the Maldives loves the world's greatest sport and yes, we probably gave it to them.

The Maldives were a British protectorate for a long time until independence in 1953 and British military personnel and administrators brought their footballs with them.

The RAF seem to have had a particular role in promoting football on the islands. During the Second World War, with the threat from the Japanese navy spreading in the east, the Maldives suddenly acquired extra strategic significance. RAF Gan was built in 1941 on Addu Atoll in the Maldives. It became a transit point and could handle flying boats like the Short Sunderland and the Catalina. Gan was abandoned after the war but was occupied again by British military personnel from the late 1950s and into the 1970s as a staging post to destinations further east.

There were already some football competitions in the Maldives in the 1940s. Plenty of football was played by Brits based at Gan, but local teams formed on Addu Attoll as well. By the 1960s and '70s a variety of football clubs were being founded. For instance, in 1979, New Radiant Sports Club, one the Maldives' most famous teams, was started in the capital, Malé. In 1969, the interestingly named Delightful Neighbours Club was also founded.

The Football Association of the Maldives was created in 1982 and a national league commenced in 1983. The national men's team has won the SAFF (South Asian Football Federation)

Championship twice, and the women's national team reached the semi-finals of the SAFF Women's Championship in 2016.

Mali

The African country takes its name from the hugely rich medieval Mali Empire. The modern country has a huge land mass but a comparatively small population. The south is where most of the people live and where the capital Bamako is located, while much of the north is desert and includes the ancient city of Timbuktu. Mali has a lot of football talent.

France was the colonial power here from 1892 to 1960, and for much of this period the country was known, somewhat confusingly, as Soudan Français, or French Sudan. Some of the earliest football was played at the start of the twentieth century in military bases, like the garrison at Kati or the Djicoroni air base at Bamako. Football was also popular among expatriates working for the colonial administration, and in 1929 some of these formed the SSS, the Société Sportive Soudanaise.

However, soon the raw talent of Malian football would show through. Makane Macoumba Diabaté was born in 1907 in Guinea but moved to French Sudan. He had experience as a boxer, but in 1930 he established Amicale, the first proper football club for players from the local population. It wasn't an easy task to build a team to take on teams with the logistical advantages of links to the military and colonial administration, but in 1938 Amicale took the Coupe de Soudan.

Mali has produced many talented footballers, including Salif Keita, one of the greatest African players of all time, and the first African footballer of the year in 1970. Some players with Malian heritage, including Djimi Traoré and Frédéric Kanouté, 2007 African footballer of the year, have contributed to the game in Britain.

At an international level, the Mali men's team have had quite a lot of success in the Africa Cup of Nations, and in 2010, they achieved one of the greatest international footballing recoveries ever. Trailing by four goals against Angola, and with just eleven minutes left, they scored four times to draw the match. Mali also have a good track record in the Africa Women Cup of Nations competition, and in 2018 Mali came fourth.

Malta

When you go on holiday as a Brit in Malta, there is so much that seems familiar from the days when Britain ruled the island that it won't come as a huge surprise that, yes, we gave the Maltese football.

It was probably the British military who first played football on Malta. Certainly, there was a British football league at an early stage, and this only allowed Maltese with military connections to get involved. This, however, did not deter the locals, who soon realised how good this new sport was and created their own teams.

Sometime in the 1880s, a bunch of young Maltese in Cospicua, a dockside area, were watching British soldiers play football and an officer gave them a ball. In 1890, St George's Football Club was founded in Cospicua.

Other clubs weren't far behind. In 1894, Floriana FC was formed, and took on St George's in the first official civilian match (St George's won 1-0). Floriana FC today play in white and green and they do so, it seems, because early in the twentieth century, before the First World War, they played a series of matches against the Royal Dublin Fusiliers, who were stationed in Malta then. At the end of the match, the teams swapped shirts and Floriana ended up with the green of Ireland on them.

The Maltese Football Federation was formed in 1900, a proper league was established in 1909, and by 1910 civilian teams were taking on military ones in the Cassar Cup. Among early team names were the Boys Empire League and, of course, Sliema Wanderers. The Wanderers went on to become one of the great forces in Maltese football.

Malta joined FIFA in 1959, and in 1964 the country became independent from Britain. Because of the small size of the country, they are unlikely ever to be one of Europe's football giants but the men's team did draw 0-0 with Switzerland in 2011 after their goalie saved two penalties, and in 2013 the women's team beat Luxembourg 6-0.

The Marshall Islands

The Marshall Islands, a Pacific island nation, have many fine features, but being a leading football nation isn't one of them.

They take the name from a Briton, explorer John Marshall, who was born in the closer to home and rather less exotic town of Ramsgate. However, the dominant foreign force in the area for a long time has been the United States.

The Spanish, Germans and then the Japanese all got involved in the islands at various times. However, in 1944, during the Second World War, US military forces seized control, and the country then administered the islands until they gained independence in 1979.

Bikini Atoll became a location for exploding US nuclear bombs, and, of course, a source of inspiration for swimwear. US influence, which has remained strong since 1979, did extend to giving the locals a passion for basketball but did not, perhaps unsurprisingly, extend to the Marshallese gaining a passion for association football, or soccer, as the Americans would call it.

The Marshall Islands are not a member of FIFA or the Oceania Football Confederation. What football has been played on the islands tends to have been played by foreigners. For instance, in the 1990s an Australian businessman tried to start a football league, but had little long-term success.

The logistical problems of constructing football leagues in nations composed of small islands separated by huge distances of water, with little strong football heritage, are evident in a number of Pacific nations, but are perhaps nowhere more obvious than in the Marshall Islands.

Mauritania

It would be fair to say that Britain probably didn't have a lot to do directly with the early years of football in Mauritania, but there again, for a long time, the country didn't have that much to do with football either.

Mauritania is a big African country with a coastline not a huge distance south of the Canary Islands. Large numbers of ships containing Brits with their footballs have passed that coastline over the decades. However, not that many of the ships seem to have actually stopped there during the years when football spread across the globe.

France was the colonial power in the area from the early 1900s until 1960, so football probably got there via that route. Some football was definitely being played in Mauritania by the late 1940s, when a few proper local clubs were being formed.

The country became independent in 1960, and in 1961 the Football Federation of the Islamic Republic of Mauritania was formed. It didn't become a member of FIFA until 1970 and, broadly speaking, it had a long period when its international track record was, frankly, not great. In December 2012, they

were 206th in the FIFA world rankings. In recent years, however, a lot of effort has been put into improving that situation
and Mauritania actually qualified for both the 2019 and 2021
Africa Cup of Nations.

Among the players who have helped Mauritania finally achieve
a degree of international success is Aboubakar Kamara.

Mauritius

It's a beautiful island nation in the Indian Ocean. Arab sailors
reached it first, followed by the Portuguese and then the Dutch,
who gave it its present name (after Maurice, Prince of Orange).
The French had a period in charge and then Britain took it off
them. The French brought in slaves from Africa and the British
brought in indentured labourers from India. A culturally
complex society was created and the complexities of that society
and the various communities that constitute it, and their rivalries,
have often been reflected in its football.

The world's greatest sport seems to have arrived in Mauritius
in the late nineteenth and early twentieth century. It seems to
have first reached there with British settlers and sailors and was
soon being played in English-administered schools. Some of the
names of Mauritian clubs, such as Arsenal Wanderers and Bolton
City Youth Club, reflect this British heritage.

The Franco-Mauritian population joined in, forming their
own clubs in the years between the two world wars. And soon
the other communities of Mauritius also adopted the sport and
formed their own clubs, too. By 1935, there was a Mauritian
League, and in 1954 the Mauritius Football Association was
formed. Among its founder members was FC Dodo, named
after perhaps the most famous product of the islands, the now
infamously dead dodo.

In 1990, rioting between fans of Scouts Club and Fire Brigade SC led to a suspension of league football and a far-reaching and controversial attempt to reorganise the basics of football in Mauritius.

Internationally they have had quite a good record in the Triangulaire – a tournament between Mauritius, Réunion, and Madagascar – and its replacement, the Indian Ocean Island Games (admittedly against a distinctly small group of competitors). The progress of women's football in Mauritius has not been that fast.

Mexico

The country, of course, has a long and distinguished football tradition and they got the sport from here.

Mexico were at the first World Cup in 1930 and, of course, have hosted the competition twice, in 1970 (*that* save by Gordon Banks and the England squad singing 'Back Home' etc.) and 1986. And in the latter year they introduced the world to what many people call the 'Mexican wave'. OK, yes, the phenomenon had actually originated in the USA in the 1970s and '80s, but it was the World Cup that introduced it to a worldwide audience.

It was, however, Britain that introduced the beautiful game to Mexico. Like neighbouring Nicaragua and Belize, the Mayan ball game of Pok-Ta-Pok and its Aztec developments had been played there many centuries before, but in the nineteenth century they got football.

Britain was one of the first countries to recognise Mexican independence, in 1810, and develop trade links. However, in 1861, along with the French, we were involved in a war against Mexico. The Mexican government had suspended debt repayments to Britain and France, so we sent in the Navy.

By 1880, we had decided, though, that there was money to be made from Mexico using our expertise in railways and mining. In the period before the First World War, Brits invested heavily in Mexican railways and mining. With the money came skilful engineers and miners, who brought in football and cricket.

It was probably miners rather than sailors who were the first to play the world's greatest sport in Mexico. When the Spanish left Mexico, many of the silver mines in Hidalgo were out of order because of flooding. The British Company of Gentleman Adventurers in the Mines of Real del Monte recruited 130 Cornish miners to use their know-how to get them functioning again. This small group was joined by more emigrants from Cornwall as British mines experienced strong competition from new ones in South America. By the end of the nineteenth century, football was being played by miners as an informal game. This has left a local Hidalgo tradition of a quick kick-around at 4 p.m., as well as a taste for Cornish pasties. Real del Monte also has an English cemetery with 750 graves aligned north-east towards England.

In 1901, the miners set up Pachuca Athletic Club, with football as one of its activities. A year later, Pachuca was a founder member of a five-team Mexican league. The town likes to think of itself as the 'cradle' of Mexican football and has a football museum.

All five teams that competed in the first league in 1902 were founded by the Brits and the players were almost universally British. The winners of the opening season were Orizaba, which developed from Orizaba Athletic Club founded by Duncan MacComish MacDonald, owner of a steel company. There was also Mexico Cricket Club, which had begun in 1894. As elsewhere, cricketers found it useful to play football as well to keep fit in the winter. Club Reforma was founded by Brits in 1894 as a sport club, while also providing a social hub. The final team was the British Football Club, founded in 1902 by Cornishman Percy Clifford. Brits dominated the league that they had set up. It continued as the Mexican Revolution started in 1910 but the outbreak of the First World War brought an end to British control as they came home to fight.

The new teams that appeared after 1914 show the influence of other countries. There are two teams named España, both with Mexican links, as well as an América and a Germania. By 1923, football was sufficiently well established in Mexico that they joined FIFA.

One of Britain's later contributions to Mexican football was that in 1935, when the Mexican national team won the Central American Championship, they were managed by Alfred Crowie from Pachuca FC.

On the international stage, Mexico has a long history of World Cup appearances after attending the first tournament in Uruguay in 1930. It was not until 1962 in Chile, however, that they won a World Cup match, defeating Czechoslovakia 3-1. Hosting the World Cup in 1970 and again in 1986 was a tremendous boost for football in Mexico. In both competitions, Mexico reached the quarter-finals, but the 1970 World Cup was dominated by Pelé and the Brazilians, while the 1986 competition starred Maradona and Argentina.

Mexico is the most successful of the CONCACAF countries and it has won eight Gold Cups. Mexican football has also been well represented in the Premier League, through talents such as Javier Hernández and Raúl Jiménez.

Mexico has a special place in the history of women's football because in 1971 it hosted an unofficial World Cup. The first women's games were played in the 1950s and in 1969 a seventeen-team league was started in Mexico City. The star of Mexican women's football was Alicia Vargas, nicknamed 'La Pelé'. She began playing the game with her brothers and against the wishes of her parents. She talked her way into the Guadalajara line-up and by 1971, she was playing for the national team in the unofficial World Cup. She scored a goal against England and was offered a contract in Italy by Real Torino. Instead of that, though, she remained in Mexico. Aged 37, she was still playing for Mexico when FIFA organised an 'official' Women's World Cup in 1991 and was named by CONCACAF as the third best women's player of the twentieth century.

An England team organised by Harry Batt also attended the 1971 unofficial World Cup. The tournament was a tremendous experience for the England team and it showed that the women's game could be a commercial success. Only two of the England players were over 20, and some were still at school when they arrived in Mexico. Good job it was during the holidays. They were stunned to find themselves regarded as stars in Mexico, and 25,000 spectators watched England defeated by Argentina after a fierce battle, which ended with one England player with a broken leg and another with a broken foot. In the match against Mexico, a crowd of over 90,000 cheered as the hosts defeated England. In 1972, the women's football association selected its first squad.

Micronesia

The scoreline 46-0 is not one you want to see when your team has the 0. Particularly when the 46 is for Vanuatu, not usually reckoned as being one of the giants of the international football world. And particularly when your previous two results were being beaten 30-0 by Tahiti and 38-0 by Fiji.

However, the Federated States of Micronesia and their Under-23 team that was on the receiving end of those scores do labour under some serious disadvantages from a football point of view.

The country consists of just over 100,000 people living on hundreds of islands with very few football facilities, spread across a vast area of the Pacific.

The Spanish were the first colonial power, followed by the Germans. The Japanese administered it between the wars, and then the USA oversaw it for decades after the Second World War. In addition to inflicting whatever indignities they did on the local population, none of those countries seem to have done much about promoting football on the islands.

In fact, it's hard to say which country should be given the credit for giving football to Micronesia and giving the world Micronesian football. British football writer and coach Paul Watson, with his friend Matt Conrad, did, famously, spend some time coaching there.

Moldova

Arguably one of the countries in Europe that Brits know least about, although many here will have admired, or at least noticed, their (sometimes somewhat eccentric) performances in Eurovision.

It's quite a small country, sandwiched today between Romania and Ukraine, and the region has had a complex history that reflects competition for control of it, between Romania (situated to the south) and the old Russian Empire and then Soviet Union (to the north). Even today the problems over the region of Transnistria reflect that competition.

When, and how, exactly football arrived in Moldova seems a little unclear. At the time when football was spreading across Europe, the influence of the Russian Empire was strong in what is now Moldova, but, strange as it may seem, it is possible that Brits may have been instrumental in taking the world's greatest sport there.

As we will see in the Ukraine chapter, Brits played a crucial role in popularising the game there in the port city of Odesa in the late nineteenth and early twentieth centuries. Odesa is only a short distance from Ukraine's border with Moldova. Even more intriguingly, in that pre-First World War period, British telegraph workers based in Ukraine are said to have played football against their Romanian counterparts in Galaţi. Galaţi is situated on the other side of Moldova from Odesa but is even closer to Moldova. It's only about 10 miles from the border.

Did British feet kick a ball on Moldovan soil in this period? We may never know. However, after the First World War, the area became part of Romania and joined its football system. Then, after the Second World War, it was part of the Soviet Union and that system. Finally, in 1991 Moldova declared independence.

The Moldovan national men's and women's teams have not exactly been among Europe's major football powers. FC Sheriff Tiraspol, based in the capital of Transnistria, have, however, emerged as something of a force in European club football. In September 2021, they even managed an away win against Real Madrid in the UEFA Champions League.

Monaco

Despite being tiny, Monaco is, yes, a genuine, separate, sovereign country and a full UN member state etc. – but it's not, for some reason, a member of UEFA or FIFA, which is why you won't have seen Monaco fighting alongside the other European mini-states of Andorra, Liechtenstein and San Marino to achieve respectable scorelines against much bigger countries.

Football does not have quite the same importance as motor racing, but the principality, despite being FIFA-less and UEFA-less, does have a national team, a Champions Promenade and, of course, a club side, AS Monaco, who play in the top French league.

The national side has somewhat limited opportunities, being, for instance, unable to play in the qualifying rounds of either the Euros or World Cups. The team is largely amateur, although there are a handful of professionals available, and this century it has played nearly thirty friendlies with mixed results. There have been victories against Vatican City, but FA Sápmi, who represent the Sámi people of northern Norway, beat them 21-1. Other interesting opponents have included Ellan Vannin, a team representing the Isle of Man. A 10-1 victory to the Manx.

While the national team is, for obvious reasons, little known internationally, the club side AS Monaco have frequently been in the limelight. They have won the French League eight times and reached the finals of the European Cup Winners' Cup and the Champions League.

It is hard to know exactly when football was first played in Monaco, but it was already well established in the region well before the end of the nineteenth century and club football had already started in Monaco by 1903. After the First World War, a bunch of local clubs teamed up to form what would become the mighty AS Monaco.

Football probably arrived in Monaco via France and Italy, rather than directly from here. It is possible that visiting sailors or public school sports enthusiasts may have played the game in the principality. One of the organisations that helped form AS Monaco was called Swimming Club.

It was in the 1980s that AS Monaco grabbed British attention with the arrival of Glenn Hoddle and Mark Hateley from the UK. At Monaco they were managed by Arsène Wenger, a then unknown French manager. Under Wenger, Monaco won the French League, the French Cup and reached the final of the European Cup Winners' Cup. He also gave Monaco a role in developing young players. Wenger brought his expertise to Arsenal in 1996 and with him came French talent like Thierry

Henry and Emmanuel Petit. Three Premier League wins and seven FA Cup triumphs later, Wenger and his compatriots were well known.

Monaco pays tribute to football stars in a Champions Promenade on the sea front where football stars have left their footprints, like Hollywood stars in L.A. The stars involved do not have to have a connection with the principality and the accolade is awarded by a public vote, for athletic achievement and personality. Alongside Pelé, Maradona and Ronaldo is Ryan Giggs.

Mongolia

It's a country that has long been big on its traditional sports, like horse racing, wrestling and archery. Football, not so much. However, that has changed a bit in recent decades.

Football seems to have first become established in Mongolia in the middle part of the twentieth century, with reports of matches being played there in 1946 and the Mongolian Football federation founded in 1959. It's a period when Soviet influence was extensive in Mongolia, and therefore it seems plausible to believe the start of its football was mostly down to the USSR. Army and police football teams played a significant role in the early period.

The 1990s saw the arrival of multi-party democracy in Mongolia, and a wider opening up to new opportunities. The period saw the creation of a range of football clubs, including Erchim FC, founded in 1994, which became a major force before merging in 2020 with another team. In 2014, football writer and coach Paul Watson played a key part in the foundation of Bayangol FC.

The first national team had been formed in 1956, but Mongolia didn't join FIFA until 1998, and in the 2014 World Cup qualifiers they earned their first three points by beating Myanmar 1-0. The women's national team played its first proper match in 2018.

But then football in Mongolia does encounter some problems that players in a lot of countries don't have. The temperatures can get so low that playing outside is impossible, and if they are using a light-coloured ball it can be hard to see in the snow.

Montenegro

Milo Milunović was a talented painter, but he also seems to have been one of the fathers of Montenegrin football.

He was born in the late nineteenth century in Cetinje, which was then the capital of Montenegro, but he crossed the Adriatic to Italy with his brother Luka to study there. And study they did, but they also experienced the fun and excitement of Italy's early British-influenced football. On their return to Cetinje in 1913, a local cobbler was allegedly prompted to make a football and the brothers teamed up with others to form FK Lovćen (named after a nearby mountain), Montenegro's first football club. Shortly afterwards, in 1914, the club that would go on to become FK Arsenal Tivat was founded on the Montenegrin coast.

After the First World War, Montenegro became part of Yugoslavia, as did its football administration. However, in 1931, the Cetinje Football Sub-Association was formed within the Football Association of Yugoslavia, and after Montenegro separated from Serbia in 2006, it became the Football Association of Montenegro.

During the Yugoslav period, Montenegrin players contributed to the success of the Yugoslav national team. Montenegro has had a fairly mixed international track record as an independent nation; however, at one stage in 2011, the FIFA ranking of its men's team was sixteenth. Goalkeeper Matija Šarkić, born in

Lincolnshire to Montenegrin parents, has played both for the Montenegro national side and a number of English clubs.

Morocco

Yes, it has the Atlas Mountains, beautiful beaches, fascinating culture and lively markets, and, yes, it also has a long and distinguished football history. In Mexico 1986, for instance, the Atlas Lions of Morocco were the first African team to go beyond the group stage in the World Cup.

Football seems to have got from here to Morocco via France and Spain. It is true that Britain did take some colonial interest in Morocco. Tangier was actually given to Charles II as a wedding present but was eventually abandoned as too expensive, and between the wars, Britain was one of the countries running what was then the International Zone in Tangier. However, the two main colonial powers in Morocco when football began to develop seriously there were France, which controlled most of the country under a 1912 agreement, and Spain, which controlled a few parts, too.

Club Athlétique de Casablanca became the first football club in 1902, and they were the first league champions in 1916. The French colonial authorities founded a Central Sports Committee in Casablanca in 1913 and a host of football clubs appeared. Union Sportive Marocaine de Casablanca, Sporting Club Cheminots des Roches Noires, Avant Garde du Maroc de Rabat, Union Sportive d'Oujda, Union Sportive de Marrakech and Union Sportive de Meknès were founded by the French, mainly for the French.

Football matches were played in Spanish Morocco before the First World War, and two parts of that territory, Mellila and Ceuta, are still Spanish enclaves in Africa and their teams play in the Spanish League. Morocco regards them as 'occupied' territories.

The French used sport, including football, to help them control Morocco. The model was based on their experience in Tunisia and there are similarities with how British colonial authorities used football in some territories.

French schools provided an education for some of what they regarded as the Moroccan elite. The curriculum included two hours of physical education and Thursday afternoon was for sport. The army also encouraged physical training and had an input into the school curriculum. Locals who wished to join the army learnt the game.

Football in some senses helped assert French control but it also provided an opportunity for locals to combine and develop their own Islamic and Moroccan identity.

Following the First World War, football spread rapidly across Morocco. In 1928, Union 14 Sportive Musulmane de Casablanca was formed. This was a club for Moroccans, giving them the opportunity to play. In 1937, one of Morocco's big clubs, Wydad (Love), was founded. Although based in Casablanca, Wydad hoped that by not using the city in its name it could attract countrywide support. The policy worked. Wydad has never been relegated from the Moroccan top league and has amassed sixteen championships. After the Second World War, another major club, Raja CA, was founded in Casablanca. It too has never been relegated and has collected eighteen league titles. Football allowed Moroccans to show their prowess against the French and promoted a sense of national identity and dignity. In 1956, Morocco became independent.

Morocco has produced many football stars. Larbi Ben Barek led the way, moving to France before the Second World War. Post-war, he was a prolific scorer for French teams and Atlético Madrid. The Premier League has hosted a number of Moroccan stars, with Hakim Ziyech of Chelsea being one of the best known in recent years.

Morocco were in the same group as England at the 1986 World Cup and ended up as group winners after England's defeat to Portugal. Morocco have also won the Africa Cup of Nations in 1976 and were runners-up in 2004. Morocco is investing in the women's game but it is quite a recent development.

Mozambique

Mozambique and football? Eusébio, of course.

Football first came to Mozambique, and the first football clubs were formed there, in the early twentieth century. At the time the country was part of the Portuguese empire, but its capital, then Lourenço Marques (now Maputo), had the British Empire about 30 miles to the west of it, and 80 miles to the south of it. In the 1930s, white Portuguese and British players took part in one football league, while the majority of Black players participated in a separate league.

Eusébio was born in 1942 to Laurindo António da Silva Ferreira and Elisa Anissabeni. The footballing world he was born into had close connections to Portugal. The first club he applied to join was Grupo Desportivo de Lourenço Marques (now Grupo Desportivo de Maputo), a team founded in 1921 and closely linked to Benfica. He didn't get into that but he was accepted into another great Mozambican club, Sporting Clube de Lourenço Marques, usually known today as Maxaquene, a feeder club of Sporting Lisbon. In 1960, however, he flew to Portugal to play for Benfica, rather than Sporting, and the rest is Mozambican, Portuguese and world football history.

After a lengthy guerrilla war against Portuguese rule, the colonial power withdrew from the country in 1975 and it became independent. Since then, Mozambique has qualified four times for the Africa Cup of Nations. The national women's team qualified for the Africa Women Cup of Nations (or as it was then called the African Women's Championship) in 1998 but then withdrew.

Myanmar

Sadly, Myanmar (Burma, as it used to be known), has become most famous in recent times for violence of one sort or another. However, like every country on earth, Myanmar has its football enthusiasts, and, yes, the great sport was taken there by a Scot; specifically a Scott.

James George Scott was born in Dairsie in north-east Fife in 1851. He was a keen sportsman, and later became a journalist, a colonial administrator and expert on Burma.

In 1878, he was temporarily teaching at a missionary school, St John's College, in Rangoon (now Yangon). He assembled a team from his college and another from the port of Moulmein. The football he had brought needed a new bladder but after that had been found the match took place.

Eventually Scott would return to Britain, where he would play for London Scottish with great success. Meanwhile, in Burma, the sport he had introduced would thrive and grow.

The Burma Football Federation was founded in 1947 and in 1948 the country became independent. In the 1960s and early '70s Burma became something of an Asian football power, winning a large number of regional competitions. For example, between 1961 and 1970, the team went to the finals of the U-19 Asian Cup no fewer than nine times, and won it seven times.

However, since then the football performance of the country internationally has been distinctly patchy. The long-term political and economic problems that have affected Burma/Myanmar have had a major negative effect on its football.

One of the most recent major news stories about football in Myanmar was not about performance on the pitch. Instead it was about Pyae Lyan Aung, who had played as goalkeeper for the national team and for Yadanarbon FC who, in 2021, after signalling his opposition to Myanmar's military, fled to Japan and was granted refugee status there.

Namibia

The first football was played by expatriates in Namibia in the period before the First World War when Namibia was a German colony called South-West Africa. Unfortunately, while football was being introduced there in the early twentieth century, at the same time an appalling tragedy was unfolding, with Germans responsible for the deaths of tens of thousands of Herero and Nama people.

In 1915, with the British Empire at war with Germany, an expeditionary force from South Africa advanced into the German colony to seize control. From then until independence in 1990 (following a long guerrilla war), Namibia was controlled by South Africa. Consequently, British-influenced South African football had a lot of involvement with the early years of the Namibian game.

A wide variety of football clubs were founded in the 1920s and '30s, including local clubs like Tigers FC, founded in 1927 in Windhoek, and Blue Waters FC, founded by teacher Daniel Shimbambi in 1936 in Walvis Bay.

A number of Namibian clubs have shown a link to British football heritage over the decades through their names.

Rangers FC has been one of the most famous of such clubs, but there has also been a Liverpool from Okahandja and a Chelsea from Grootfontein. Mighty Gunners FC actually *are* gunners, since they are the Namibian Army's 4 Artillery Brigade club.

The Namibia national men's side, known as the Brave Warriors, have qualified for the Africa Cup of Nations three times. The national women's team went to the Africa Women Cup of Nations in 2014.

Nauru

This isn't going to be a big chapter, partly because Nauru is the third smallest sovereign state in the world, with a population of about just 10,000 and partly because it hasn't ever really played that much football.

Before the First World War, Germany was the colonial power, but Nauru is in the Pacific, east of Papua New Guinea, and while the little island is a huge distance from Germany, it is a lot closer to Australia. In November 1914, shortly after the start of the war, Australian forces landed and seized the island.

Since then, with the exception of a period of Japanese occupation during the Second World War, Australia has been the main outside influence on the island. Consequently, a lot of the football that has been played there has been of the Australian rules variety, or of the rugby type.

There does seem to have been a period in the 1960s when workers from other Pacific island nations played a bit of football and there is still some interest, but in such a small country even space for a pitch is in short supply.

Nepal

Football seems to have come to the country in the period after the First World War.

The influence of Britain and British-controlled India was strong in the country at the time and it seems reasonable therefore to assumed there was at least some sort of British involvement in the commencement of the Nepalese game. However, Nepalese returning from abroad with a passion for the sport do seem to have played a major role in the start of organised football. Kathmandu's New Road Team, founded in 1934, is one of the oldest and best-known clubs.

The All Nepal Football Federation was formed in 1951, and in 1970 Nepal joined FIFA.

In 2021, the Nepal men's national team lost to India in the final of the SAFF (South Asian Football Federation) Championship. The women's national team have regularly been runners-up in the SAFF Women's Championship.

Netherlands (and Overseas Territories)

Who was the greatest Dutch master? Does the honour belong to Rembrandt and Vermeer, or is the artistry of Johan Cruyff or Rinus Michels actually even rarer? The Premier League has often looked to Dutch players (so many of them, but Dennis Bergkamp, Edwin van der Sar, Robin van Persie and Ruud van Nistelrooy definitely need a mention here) and managers for innovation. However, Dutch clubs, too, have often looked across the North Sea for inspiration.

Brits did not have to try very hard in order to start the game in the Netherlands. In the nineteenth century, the Dutch admired British culture and cricket clubs began before football ones. As elsewhere, cricketers chose football as a way of keeping fit in winter. Dutch student Pim Mulier started the earliest football club, Haarlemsche FC, in 1879. At boarding school in Noordwijk, Pim saw Brits playing football. He went home, bought a ball and encouraged his friends to play. At first, they played rugby, but in 1883 switched to football. Haarlemsche FC played its first match against the predominantly English side Amsterdam Sport in 1886. Sport won 5-3.

While Haarlemsche was the first club, the first match was organised by Jan Bernard van Heek, who had come across the sport while doing business in Burnley. In 1885, Enschedese Football Club took on Lonneker.

Football spread rapidly, with new clubs being founded. Some of these were multi-sports clubs and others were cricket clubs, where younger members found themselves more attracted to football than cricket. One of them, Sparta Rotterdam, was founded in 1888.

Initial development was slightly chaotic, but in 1889, Pim Mulier founded a Dutch Football Association. Three of the eleven early clubs still exist: Haarlemsche FC, HVV of The Hague and Rotterdamsche Cricket en Football Club Olympia. By 1899, the Netherlands had both a football league and a cup.

Corinthians toured in 1906 and defeated both Dutch champions HVV Den Haag and a Holland XI. At international level, Holland won bronze at both the 1908 and 1912 Olympics.

Between 1900 and 1914, the three best-known Dutch clubs were founded. FC Ajax started in Amsterdam in 1900, while Rotterdamsche Voetbal Vereeniging Feijenoord (Feyenoord) began life in 1912. Feyenoord saw themselves as a working men's club and as such their formation marks a turning point for Dutch football. The game was spreading from the wealthy 'gentlemen's clubs' to ordinary people. The following year, Philips Sport Vereniging started in Eindhoven. It was a works club and only those with connections to the Philips company could join. It's now, of course, better known as PSV Eindhoven.

The First World War provided a boost for football. The Netherlands did not fight in the war, but a lot of young men had to join the army as a precaution. As they weren't actually fighting, there was plenty of time for football. In 1916, Sparta Rotterdam opened the first purpose-built football stadium in the Netherlands, the intimidatingly named Het Kasteel (The Castle).

Some British soldiers were interned in the Netherlands after fighting alongside Belgians to defend Antwerp. Defeated, they crossed into the Netherlands rather than surrender to the Germans. The camp in Groningen contained many good sportsmen, who used the war to improve their skills and play local sides.

Corinthians toured the Netherlands again in 1922 and 1923 with rather more mixed results than their earlier visit.

After the Second World War, there were big changes to football in the Netherlands. Dutch football went professional in 1954.

The 'Big Three', Ajax, Feyenoord and PSV, have dominated Dutch football. However, FC Twente did win the Eredivisie title in 2010, when they were managed by English coach Steve McClaren.

The modern Dutch game has been credited for inventing 'Total Football', a system where any player can play in any position. Rinus Michels, FIFA's Coach of the Century, introduced the idea at Ajax with players like Cruyff, Neeskens and Rep. Ajax became European Cup winners in 1971, 1972 and 1973.

Brits have played a supporting role in defining recent Dutch football. Vic Buckingham was the Ajax coach before Michels. He gave Cruyff a first team debut and instilled that 'the best form of defence is attack'. At PSV, it was Bobby Robson who led PSV to back-to-back league titles in 1991 and 1992. At club level, Ajax, PSV and Feyenoord have all won the European Cup or Champions League. The 'Oranje' (national side) have been runners-up in the World Cup three times, in 1974, 1978 and 2010. Their sole major triumph was the 1988 European Championship. However, they remain much admired and copied for their talent and tactics.

The Netherlands has a reputation as a tolerant society, but sadly this has not always been true of attitudes to the women's game. The first women's football club, Oostzaanse Vrouwenvoetbal Vereeniging, was formed in 1924, but as recently as the 1950s, the KNVB banned the women's game. Despite this, Dutch women won the European Championship in 2017 and were runners-up in the 2019 World Cup. Since 2007 there has been a professional women's league and the KNVB now has over 150,000 women on its books.

Curaçao, Aruba, Bonaire and Sint Maarten comprise the Netherlands Antilles in the Caribbean. It was mainly the Dutch who spread football here, though there was contact with Caribbean islands then controlled by Britain. In Curaçao, the first club was Republic, founded in 1909. In Aruba, Vitesse, Wilhelmina and Be Quick all show their Dutch link in the name choice. In Bonaire, Hercules and Brion played a match in 1923. Curaçao have more recently hired Patrick Kluivert to be their manager. His mother was born in Curaçao.

New Zealand (plus the Cook Islands)

This small country with only 5 million inhabitants has the most feared rugby football team in the world, the All Blacks. Its soccer team, the All Whites is rather less successful, and rather less well-known, although they have qualified for two World Cups. And yes, we did, of course, give them both rugby and football.

Nelson Football Club played a game in 1868 using a round ball, but with a mixture of Football Association and Australian rules.

On South Island, Canterbury Association Football Club played its first game in 1882 against Christ College. On the North Island, North Shore United was formed in 1882 and is the oldest Kiwi club still playing.

By 1887, there were thirteen football clubs in Auckland. A number of local football bodies were formed and then a national New Zealand Football Association was created in 1891. By 1892, there was also a national competition, the Brown Shield, started by Scottish whisky magnate Robert Brown. Wellington defeated Otago 6-2 to win the first one.

In 1922, Captain C.B. Prickett of HMS *Chatham* gave the New Zealand FA a silver replica of the FA Cup to thank them for their hospitality. The Chatham Cup, as it was known for fairly obvious reasons, has become New Zealand's longest-running national club competition. Seacliff, based in Otago, defeated Wellington YMCA 4-0 in the first final in 1923.

Football in New Zealand found itself unable to compete with rugby in major schools and universities, so instead, it drew support from industry and job-based teams. In Auckland, for example, there was a Harbour Board team and Wellington had a Tramways club.

The women's game also made an early start. In 1888 in Wellington, the Girls' High School took on the Hallelujah Lasses. While the Lasses prepared with physical exercise, the Girls' High brushed up on the rules in the classroom. In the 1920s, Auckland, Wellington and Christchurch all formed women's clubs.

At an international level, getting to the 1982 World Cup in Spain was a major achievement. The team was masterminded by two Brits: John Adshead was the charismatic leader and Kevin Fallon the coaching expert. There was also an English captain, Steve Sumner. In 2010, New Zealand qualified again and went to the South Africa World Cup, returning undefeated after three draws. The men's team has also been Oceania Football Confederation Nations Cup champions five times.

Women's football was rejuvenated in the 1970s with local competitions like the Royal Oak Cup and Kelly Cup. There is now a national league and youth development programme. The Football Ferns, as the women's national team are popularly known, have qualified for the last four World Cups and have won the Oceania Football Confederation Nations Cup six times.

The Cook Islands, self-governing since 1965, is FIFA's smallest member with a population of just 17,000. In 2018, they defeated both Tonga and Samoa in World Cup qualifiers.

Nicaragua

The country is perhaps better known over here for its coffee, or the bitter fighting between the Sandinistas and Contras, or as the birthplace of Bianca Jagger. However, while football is not as popular as baseball, it is the country's second most favourite sport.

The United States occupied Nicaragua from 1912 to 1933. This had a wide range of effects, one of which was creating the context for General Sandino's long-running guerrilla campaign against American and local allied forces, which would bring him widespread fame and make him the inspiration for the left-wing Sandinista movement later in Nicaragua's history.

Another side-effect was that baseball became the most popular sport in the country rather than football. It could all have gone in a different direction entirely, because we actually had a significant early involvement in Nicaragua.

Britain's main interest was in an area on the east coast, and they tried to establish a colony. However, the attempt was abandoned in 1860, before there was any chance that football could be established there.

Nevertheless, some British influence persisted, and, by the late nineteenth century, a number of cricket clubs were playing regular matches in the area. As we have already seen, cricket clubs around the world were frequently involved in introducing football to an area as well. In Nicaragua, however, instead of becoming a precursor to football, some of them became a precursor to, yes, you guessed it, baseball. An American persuaded a couple of the cricket teams to switch to baseball and the rest is Nicaraguan sport history.

Football mainly seems to have arrived from neighbouring Costa Rica in the first decades of the twentieth century. Other wealthy families sent their sons to Europe and they too returned with a passion for the beautiful game.

Many early matches were fundraisers, attended by the wealthy of Nicaraguan society. By 1920, there were teams in Managua, Granada, León and Diriamba. The arrival of the railways enabled the game to spread, but, slightly unusually in terms of wider South American history, there doesn't seem to have been much British involvement with the Nicaraguan railways.

The Royal Navy cruiser HMS *Cambrian*, during her assignment to the North American and West Indies Station, did visit on New Year's Eve 1920, and a football match was arranged with a Nicaraguan XI.

There was some more British involvement after Thomas Cranshaw arrived from Manchester in 1917. Having established himself as a successful businessman, he turned his attention to promoting sport. He was multi-talented, refereeing football matches, judging swimming competitions and playing international tennis. In 1926, he tried to establish a national football league in Nicaragua and there is a football stadium in Managua bearing his name. His position was recognised in 1995 when he was inducted into the country's sports hall of fame.

At an international level, Nicaragua has slightly struggled to exert much influence after a promising start. In 1920, there was an international game between a team representing Costa

Rica and a selected Nicaraguan side. A local newspaper saw it as a matter of national pride and recommended extra training and abstaining from alcohol and tobacco. The result of the match was a creditable 1-1 draw. However, the following year the Costa Rica national team defeated a team formed by two Nicaraguan clubs 11-0. The Costa Ricans were so confident that they offered $5 for every goal scored against them.

In 2009, Nicaragua did qualify for the CONCACAF Gold Cup, so maybe one day soon they will qualify for the World Cup finals.

The US organisation Soccer Without Borders has been working to help develop the women's game in Nicaragua.

Niger

It's a country that sometimes gets confused with its southern neighbour Nigeria, particularly since the demonym of Niger is Nigerien. Niger is actually a bigger country than Nigeria but a lot of it is desert and the country's population is little more than a tenth of Nigeria's. Consequently, while Nigeria is an African football superpower, Niger … not quite so much.

From 1900 to 1958 Niger was under French colonial control, so it seems most likely that football came to the country not directly from Britain but via France, and perhaps partly via other French colonies as well. A number of proper football clubs were formed in the 1940s; for example, Renaissance Elmina, a major force in Nigerien football in the early period, was formed in 1947 by workers from Togo and Benin.

The Nigerien football federation was founded in 1961 and joined FIFA in 1964. By 1966, the country had a national football competition. Niger's national team is known as the Ménas, a local name for a gazelle.

Domestically the professional game is less developed than in a lot of other African nations; however, the Ménas have occasionally scored some surprising triumphs, including going twice to the Africa Cup of Nations. In qualifying for the 2012 competition, they even won their group, beating some major teams.

By contrast, the development of women's football in Niger has somewhat struggled.

Nigeria

There is plenty of Nigerian talent in the Premier League and the list of names includes John Obi Mikel, Shola Ameobi, Wilfred Ndidi and Alex Iwobi. But then Nigeria is the most populous of African nations with over 200 million inhabitants, and, yes, it was Brits who introduced football here.

In 1904, a game was played in Calabar. Students from Hope Waddell Training Institute, a Presbyterian missionary school, took on sailors from HMS *Thistle*. The students beat the sailors 3-2. It is likely that the students had already played several games or it was really not one of the Navy's better days. The students went on to play against teams from the Southern Nigeria Regiment.

Games between the regiment and school teams were encouraged by Captain Beverley, who organised the Beverley Cup. The regiment won in 1906 and 1907, Duke Town School were victors in 1908 and Hope Waddell in 1909. Football thrived in Calabar. By 1911, nine teams had joined the competition, including Roman Catholic Mission, Creek End School, Christ Church and East End Lions.

Further west, in Lagos, it was Frederick Mulford, who worked at the Lagos Stores, who spread the game. From 1906 he organised games on the race course between European traders, soldiers and civil servants. He also invited Nigerian teams to play and a Calabar XI featured heavily. He coached football at King's College, St Gregory's College and Igbobi College.

Colonial Nigerian football was dominated by teams from government agencies and services. The idea of the authorities at the time was that providing entertainment would help Brits control the country, and, at the same time, football would also instil values of teamwork and fair play.

The Police Force, Nigeria Regiment, Public Works Department (PWD) and Nigerian Railway all had football teams. PWD Sports Club in Lagos was open to both Black and white workers. Architect H.A. Porter established a PWD football team in 1929. He became first president of the Lagos League and president of the Nigerian FA.

Football, however, would also become a tool for Nigerians seeking self-determination. Nnamdi Azikiwe ('Zik') was a footballer, journalist and press magnate, who became Nigeria's first president. He played football at Hope Waddell and won the Lagos City championship in 1923 with the Diamond Football Club. He continued his studies in Pennsylvania, where he captained the Lincoln University soccer team. Back in Nigeria, he started Zik's Athletic Club in 1938. ZAC, open to men and women of all ethnic heritages, was the first sports club not controlled by Brits.

Zik used money from his press empire to build facilities, including a small stadium. In 1942, ZAC won a league and cup double. The Second World War gave Zik something of a footballing opportunity. Brits were worried about the growth of Nigerian nationalism so they placed some restrictions on movement, but they also wanted to encourage the war effort. Zik took his team on two nationwide football tours, raising some funds for the war effort. Matches were well attended and Zik mixed with other nationalists, developing a Nigerian identity.

After the war, a Nigerian team toured Britain in 1949. These 'Ambassadors of Friendship' impressed English spectators. They also spread national pride in Nigerians. Consequently, Okere and 'Thunder' Balogun became the first Nigerians to sign professional contracts in England.

In 1960 came independence and membership of FIFA. Zik became President of Nigeria in 1963.

Independent Nigeria has not had the easiest of histories. The country has, for instance, experienced occasional periods of political and military turmoil and recently there have been terrorist attacks by Boko Haram. Nigeria's love of football is, however, undiminished.

The 'Super Eagles' (men's national team) won gold at the 1996 Olympics. They have won three African Cup of Nations, in 1980, 1994 and 2013, and qualified for three World Cups.

Women played football in Nigeria as early as 1943, and by 1960, there were teams in Lagos, Calabar and Kano. The Sugar Babes FC was formed in Lagos in 1978. The only opposition then was boys' teams but now Nigeria has a women's league. Pelican Stars have been the most successful team with seven titles, followed by Delta Queens with five. The national side, 'Super Falcons', have dominated the Africa Women Cup of Nations, winning eleven times.

North Macedonia

This is a part of the world that has gone under a few different names in recent years.

At the beginning of 1991, it was the Socialist Republic of Macedonia, which in turn was one of the territories that made up Yugoslavia. In late 1991, after Slovenia and Croatia had already declared independence from Yugoslavia, the Socialist Republic of Macedonia declared itself independent as the Republic of Macedonia. This hugely upset a lot of Greeks, who regard the name 'Macedonia' as part of Greek heritage, and Greece objected to international use of the name for the new country. For a long time, the country, therefore, was referred to internationally with the rather cumbersome term Former Yugoslav Republic of Macedonia; a bit of a mouthful often shortened to FYROM. Finally, a compromise deal was reached with Greece and in 2019, the country became what it is today, North Macedonia.

In 2009, the centenary of football in the area was celebrated, which, since there wasn't a huge British presence in the area at the time, would suggest football arrived indirectly from here rather than directly.

However, it does seem to be agreed that there was some significant involvement from the United Kingdom in the early development of football there, because the first major match played in what is now North Macedonia took place in 1919 between a British Army team and a Skopje youth football team. A monument was erected in 1978 to mark this major event. A bunch of football clubs in the area were also formed in 1919.

You might ask what the British Army had to do with the region in that period, which would bring us to one of the British Army's less well-known campaigns of the First World War. The Macedonia Front or Salonika (a shorter version of the name Thessaloniki) Front saw British troops, alongside other Allied troops, fight a bitter, but in the end, victorious campaign, in this part of the Balkans, against Germans and their Bulgarian allies. By 1919, with the war ended, British troops in Skopje were in a position to show off their football skills rather than risking their lives any more.

The locals embraced football with enthusiasm, and a variety of clubs were soon in competition with each other, representing various local communities. Vardar Skopje, founded after the

Second World War, in 1947, is perhaps the best-known and most successful local team.

Since independence in 1991, it's been a bit of a mixed picture for North Macedonian football internationally. For instance, in 2006, Andorra beat the national team 1-0. However, 2021 was a big football year for North Macedonia, as they made it to the 2020 Euros. It may be best not to say too much about the results once they got there, but they were *there* and that is important. As every football fan anywhere would agree – if your team is going to lose, then better they lose at the Euros against the Netherlands, Austria and Ukraine, than they lose against Andorra in a World Cup qualifying round. And in 2022 North Macedonia put mighty Italy out of World Cup qualifying!

In 2021, in the qualifying rounds for the 2023 Women's World Cup, England beat North Macedonia 8-0, and Northern Ireland beat them 9-0.

Norway

Norway is one of those countries where, despite the obstacles put in the way of the development of the women's game globally, the national women's team has decisively outperformed the men's team on the international stage.

While the men have only qualified for the World Cup twice and been eliminated in the group stages on both occasions, the women have been world champions once, runners-up once and fourth twice. The women were European champions twice in 1987 and 1995 and runners-up four times, in 1989, 1991, 2005 and 2013. The men have only qualified for one Euro, in 2000, and were eliminated at the group stage. The women have also won both gold and silver medals for football at the Olympics.

Norway was a late starter in women's football compared with neighbouring Denmark and Sweden. However, in terms of the world as a whole, it was still pretty early, playing its first game in 1978. The 1995 World Cup, which was conveniently staged in neighbouring Sweden, was perhaps Norway women's greatest football triumph. En route to the semi-final, the Norwegians defeated England, Canada, Nigeria and Denmark. In the semi-final they got revenge on their great rivals the USA, who had defeated them in the final of the previous World Cup. In the final they beat a German side that they had not defeated for ten years. Over the whole tournament, the Norwegians conceded only a single goal while scoring twenty-three. Ann Kristin Aarønes was the top scorer in the tournament and Hege Riise was voted the best player.

The earliest football in Norway, though, started with the men rather than the women. And, as in Denmark and Sweden, the Brits were heavily involved. Some Norwegians adopted the game after an education in Britain, in other matches British migrants played, and then, of course, there were the sailors.

The first teams started in the 1880s and 1890s. Johan Salvesen and John Dahl returned from studying in Scotland and England to start Christiania football club in 1885. They recruited between twenty and thirty students and pupils at a local high school and translated the Football Association rules into Norwegian.

In 1886, a big crowd turned up to watch a game between sailors from two visiting British warships and Christiania. The Norwegian King Oscar II (who also happened to be King of Sweden as well, and would support Britain during the Boer War) visited the warships to help recruit the opposition. Sadly, only four British sailors were available to play and the 'British' team had to recruit Norwegians to make up the numbers. Christiania won 3-0, but the following day the Royal Navy demanded a rematch. So many sailors volunteered, determined to restore British pride, that the game ended up thirteen per side.

A second early side was Odds in Skien. The club took its name from the character in a novel where one of the characters is a Norwegian athlete called Odd. The club began as an athletic and ski club, but took up football in 1894. Some of the original players were Brits working nearby. There was also Grane in Nordstrand, Oslo, where early players included Scottish cousins Patrick Moyer and Charles Semper.

By 1902, there was sufficient support for football to form the Norwegian Football Association and to organise a cup competition. Grane were the first winners of the Norway Football Cup, but Odds were to dominate the early years. Interestingly, Odds still exist and they won the Norwegian Cup again in 2000.

Norway joined FIFA in 1908, but made a slow start in international football. The first international was against Sweden (the union between the two countries had ended) in 1908. Not a great start. Sweden beat them 11-3.

A major achievement for the men's national team in the early years came at the 1936 Olympics in Germany. Adolf Hitler was not a football fan but he did appreciate the propaganda potential of sport. The only game he watched was the quarter-final between Germany and Norway. It was not fun viewing for Hitler as Norway took the lead after seven minutes and he walked out when the Norwegians added a second after eighty-three minutes. Norway went on to finish third.

In 1940, Hitler invaded Norway and put Vidkun Quisling in charge of the country. Resistance to Quisling and the German occupiers was widespread, and when Quisling assumed control of sport, including football, Norwegians reacted. Players found excuses not to play, coaches didn't coach and spectators stayed away. The Ullevaal Stadium, with a capacity of 40,000, hosted games with fewer than 100 spectators. Instead, players and crowds gathered in isolated villages to play, celebrate the game and discuss resistance.

There have been some great Norwegian footballers and Britain has been privileged to watch them at work. While there is disagreement about the value of Ole Gunnar Solskjær during his time as manager of Manchester United, there is no escaping his contribution to the club during his playing career. And names like John Arne Riise, John Carew and Tore André Flo are now part of our football history over here.

Oman

Oman was a British protectorate between 1891 and 1951 and football began under British rule. Local tradition has the first game being played in Muscat by British sailors from HMS *Crocus* in 1919 and this was followed by further demonstrations of football by sailors. The details of this first game may not be entirely accurate but it is likely that some British sailors did bring football to Oman.

Maqboul Sports Club was established in 1932, but it was mainly for hockey and cricket. In 1942 the Maqboul Club was renamed the Oman Club. It added football to its sporting activities and set about publicising the game. Saidia School in Muscat helped spread the game among young people and provided a stadium.

However, the sport really started to take off in Oman in the 1970s, after a new Sultan, Qaboos bin Said, came to the throne and, with British help, defeated a rebellion in Dhofar in the south of the country. A lot of Oman's football clubs were founded in that decade and, in 1978, the Oman Football Association was formed.

Oman has had a vigorous domestic league and some success with its national team, including qualifying four times for the Asian Cup and winning the Arabian Gulf Cup twice.

Goalkeeper Ali Al-Habsi had a long career with the Oman national team and also played for a number of English clubs.

Pakistan

Pakistan has over 200 million inhabitants, many of them massive sports enthusiasts. The country's cricket team have been world champions, as have its hockey team, and Jahangir Khan dominated squash in the 1980s. The Pakistan Football Team has yet to quite match such achievements. Nevertheless, football is hugely popular.

The British Army introduced football to what is now Pakistan while it defended the north-west frontier of the Raj. The Army used football to improve teamwork and encourage physical fitness. There were games between units based in Peshawar in the late nineteenth century. It is likely that some of these involved local soldiers working for the Army.

In 1893, surgeon Theodore Leighton Pennell became principal of a school in Bannu and led pupils on football tours of other local missionary schools. Soon football had spread across the local population. Kohat FC was the first club in 1930 and in 1937 they won the North-West India Football Competition.

The partition of India, in 1947, created a divided Pakistan. There was Western Pakistan, and Eastern Pakistan, which is today Bangladesh, with Indian territory between. The Pakistan Football Association was soon established. In 1948, Pakistan joined FIFA, and international football followed. However, the split nature of Pakistan made national competitions and sponsorship somewhat more difficult and this hindered the development of the game.

In 1971, war in Bangladesh and the Indo-Pakistani War led to East Pakistan becoming Bangladesh.

Big organisations like the Army and the Water and Power Development Company have played a role in the development of Pakistani football. Brits have also provided some support. Dave Burns, John Layton and Graham Roberts, for instance, have all coached the national side. And in return players of Pakistani heritage, including Zesh Rehman, have made their own contribution to football here.

The Pakistan men's national team has had some successes in the South Asian Games.

Women's football in Pakistan has made some progress recently with the appearance of a number of teams such as Diya WFC Karachi and the arrival of a National Women Football Championship. In 2010 the women's national team reached the semi-finals of the SAFF (South Asian Football Federation) Women's Championship.

Palau

This Pacific island nation had a fairly chaotic colonial history. First, the Spanish took control. Then they sold it to the Germans. Who lost it to the Japanese in the First World War. Who lost it to the Americans in the Second World War. Finally, in 1981, it became the Republic of Palau and, in 1994, fully independent.

It's difficult to be sure exactly who first played football in the islands; however, it can reasonably be said that football came late to Palau. It has only really been in the twenty-first century that football has become properly organised in the country. Palau is not a member of FIFA nor of the Oceania Football Confederation, but teams from Palau have played in the Micronesian Games. Members of the Bangladeshi community in Palau have been influential in popularising football there.

Palestine

While, in terms of the United Nations, Palestine is a 'non-member observer state', which is a bit of a mouthful, it has been accepted as a FIFA member since 1998, and plays in the Asian Group.

This chapter looks at the development of Palestinian Arab football within the territory that would be British controlled under the Palestine Mandate and then, after 1948, looks at football in the territory that is now recognised by some nations as the state of Palestine. The chapter on Israel looked at Jewish football within the territory that would become British controlled under the Palestine Mandate and then, after 1948, within the state of Israel. In both stories, Brits played a central role.

Organised football was introduced to Palestinian Arabs by missionary schools like St George's School. Established in Jerusalem in 1899, the school took up the game in 1908. The following year it was strong enough to defeat the American University in Beirut. One player, Izzat Tannous, went on to be a medical doctor and member of the Arab Higher Committee, helping Britain administer Palestine.

Under the British mandate after the First World War, sport, and football in particular, spread rapidly. Brits wanted to open up the game to Palestinian Arabs as well as Jews, hoping to avoid the problems they had experienced in Egypt, where football had encouraged nationalism.

Brits established some clubs like Jerusalem Sports Club in 1920, which were open to all. Other clubs were established by socially minded Palestinian Arabs, like the Islamic Sports Club in Jaffa in 1926. By 1930, there were about twenty Arab sports clubs in Palestine and many of these played football. Orthodox Christian clubs, such as one in Jaffa, were also open to Palestinian Arabs and also played football. The British Army, Royal Air Force and police also fielded teams.

Josef Yekutieli, from the Jewish community, a leader of Maccabi Athletic Association, formed a Palestinian Football Association in 1928 and the following year Palestine was admitted to FIFA.

While British teams played in the PFA championships, some Palestinian Arabs felt excluded and responded in 1931 by forming the Arab Palestinian Sports Federation with ten clubs. Shabab al Arab (the Arab Youth) club in Haifa won the championship in 1933 and 1934. However, the APSF only lasted for a short time, and the British authorities regarded it as seditious.

Palestinian Arab football did not stop though. By 1942, five Arab teams, like, for instance, Islamic Sports Club, played in the PFA League. Other teams played in smaller local leagues. In 1944 there was another attempt to form an Arab Palestinian Sports Federation.

In 1948, amid political and ethnic violence and turmoil, the independent state of Israel came into existence. Some Palestinian Arabs fled to Lebanon, Syria or Jordan. Others sought safety in the refugee camps in Gaza or on the West Bank and some remained within Israel. Palestinian football was thrown temporarily into chaos but did not die out. A Palestinian team, Al-Wehdat, played in the Jordanian League and helped keep the idea of Palestinian identity alive.

Palestinian football in Gaza and the West Bank had to deal with the effects of Israeli control after the Six-Day War in 1967 and the sport inevitably came to something of a halt during the intifadas of 1987–93 and 2000–2005. Despite all these problems, Palestinian football has both continued and flourished.

In 2014, in the Maldives, the Palestine national team actually won an Asian Football Confederation tournament for some of those countries where the AFC was trying to encourage more football development. Women, too, are playing football in Palestine. Many start playing against boys in the street, but there are now women's teams, like Ramallah WFC.

The Beginnings

Bramall Lane, where Sheffield FC played Hallam FC in 1862.

Plaque marking the foundation of the FA in 1863, London.

Spreading the Sport

Edinburgh University. Among others, Alexander Hutton (see Argentina) and William Mackay (see Spain) studied here. Schools and universities played a key role in spreading football around the world.

Scottish footballer John Dick, an Arsenal legend who then helped make Sparta Prague one of the best clubs in Europe.

Famous sports goods supplier Lillywhites. The export of footballs, including Lillywhites' footballs, from Britain was a major element in spreading the sport.

Monument to the Imperial Camel Corps, London. The Empire's forces – army, navy and air force – took footballs with them to many parts of the world.

A western instructor taking part in western sports at the Japanese Naval Academy in about 1931. Japan got football when a British naval mission introduced the game to the Japanese navy. (G.K. Laycock)

Brits go on Tour

Exeter City football tour of Brazil, 1914. British teams touring overseas helped spread a passion for the game far and wide. (With thanks to the Grecian Archive)

The World Game

Original members of Oneida FC, Boston Common, USA. As association football spread around the world, it absorbed many local football traditions, including 'Boston Rules' football, as played by Oneida FC.

A stadium that marks the centenary of the Malta Football Association, founded in 1900. Britain helped spread the administration of the sport around the world, as well as the sport itself.

Sliema Wanderers of Malta on the pitch. Many football club names around the world still show signs of British football heritage.

Early football legend Walter Tull, whose father was Barbadian. Almost as soon as Britain started exporting football to the world, talent with overseas heritage would start playing the sport here.

Stamford Bridge. Football today is a vast international cultural and economic phenomenon.

Women's Football

A plaque marking the founding of the legendary Dick, Kerr Ladies club, pioneers of women's football.

The Preston home of Dick, Kerr rail and tram works. Workers and engineers in the rail industry, both men and women, played a huge role in spreading football.

The FIFA Women's World Cup, 2019, as England and Scotland prepare to meet at the Allianz Riviera Stadium, Nice.

The Magic of Football

British schoolboys take on Soviet Pioneers (the communist version of Scouts), west of Moscow, in about 1977. Football can bridge huge political and cultural divides. (Stuart Laycock)

A boy playing with a football in a refugee camp in Croatia, 1994. Almost wherever you are, you can get fun from a football. (Stuart Laycock)

London Tube station temporarily renamed after the Euros in 2021. The passion and excitement of football can lift an entire people.

Panama

British interest in Panama hats may have helped football develop in Colombia (see the Colombia chapter for the details), but, somewhat ironically, British influence probably had rather less effect on the early development of football in Panama itself – a country, incidentally, that has a lot more to it than just that canal.

It is likely that football was first played in Panama by assorted sailors on shore leave. Until 1903, Panama was part of Colombia, where sailors, some of whom were British, introduced football in the early twentieth century.

In the end, though, it was the USA rather than Britain that would dominate developments (including sports developments) in Panama. It was the Americans who built the railways and who bought out the French to complete the Panama Canal. Consequently, it is no surprise that the most popular sport in Panama today is baseball rather than football.

Football really came quite late to Panama. It was not until the 1960s that clubs like Alianza were founded and it was not until 1998 that a professional league was started.

Even today the Panama domestic league is small scale, with crowds numbering only a few thousand. The best Panamanian footballers tend to play in either the USA or Colombia rather than their own country.

The passion for football in Panama tends to be for the national team, which is known unsurprisingly as 'Los Canaleros' (the Canal Men) rather than for domestic sides. When Panama qualified for the 2018 World Cup in Russia by beating local rivals Costa Rica 2-1, President Varela gave the country a national holiday. Panama's first goal in the World Cup in Russia was scored against England by Felipe Baloy. However, the match itself was (fortunately for England fans) a 6-1 English victory.

Many people in Panama credit some of the recent success of Los Canaleros to the work of Englishman Gary Stempel. He was born in Panama and his father played professional baseball, but his mother was English and he moved to England as a young boy. He went on to work with Millwall and their outreach programme, before returning to Panama in 1996 to see what he could do to develop football there.

Domestically he led San Francisco to five Panamanian League titles and Panamá Viejo to a further two. At international level he succeeded in taking the Under-20 Panamanian team to the 2003 World Cup and in 2009 he led the senior squad to a Copa Centroamericana title.

In 2018, the women's national team finished fourth in the CONCACAF Women's Championship.

Papua New Guinea

Britain and Germany were the colonial powers in the area in the late nineteenth century. However, Britain largely ceded its influence to Australia, and Australia then captured the German-controlled area in the First World War. There was also fighting in the region during the Second World War after the Japanese invaded. Basically, though, from the 1920s until independence in 1975, Australia was the main foreign power in the country, which may explain why it seems to have taken quite a long time for association football to become popular there.

In some of the more remote parts of Papua New Guinea, Australian colonial administrators did make occasional efforts to introduce football as a means of inter-tribal competition to replace actual warfare.

However, when football did start to develop, perhaps inevitably, club football seems to have emerged fastest in the cities. Some of the area's German heritage may be visible in the name of the Port Moresby club, Germania, which had some success in the early years of a national football league in the 1970s.

The Germania club also hosted most of the football in the 1969 Pacific Games, in which Papua New Guinea came third.

And in 2016 the Papua New Guinea national men's team were runners-up in the OFC (Oceania Football Confederation) Nations Cup. The national women's team have had rather more success, though, coming second in the OFC Women's Nations Cup three times and winning the Pacific Games Football Tournament four times.

Paraguay

It is one of only two landlocked countries in South America, which may be why our involvement in the introduction of football there was somewhat less marked than in some of the neighbouring countries. Nonetheless, there was involvement.

By 1886, British railway workers had made it to the capital of Paraguay, Asunción, and were showing off their skills with a ball. Some of them played under a familiar name, Everton. However, rather than British players, Paraguay seems to be one of those countries where it is a proud British football from a chain of British shops that is the real hero of the birth of the sport.

The Buenos Aires branch of Harrods was selling McGregor footballs, endorsed by no less a personage than the founder of the English Football League, William McGregor, himself. A passing Dutchman, Wilhelm Paats, then a resident of Asunción, bought a ball and took it home to Paraguay with him. A different version of the story has Paraguayan writer and intellectual Juan Silvano Godoi buying the ball and giving it to his son. Then in 1902, both Paats and Godoi became founder members of the oldest football club in Paraguay, Olimpia, which went on to become a massive force in the domestic game.

Whoever actually carried that first ball, though, it had done its job. By the time HMS *Petersfield* sailed up the river to Asunción to pay a courtesy visit in August 1920, landing both Admiral Sir Charles Madden (veteran of the Battle of Jutland) and a football party, Paraguayan football was a national passion.

Paraguay has won the Copa América twice, picked up the football silver medal at the 2004 Olympics and qualified for the World Cup finals eight times. In 2006, after England spent much of the match defending a 1-0 lead (an own goal from a Beckham free-kick), Paraguay gave England fans some distinctly uncomfortable moments, and in 2010 the Paraguayans reached the quarter-finals. The women's national side came fourth in the Copa América Femenina in 2006.

And it all started with a British McGregor football.

Peru

It's on the other side of South America from here, but, yes, we did bring football to Peru. In fact, the early years of football in the country were strongly influenced by the British. Involved were visiting British sailors trading guano along the coast, a small but influential community of British residents, and some members of the Peruvian wealthy who were educated in British schools before returning to Peru.

At first football was slow to catch on. Alejandro Garland, who had encountered the game as part of his education in Britain, tried to organise meetings and games in the 1870s. However, the Pacific War of 1879–84, in which Peru and Bolivia were defeated by Chile, gave Peruvians some rather urgent matters to deal with and it was not until 1892 that the development of the world's greatest sport restarted.

That year, Lima Cricket Club hosted a football game between a team from Lima captained by Mr Pedro Larrañaga and one from the neighbouring port of Callao captained by Mr Foulkes. Both sides were predominantly British.

It was the two cricket clubs, Lima Cricket Club and its rival Union Cricket Club, that would develop football in Peru at the end of the nineteenth century.

Lima Cricket Club was mainly for the British community. Union Cricket, by contrast, had both European and Peruvian members. There were regular football games between the two and some between British and Peruvian teams.

The growing enthusiasm for the best sport in the world was evident when HMS *Leander* visited in 1897 and more than 2,000 spectators turned up to watch the game.

Union Cricket took football seriously and in 1896 was even prepared to import turf from Britain to improve its playing facilities. In 1912, a Peruvian football league was established and Lima Cricket were the first champions.

By the 1920s, some violence had entered the Peruvian game. In a match between Atlético Chalaco and Alianza Lima, the Alianza goalkeeper was stabbed in the back through his net by a spectator. Chalaco fans were also accused of throwing dynamite at an opponent while he took a throw-in.

And the 1936 Olympics would be chaotic and controversial, too. In their quarter-final match against Austria, the Peru team were leading 4-2 with almost no time remaining. At this point the game was abandoned due to Peruvian fans storming the pitch. Peru withdrew from the Olympics at this point rather than replay the match, claiming that they were experiencing racial discrimination.

It's worth mentioning here one more aspect of British involvement with the early Peruvian game. Jack Greenwell had an extraordinary football career. While he played amateur football for Crook Town, he never made it into the professional game in England. However, he left for Spain in 1912 and ended up first as a player and later manager of Barcelona, winning the Copa del Rey in 1920 and 1922. In 1938, he became manager of Peru and led the team to a gold medal in the Bolivarian Games in Colombia in 1938 and victory in the Copa América in 1939 after a 2-1 victory against Uruguay. Greenwell was consequently hailed as a hero in Peru.

Peru had attended the first World Cup in Uruguay in 1930, but they did not go to another competition until 1970, where they reached the quarter-finals. The men had the same success in 1978 but in 1982 and 2018 they failed to get beyond the group stage.

Women's football is somewhat less developed, although the national team achieved third place in the Women's Copa América in 1998, and a football league was founded in 1999.

Nolberto Solano is one of the Peruvian footballers who have displayed their talents playing for clubs in Britain.

Philippines

The Philippines are not usually thought of as an area of major British influence, but actually over the centuries we have had more involvement there than you might think – and yes, that does include involvement in the introduction of football.

In 1762, for instance, a British invasion force actually seized Manila and we held it for a couple of years before swapping it for real estate elsewhere in the world.

English artist Charles Wirgman witnessed locals in Manila playing some kind of ball game as early as 1857. However, in terms of association football, one story goes that English sportsmen first brought the game to the islands in the 1890s. Another version is that it was Filipinos who played the game in China or in British Hong Kong who introduced the sport. Maybe it was a combination.

Certainly the game seems to have made some major advances in the Philippines in the early years of the twentieth century with the founding of a number of clubs and, in 1907, the establishment of what was then the Philippine Amateur Football Association, and is now the Philippine Football Federation.

The British community was well established in Manila, with its Manila Club already in existence by at least 1877. In 1914, Brits formed their own sports club, the Manila Nomads Sports Club, which developed an impressive proficiency in both football and rugby. That same year, Manila Nomads won their local league, becoming some of the earliest football champions in the Philippines.

And soon there was international football, too. In 1917, in the Third Far Eastern Games, the Philippines achieved its biggest ever international win by beating Japan 15-2. Unfortunately for the Philippines, this was followed by a game against China. With China already leading, they scored a penalty. The Philippines goalkeeper then punched the scorer, a fight started and the match was abandoned.

However, for much of football history, the Philippines has not achieved quite the success in international football that its early history in the game might have suggested, and the domestic game has had pretty major problems, too.

Some of all this, at least, has been down to strong American influence in the country and the consequent popularity there of sports like basketball and baseball.

However, recent years have actually seen some significant football successes for the men's national team, including a number of appearances in the semi-finals of the ASEAN Football Federation Championships. In a major international achievement for them, the Philippines did also make it to the 2019 AFC Asian Cup. And some of all that is down to the star player and captain for some years, Phil Younghusband, who was born in Surrey to an English father and Filipino mother and trained in the Chelsea youth academy.

The Philippines hosted the AFC Women's Asian Cup in 1999, and, in the 2018 tournament they reached the knockout stages.

Poland

Older English fans will be aware of the magnificent goalkeeping of Poland's Jan Tomaszewski at Wembley in 1973. Magnificent from a Poland fan's point of view, that is. Bit of a disaster from an England fan's point of view. The 1-1 draw prevented England from qualifying for the 1974 World Cup, which, so soon after 1966, was a calamity.

When football was first played in Poland, in the late nineteenth century, Poland itself did not exist as an independent state. It was just the dream of romantics and revolutionaries. Modern-day Poland had been divided between the great powers of Austria, Russia and Prussia in 1815. Consequently, the early development of football was very fragmented.

In Austrian-controlled Poland, Kraków was a centre for the early development of Polish football. Two local doctors, who had seen the game in Britain and elsewhere, promoted the sport's health benefits. One of them, Dr Edmund Cenar, returned from England with a football, which helped, and wrote a teachers' handbook for use in schools.

In 1894, a team from Lwów (now Lviv in Ukraine) took on a team from Kraków. Włodzimierz Chomicki scored for Lwów but the game came to an abrupt end after six minutes, because it was part of a sports jamboree and they were out of time.

In 1906, Brits and Americans from a touring Buffalo Bill show took on a Kraków gym club at football and lost.

When football stepped up from gym clubs to specific football clubs, two Brits were to star for Cracovia in 1908. One of them was William Calder, who had played for Fulham and was a master of the long throw-in.

In Russian-controlled Poland, Łódź was the centre for football. A booming textile industry attracted workers, many of them Brits, who will probably have brought footballs to the town and organised kick-arounds.

LKS (Łódzki Klub Sportowy) was the first Polish football team in the city and, in order to persuade the Russians that the team was not a threat, it included Brits James Galaway and Thomas Horrocks as honorary members.

Robert Smith and Alexander Gilchrist contributed the Łódź Championship Cup for local teams. A Newcastle Łódź club was started in 1911, founded by a Brit but with a largely German team. Football in Łódź was a cultural mix.

In German-controlled Poland, conditions for football were even more difficult, as the Germans waged a culture war against Polish nationalism.

Some clubs such as Deutsche Sportverein Posen were for Germans only, but others had a mixture of Poles and Germans, although the Poles often felt unwelcome. The largest of these took the English names Britannia Posen and Victoria Posen as something of a link to football's British heritage. However, by this stage the day of Polish independence was not far off.

Józef Piłsudski saw 1914 as an opportunity to form a Polish legion to help Austria fight the Russians. He hoped when Russia was defeated, he could join the allies and form an independent Poland. In 1916, Master Sergeant Zygmunt Wasserab started a football club, Sporting Team Legia, who played other army units and civilian teams. Legia went on to become Legia Warsaw, Poland's most successful team, while Piłsudski emerged from the chaos and confusion of the war as chief of state of an independent Poland.

Poland suffered terribly under Nazi occupation during the Second World War, and the decades as part of the Warsaw Pact often weren't much fun either.

However, at least football has often given Poles hope. In all, Poland has been to eight World Cups and four Euros, and they have an Olympic gold medal and two silvers. Among the stars of recent Polish football have been the mighty Robert Lewandowski, and Łukasz Fabiański, who has also played here for Arsenal, Swansea and West Ham.

Women in Poland have had a league since 1979–80, with Czarni Sosnowiec and AZS Wrocław among the most successful clubs. Polish women are yet to qualify for a major championship but stars such as Ewa Pajor play in the Bundesliga, which may help raise standards. Ewa Pajor, voted Poland's best player in 2018 and 2019, plays for Wolfsburg, where she has won four German championships and played in three Champions League finals.

Portugal

Portugal is known as England's oldest ally, with a friendship that dates back hundreds of years. Having said that, if you're an England fan, the thought of 2004, for instance, when England lost in the semi-finals of the Euros to Portugal on penalties, or 2006, when England lost on penalties to Portugal in the World Cup quarter-finals, may still sting a bit.

Of course, in recent years the Premier League has been lit up by Portuguese stars. On the field, Manchester United have benefited from Bruno Fernandes, Cristiano Ronaldo and Nani. Manchester City have starred Bernardo Silva, João Cancelo and Rúben Dias. Liverpool have Diogo Jota and Wolves have played Rúben Neves and João Moutinho. It all seems to have been aided by José Mourinho, and Chelsea's winning teams have often included a Portuguese element. This seems a fairly good return, in some sense, for the role Brits have played in developing the game in Portugal.

There is now a monument to the first football played in Portugal, a kick-around in Camacha, Madeira, in 1875. The game was organised by an Anglo-Portuguese teenager, Harry Hinton, who had encountered the game while studying in Britain. His family ran businesses in the sugar and banana trade and, with visiting British sailors, there may well have been many kick-arounds. However, Madeira was not to become a hotbed for Portuguese football (even though it would later be the birthplace of one Cristiano Ronaldo).

The first football in mainland Portugal was down to the Pinto Basto brothers in Cascais in 1888. They were Portuguese but had played the game while studying in Britain and brought a ball home with them.

The following year, there was a more organised eleven-a-side match in Lisbon between a Portuguese XI and a British team made up of workers from Carcavelos, where they were building the electric trans-continental submarine cable. The Portuguese won 2-1. However, the British Carcavelos team went on to be the best in Lisbon, being undefeated between 1894 and 1907.

The Portuguese in Lisbon were also quick to form their own football clubs. Benfica was established in 1904 for Portuguese players and, obviously, went on to become one of the country's most successful. Sporting Clube de Portugal (Sporting Lisbon to you and me) also began life in 1906 with the ambition of becoming 'one of the greatest' and not just a social club. Mission accomplished as one of Portugal's 'Big Three'.

Further north, in Porto, the British contributed Oporto Cricket Club. The founder of Portugal's third great club, FC Porto, was the wine merchant António Nicolau d'Almeida. He had visited England and through his trading contacts would have been familiar with the English game. Boavista FC, who were one of the few clubs outside the 'Big Three' to win the Portuguese League in 2000–01, were also founded by Brits. Harry and Dick

Lowe took time off from making port to start this combined Anglo-Portuguese venture.

For many years, Portuguese football was a bit of backwater dominated by Benfica, Sporting and Porto. However, in the 1950s that changed as the country modernised and new managers were introduced. The most successful was Hungary's Béla Guttmann, who led Benfica to back-to-back European Cups in 1961 and 1962, defeating Barcelona and Real Madrid in the two finals. Sporting Lisbon were league champions every year from 1946 to 1954, except for 1950. The English coach Bob Kelly led them to their first title and another Brit, Randolph Galloway, was in charge for a hat-trick of titles between 1950 and 1953. The Portuguese also benefited from African players like Eusébio recruited from their colonies.

Brits coaching in Portugal continued in the 1990s, with the English manager Bobby Robson working at both Sporting Lisbon and FC Porto. Robson led Porto to the league title in 1994–95 before leaving Porto for Barcelona. When Robson arrived in Lisbon in 1992 he got José Mourinho as his assistant. Robson took Mourinho to Porto when he moved there and it was Mourinho who would lead the club to success in the Champions League in 2004 before taking charge at Chelsea.

Considering Portugal is a country of only about 10 million people, it has had huge success in international football. Both Benfica and Porto have won the European Cup or Champions League twice. Sporting Lisbon won the European Cup Winners' Cup in 1964. Porto have also won the Europa League twice, in 2003 and 2011. The national side won the Euros in 2016, defeating the French in Paris 1-0, and were runners-up at the Euros in Lisbon in 2004. In the World Cup, Portugal has usually disappointed, but they did finish third in the 1966 tournament in England.

There has been a national Portuguese women's competition since 1985. The most successful team is Sociedade União 1º Dezembro from Sintra with twelve titles, closely followed by Boavista with eleven. Sporting and Benfica have two each. Portugal has never qualified for a World Cup but it did reach both the 2017 and 2022 European Championship.

Qatar

It would probably be fair to say that when most people think of Qatar and football, they think of the 2022 World Cup, with its assorted controversies, rather than thinking of people actually booting a ball in Qatar when there's not a World Cup on. However, balls have been booted and, yes, we have been involved.

Football first really seems to have taken off in Qatar in the period around the Second World War when British influence was strong. British oil workers like Tom Clayton, who arrived there in 1948, and their Indian colleagues, were among the first to show the locals what they had been missing. The oil workers used sacks for goalposts, instead of the traditional jumpers. Considering how hot it often is in Qatar, jumpers may have been in short supply.

Soon the Qataris acquired a passion for the sport, too. The oldest football club in Qatar, Al Ahli, was founded as the Al Najah Sports Club in 1950.

Frank Wignall, of (among other teams) Nottingham Forest and England, took control of the Qatar national squad from 1975–77, and in 2019 the team celebrated their biggest achievement so far by winning the Asian Cup, beating Japan 3-1 in the final. The national women's team was launched in 2010.

Romania

Not perhaps in the front rank of world football these days, or even in the front rank of European football, but they have certainly had their moments, like being one of only four countries to be in all three of the first World Cups. And, of course, you can't really mention Romanians and football without also mentioning the colossus of the game that is the great Gheorghe Hagi, who, among his other epic achievements, led Romania to the World Cup quarter-finals in 1994.

There were various pioneers of Romanian football. The earliest football match on Romanian soil may have been played by sailors from HMS *Cockatrice*. It's a story made slightly complicated by the fact that a big chunk of Romania, Transylvania (yes, it's a real place), didn't become part of modern Romania until after the First World War. In addition, as in Azerbaijan, some of the earliest football teams were being organised by English and German workers in the oil fields (yes, Romania has oil fields, which the Allies spent quite a lot of time bombing during the Second World War when Romania was a German ally).

However, Iuliu Weiner definitely came to England in the late nineteenth century to become a dentist and he definitely returned home in 1890, perhaps with drills, but also with a football and a set of football rules, and would, thanks to his evangelising efforts, eventually become widely acknowledged as the father of Romanian football.

A football club was established in Arad in 1899 and the first match had four referees, which makes you slightly wonder about the rules in use in Romania at the time. In 1902, Timişoara took on Lugoj in the first inter-club match. Not a great day, however, for Timişoara, who lost.

Nevertheless, the future of Romanian football was bright. The aging King Carol I became a football fan, and with royal support, the Romanian FA came into being in 1909. And England continued to be involved. One of the major early Bucharest clubs, Colentina FC, which won the Romanian championship in the 1912 and 1913 seasons, was based at a textile factory and was manned almost entirely by English players.

The First World War would, however, follow shortly. Most wars involve a lot of confusion for those who participate, but this was a particularly confusing war for Romanians. The country remained neutral until 1916, then joined the war on the Allied side, but then left the war (in early 1918 after the Russian revolution and withdrawal from the war made Romania's position extremely difficult) and then rejoined the Allied campaign in late 1918.

The Romanian club that would become internationally famous as Steaua Bucharest developed during another rather complicated part of Romanian history, as after the Second World War Romania turned communist. In 1947, the Romanian Army formed its own team called Armata, which then became CSCA Central Sports Club of the Army, and then Steaua.

The most successful women's team is FCU Olimpia Cluj, which has an impressive array of league titles.

Every footballer and football fan in Romania today, however, owes a debt of gratitude to Iuliu Weiner, and his long-ago English dentist tutors.

Russia

During the Cold War, Russia seemed, in many senses quite a distant place. And now with the West and Russia in fierce disagreement over Putin's war with Ukraine and other matters, Russia seems distant again. It is, therefore, almost something of a surprise to find quite how involved Brits were with introducing the world's largest country to the world's greatest sport.

Russia has been through many changes since football was first played there in the nineteenth century. Inevitably these political changes have each left their mark on the development of football.

In St Petersburg, British expats were playing the game by 1868. However, Russian aristocrats were not instantly attracted to the game, seeing it as too rough and physical. They preferred their sport to be expensive and exclusive, choosing yachting, riding or tennis to display their wealth and physical prowess.

The first football clubs in the country were in St Petersburg, Russia's 'window to the West'. In the 1890s, Scots formed the wonderfully named Scottish Circle of Amateurs, the English formed an English Football Club, and the Germans formed Germania. Victoria was a joint Anglo-German venture and the first to admit some wealthy Russians. The French were also involved. Georges Duperron, with French heritage but born in Russia, published football rules in Russian and established a Russian team, the St Petersburg Circle of Amateur Sportsmen (Sport for short). The first officially recognised game on Vasilyevsky Island saw a side featuring many Brits beat Sport 6-0, in 1897.

Football in St Petersburg expanded rapidly, and in 1901 there was a formal competition, the Aspeden Cup. The competing teams were Nevsky, an English team from the Neva spinning mill, Nevka; a Scottish team from the Sampson weaving factory; and the Anglo-German outfit, Victoria. Three years later there were six teams in the league, as new Russian teams had joined. By 1911, the Russians were on a par with the Brits.

In Moscow, football developed rather more slowly. Harry Charnock, from Chorley, was manager of a textile factory in Orekhovo-Zuevo near Moscow. He set up a football club for his workers in 1893, hoping to persuade them to drink less vodka. The players wore the blue and white of Blackburn Rovers, Charnock's favourite club. The team were Moscow champions between 1900 and 1914, with Harry as manager and his younger brothers Ted and Billy as players. The captain was Harry's cousin – a real family affair. In 1903, the team became OKS Moskva. Harry would flee to Finland in 1917, the year of the Russian Revolution. In the 1920s, OKS would become Dynamo Moscow.

Brits organised other football opportunities. William Hopper built pitches for his metal workers. John Gibson organised a facility at his candle factory. Arthur Thornton organised a pitch for Sokolniki Sports Club. Brits also helped to structure Russian football. Arthur Davidovich MacPherson, born in Russia to Scottish parents, became first chairman of the St Petersburg Football League in 1901. In 1912 he established the All-Russian Football Union, becoming its president. However, the Olympics that year showed Russia still had ground to make up. The Germans inflicted a humiliating 16-0 defeat on Russia.

Russia emerged from defeat in the First World War, then a revolution and a subsequent civil war to become the USSR in the 1920s. McPherson, who had been decorated by Tsar Nicholas II, died of typhoid in a Moscow prison.

Football between the wars was dominated by Dynamo Moscow and Spartak. Dynamo, supported by the NKVD (Secret Police) and the ministry of the interior, represented the Soviet ruling class. Spartak, founded by Nikolai Starostin, took its name and ethos from Spartacus, the leader of the Roman slave rebellion. They were patriotic and communist but outsiders. Rivalry between the two teams was intense and political. In 1939, Spartak won a league and cup double and Beria, head of the NKVD, wanted Starostin to be arrested. Starostin had sufficient political support on this occasion, but Beria was to get revenge later, with Starostin spending eleven years in the gulags until Stalin's death and Beria's execution in 1953.

After the Second World War, the USSR opened up to international football. In 1960, the Soviet Union were European Champions and four years later they were runners-up. They were quarter-finalists in the 1958 and 1962 World Cups, before finishing fourth in 1966. While these were creditable achievements, particularly the Euros win, they fell short of the domination their political leaders were hoping for.

Since the break-up of the Soviet Union, the biggest achievement for Russia has been staging the 2018 World Cup. Russia reached the quarter-finals and finished third in the 2008 Euros. At club level, a UEFA Cup victory for CSKA Moscow in 2005 was the greatest triumph. Now, due to international sanctions in response to Putin's invasion of Ukraine, it seems unlikely Russian teams will be achieving much internationally in the near future.

Russian women played football in public in 1911 and comprised about 30 per cent of the crowd at early matches. Progress has been limited by many Russians refusing to accept football as a suitable women's game. There is a small professional league with eight teams and about 200 professional players. Internationally, Russia's women reached the quarter-finals of the World Cup in 1999. While they have qualified for most Euros, they were replaced in the 2022 competition by Portugal, following the invasion of Ukraine.

Rwanda

When the average Brit thinks of football and Rwanda they probably think of the Visit Rwanda message on Arsenal shirts. However, Rwanda does, of course, have its own football history.

Like Burundi, Rwanda was at one stage part of a German colony and then after the First World War it was, with Burundi, part of the Belgian colony of Ruanda-Urundi.

Football was probably mainly established in Rwanda in the 1920s and it probably reached Rwanda via Belgium, rather than directly from here.

Rwanda became independent in 1962, and the 1960s and '70s saw a number of major clubs founded. In the 1970s, the Rwanda Football Federation was formed and it joined FIFA.

The appalling massacres of 1994 in Rwanda saw vast numbers of people horrifically slaughtered, some of them in football stadiums. However, since then there have been attempts to use football to heal some of the wounds.

Rwanda has had some successes, including, for instance, qualifying for the Africa Cup of Nations in 2004. The women's national team is nicknamed the She-Wasps.

Saint Kitts and Nevis

So, to begin with, if you go looking for the story of Saint Kitt in books about saints, you probably won't find him. Kit or Kitt is an old abbreviation of Christopher and this small Caribbean nation of two islands is also officially known as Saint Christopher and Nevis, though actually we have never heard anybody call it that.

Football first came to the islands during the days of the British Empire. During the period of slavery, it is said that slaves played a form of football on the island, using bladders taken from dead animals.

The Saint Kitts and Nevis Football Association was formed in 1932, with the first four teams being the Rovers, Rivals, Eagles and the Grammar School. And British heritage still appears strongly in the names of some of the domestic clubs: there are, for instance, Garden Hotspurs, one of the nation's older teams, and Village Superstars.

The women's league is the Elvis Star Browne league.

Internationally, Saint Kitts and Nevis haven't had a huge amount of consistent success, but they have had their moments. They dominated the Leeward Islands FA competition for a while, and in 2015 the men's national team travelled to Andorra and beat them 1-0, with Devaughn Elliott scoring the vital goal early in the game.

A number of Premier League players have also played for the Saint Kitts and Nevis national team, and Marcus Rashford has family heritage from Saint Kitts.

Saint Lucia

A very beautiful island, but quite small for making it big on the international football stage.

When a love of football was spreading across the Caribbean in the late nineteenth and early twentieth centuries, Saint Lucia was part of the British Empire and the sense of a link to British football can, again, be seen in some of the team names. For instance, Rovers United FC sounds about the most British football team name ever, even though, in reality, they are based in Mabouya Valley, Saint Lucia.

Saint Lucia didn't join FIFA until 1988, but they have had some success, internationally, like their 2001 14-1 demolition of the US Virgin Islands. And the women's national team beat the British Virgin Islands 8-0 in their first proper international.

And we can't mention St Lucian football without mentioning Keith Alexander. Born in Nottingham with Saint Lucian heritage, he played for a large number of teams, including the Saint Lucia national team, but he is perhaps best known now for his pioneering role as the first full-time Black manager of a professional club in England.

Saint Vincent and the Grenadines

The national team is nicknamed Vincy Heat. Internationally, though, the country has a fairly mixed track record.

Football in this small Caribbean country is, again, a product of the British Empire years. For instance, between the wars, the light cruiser HMS *Dauntless* dropped in to play football against a local team in Kingstown on Saint Vincent. The Navy team played two matches and won the first 6-0 and the second 5-1.

Among the teams that now take to the pitch are Camdonia Chelsea FC and Awesome FC.

And Saint Vincent and the Grenadines is a part of the world that has made its own contribution to British football. For instance, Jesse Lingard's grandparents are from there.

Samoa

Samoa had a complex colonial history in the late nineteenth century in which Britain, Germany and the United States competed for control of the Samoan Islands. Germany eventually ended up in control of what is now called Samoa, but not for long.

During the First World War, troops from New Zealand seized the territory. Many of the Samoans had, not surprisingly, by then had enough of being controlled by bickering foreigners, and from 1908, the Mau movement campaigned for independence. Samoa would finally get that in 1962.

Somewhere amidst all this, football came to the islands. The Royal Navy, as so often elsewhere, played some part in that. For instance, in 1928 HMS *Diomede* turned up on a sporting visit. By 1936 a report indicates that football was being played in Samoa, but only westerners were being signed up to play.

As elsewhere on a lot of the smaller Pacific islands, the locals didn't take up the game that speedily. However, in 1968 the Football Federation Samoa was founded. In 1977, Samoa's most successful team, Kiwi FC, was founded, and in 1979 the national team played its first international. OK, it lost to the Solomon Islands, but still, Samoa was on the international football stage at last.

In the 2019 Pacific Games, held in Apia, the capital of Samoa, the Samoa women's team made it to the football final. There, Papua New Guinea beat them 3-1.

San Marino

There's something that seems almost a bit mythical about San Marino, even when compared to other tiny European countries. A lot of Brits have been skiing in Andorra and know roughly where it is. When Liechtenstein comes up, some people will think of business and banking, but San Marino? Stamps maybe? Eurovision?

Yes, it is small and totally surrounded by Italy but it is a proud little country with a long history of democracy and a Crossbow Corps founded in 1295. Its national football team was founded somewhat more recently. San Marino's record at international level has not been that great, but then they don't have that many people to choose from, and they have had some success recently in the UEFA Nations League, including a draw against Gibraltar.

It's hard to know exactly when and how football arrived in San Marino. However, the Italian city of Rimini is only a few miles from the borders of the 'Most Serene Republic' and, there, the football club Libertas Rimini, now Calcio Rimini, was founded in 1912, and in the 1920s adopted red and white as its colours. What was perhaps the first Sammarinese football club was founded just sixteen years later and called Associazione Calcio Libertas, and it also plays in red and white.

It would be fair to say that Britain hasn't had huge involvement with Sammarinese football; however, Admiral was the kit supplier to the national team in the early 1990s. And coincidentally it was in the same period that England helped San Marino make football history.

In 1993, San Marino's Davide Gualtieri scored against England what was for twenty-two years the fastest goal in World Cup qualifying history, when he put the ball in the England net after just 8.3 seconds. OK, England still went on to win 7-1, but, for a long time it was a very big claim to fame for a very little country.

Development of the women's game in San Marino has been slow.

São Tomé and Príncipe

These are the Portuguese names for two islands. If you translate them into English, you get Saint Thomas and (the) Prince, which sounds like some mysterious historical play. In fact, it's an island nation state off the west coast of Africa, near Gabon.

As the country's name suggests, it was the Portuguese who seized the islands in the fifteenth century. These became a major transit point for the Atlantic slave trade. Later the country became a major producer of cocoa, which it still is today.

Football seems to have been introduced to the islands sometime around 1900, second-hand via Portugal rather than directly from the UK.

São Tomé and Príncipe is a tiny country with a population just over 200,000 and perhaps not surprisingly it has not had a hugely distinguished record on the international football stage.

Having said that, there is still plenty of passion for the sport on the islands and, as elsewhere, team names reflect plenty of local pride. One of the most successful local clubs in recent years has been UDRA, or União Desportiva Rei Amador, named after King Amador, who led a major slave rebellion against the Portuguese in the islands in 1595.

Saudi Arabia

Football seems to have arrived in Saudi Arabia in the 1920s, and the country's main port, Jeddah, played a key role in the start of the Saudi game.

A few years earlier, during the First World War, Arab rebels had attacked Turkish forces in Jeddah with the help of the Royal Navy, and the port had been used by the British to get Egyptian artillery and crews into the country to help the rebels. In 1927, Britain signed the Treaty of Jeddah with Ibn Saud, who by then was king of the territory that would become known as Saudi Arabia.

Also that year in Jeddah, a group of local football enthusiasts teamed up and founded Al-Ittihad, the oldest and one of the most successful football clubs in Saudi Arabia. Ten years later, another club was formed in Jeddah: Al-Ittihad's great rivals, Al-Ahli Saudi FC.

Jeddah was a busy trading port but it was also the entry point for huge numbers of Muslim pilgrims travelling to Mecca. A significant proportion of these pilgrims in the early twentieth century came from within the British Empire, because at that time about half the world's Muslim population lived under British administration. Many Muslims making Hajj will have brought their passion for football with them to Saudi Arabia. There is, for example, an early request from Indonesians in the country to be allowed to play football.

Saudi Arabia has had close links to Britain for most of its existence. The Saudi national side played its first international matches in 1953 and for most of the 1970s it was assisted by English trainers and coaches. Football is hugely popular in Saudi Arabia and at international level the Saudis have had quite a lot of success, including qualifying for the World Cup on a number of occasions and getting beyond the group stage in 1994. They also have an impressive Asian Cup record. The first Saudi Arabian women's football league started in 2020.

Senegal

At the time football was introduced into the region, Senegal was part of a bigger French colonial territory, French West Africa. Dakar, the capital of Senegal, was one of the first places to have properly organised football, and it seems to be agreed that Brits played a key role along with the French in introducing football.

The date of some of this is slightly in dispute but by 1913 some French, particularly military personnel, and other Europeans, probably including Brits, were playing football in Dakar and sometime around 1920, or a little before or a little after, clubs like Union Sportive de Dakar and Jeanne d'Arc, also in Dakar, were taking to the football pitch.

The École Normale William Ponty was founded in Dakar in 1918 and would also soon have football on the curriculum. It would also educate a lot of those who went on to lead the struggle for freedom from France. In 1929, the Union Sportive Indigène was created, again in Dakar.

Senegal became independent from France in 1960, and the Senegalese Football Federation was formed the same year.

The national men's team have for some time been one of the strongest sides in Africa and in 2022 won the Africa Cup of Nations. In 2002, they also made it to the quarter-finals of the World Cup, losing to Turkey. Senegalese players have also made a huge contribution to European football. Names familiar to football fans over here include, of course, Sadio Mané.

The national women's team has qualified for the Africa Women Cup of Nations once.

Serbia

The father of Serbian football was Hugo Buli. He came from a prosperous Jewish Serbian family in Belgrade, and was sent when young to study in Germany. Along with his studies, he also got involved in the sport that Brits had brought to Germany: yes, football. He showed quite a talent for it and ended up on the team at BFC Germania 1888.

Here he would presumably have played against their local rivals, BTuFC Britannia 1892. BTuFC stood for Berlin Thorball and Football Club, because at the time cricket in Germany was called *Thorball*. Buli would therefore presumably have been very much part of the British sports invasion of Germany that was football. In 1892, BFC Germania 1888 took on English FC and beat them 3-1.

In 1896, Buli returned to Serbia and, of course, he took a football and his passion for the sport with him. On 19 May 1896 he held Serbia's first ever football match in Kalemegdan Park, in the capital Belgrade, with friends and members of the Soko gymnastics club. It has to be said that football wasn't an immediate success with the Belgrade public as only fifty people turned up to watch. Few of the spectators seem to have been that enthusiastic about the new game, and there was puzzlement that the players were only using their legs and feet to move the ball.

Despite this slightly unprepossessing start, Buli bravely persisted with his efforts to promote the game. In 1899, he helped form a proper, independent football club, the First Serbian Society for Playing Ball. Other clubs soon followed and before the First World War interrupted it is reckoned there were about 3,000 people regularly playing football in the country.

Buli continued to be involved in Serbian football during the inter-war years. Tragically, after the German invasion of Yugoslavia in 1941, he was seized by the Nazis and killed.

Serbia, of course, has gone on to be a significant footballing force. Serbs played a key role in some of the great Yugoslavia sides and Serbia has qualified for the World Cup on a number of occasions. Clubs like Red Star Belgrade and Partizan Belgrade are well known beyond the country's borders. The Serbian national women's team has had a slightly tougher time.

Seychelles

It is probably fair to say that the Seychelles are better known to most people over here as a tropical paradise holiday destination than as a sports venue. But even tropical paradises need a bit of football.

In the eighteenth century, France and Britain fought over control of the islands. By the time football was spreading across the world, we had decisively won the competition and would remain the colonial power until independence in 1976.

By the early 1930s, people had already been kicking a ball in the islands for some time, occasionally with teams from visiting Royal Navy ships.

A certain Dr John Thomas Bradley decided that what was needed was a competition to really get football moving, so in 1936 he sponsored a football cup. A Dr John Thomas Bradley also happened at the time to be Chief Medical Officer of the Seychelles, so I think we can assume they were the same man. How many Dr John Thomas Bradleys are you going to find in the Seychelles at the same time in the 1930s?

Five teams fought to win the Bradley Cup in a match played in Gordon Square (now Freedom Square) in Victoria, the capital. Just like the name of the capital, the names of the teams reflect the British heritage of football on the islands: Ascot XI, Royal Mission XI, Police Team, St Louis College Team and Seychelles XI.

By the 1950s, the league had expanded to nine teams and, in the 1960s, women's football matches started on the islands as well.

And when the Seychelles started wanting to make their mark with an international team, they looked to English football coach Adrian Fisher to make it happen. In 1970, he took the Seychelles team to a friendly tournament in Kenya.

The national team is known as The Pirates – the Seychelles were once known as a pirate base. The team are not the most successful pirates in history, but at least nobody walks the plank at the end of their games.

Sierra Leone

The land of the Lion Mountains has a name given to it by early Portuguese and Italian explorers, but, despite this, its early history is very much tied up with Britain and so is the early history of its football.

The origins of Sierra Leone are complex but a key element is the British experiment of resettling freed slaves from America and elsewhere in Africa. The experiment involved a lot of suffering both among the freed slaves and among the existing local population; however, eventually a new society was created on the west coast of Africa.

And late in the nineteenth century or early in the twentieth, into this new society came football. As in other parts of the Empire, British educationalists saw sport as a key component of a good school, so major schools in Sierra Leone like Fourah Bay College and the Church Missionary Society Grammar School, in the capital Freetown, soon had football teams.

The Sierra Leone Amateur Football Association was formed in 1923, and the 1920s saw a number of football clubs established. Some of the most well known have had names that reflect early

British influence. There are, for example, the East End Lions, Old Edwardians, and yes, Mighty Blackpool.

When the club that became Mighty Blackpool was founded in 1923, it wasn't called Mighty Blackpool. However, in 1954, in the middle of the mighty Stanley Matthews's time with Blackpool in England, the Sokro Eleven Club renamed themselves in honour of this powerful force in English and world football.

The years since then have been far from easy for the people of Sierra Leone. In the 1990s, a civil war devastated parts of the country. However, the passion for football remains strong and the national team has qualified for the Africa Cup of Nations a number of times. Sierra Leone went to the African Women's Championship (as the Africa Women Cup of Nations was then called) in 1995.

Singapore

A lot of people know that, in the days of the British Empire, Singapore was one of its most important cities. So it won't come as a surprise to many people that, yes, we gave it football.

The first football match of which we know seems to have been played by teams made up of British engineers on a pitch somewhere near Tank Road in 1889. A few years later, in 1892, the Singapore Football Association was founded, and, in 1904, the YMCA started the Singapore Football League with twelve teams.

At first, British teams were a major element in the league. The team of the 1st Battalion, Manchester Regiment, for instance, won it in 1904. Soon, however, local teams were showing a lot of talent on the pitch, too. The Singapore Chinese Football Association won the league in 1925, and in 1934 the title was taken by the Singapore Malay team.

From early on, teams from Singapore took part in what was originally the Malaya Cup and which then became the Malaysia Cup, and Singapore has, on a number of occasions, won the ASEAN Football Federation Championship. The Singapore men's team are known as the Lions and the women's team are, yes, the Lionesses.

One of Singapore's most distinguished international players is Daniel Bennett, who was born in Great Yarmouth but moved to Singapore at a young age. He also plays in the Singapore Premier League, and a number of Singaporean clubs over the years, like Sembawang Rangers, have shown a link to British football in their names.

Slovakia

Slovakia used, of course, to be the other part of Czechoslovakia. It's a bit unfair to Slovakia really, but when a lot of Brits think of what became of Czechoslovakia, they tend to think of the Czech Republic first, perhaps because they have been to Prague, or because Slovakia is smaller than the Czech Republic, or because even during the Czechoslovakia period Czech was often used here as a convenient, shortened version of Czechoslovak.

Having said all that, Slovakia does have a rich football history itself. And part of that has involved Britain, with, for instance, Martin Škrtel making hundreds of appearances for Liverpool, while there is also Martin Dúbravka in goal at Newcastle and Juraj Kucka at Watford.

When football started in the 1890s, Slovakia was part of the Austro-Hungarian Empire and handily placed between Vienna and Budapest, both then being locations where football was spreading rapidly. A Hungarian engineer who had taken up football while studying in Switzerland, brought an English football to what was then Eperjes and is now Prešov, in Eastern Slovakia, in 1896. Two years later, the town had its own football team, when Eperjes Sports Club added it to a list of activities that included fencing and gymnastics. A local Latin professor, František Pethe, took an interest in football, and in 1898 Eperjes held the first organised game. Locals cleared molehills and cow dung from the pitch and built wooden benches. Two Hungarian sides provided an exhibition match.

Football also developed along the Danube in Bratislava. Visitors from Vienna or Budapest may have had kick-abouts earlier but in 1898 football became one of the activities of the Bratislava Gymnasium Association. The following year, players from Eperjes took on a team from Bratislava in the first match between Slovak sides. The Bratislava side ran out 2-1 winners.

Before the First World War regular games took place between Slovak teams and their neighbours in Vienna and Budapest.

Slovakia emerged from the First World War as part of a new nation: Czechoslovakia. In 1919, Slovakia's most successful football team, Slovan Bratislava, was founded. They began life as Čs.Š.K. Bratislava. Bratislava made rapid progress and were very proud of an 8-1 victory over a professional Newcastle United in 1929 (not the Magpies' finest ninety minutes!). However, perhaps their greatest performance was in 1969 when they defeated Barcelona 3-2 in the European Cup Winners' Cup Final. They are the only Slovak club to win a European competition.

Slovaks were part of the Czechoslovakian team who were runners-up in the 1934 World Cup, but they played their first game as Slovakia in 1939 after the Nazi takeover of Czechoslovakia. On 27 August, Slovakia defeated Germany 2-1 in Bratislava.

The Slovaks can also claim a major share of the glory for Czechoslovakia's triumph in the 1976 European Championship. Six of the eleven players who defeated West Germany were Slovak but Panenka, scorer of the winning penalty, was Czech.

Since 1993, Slovakia has qualified for the 2010 World Cup in South Africa and for the 2016 and 2020 European Championship.

There has been a women's football league in Slovakia since 1994, which has been dominated by Slovan Bratislava, who have won it fourteen times. The national women's team is yet to qualify for a major championships, but as Slovaks experience playing football in Germany and Italy, the standard will rise. Dominika Škorvánková, who started with Slovan Bratislava, has played for Bayern Munich and been Slovak player of the year nine times.

Slovenia

Slovenia declared its independence from Yugoslavia in June 1991. It's a small country with only 2 million people, with Austria to its north, Hungary to the east, Croatia to the south and Italy to the west. While Croatia has a long coastline with lots of beautiful beaches, Slovenia has a very short coastline, which is one reason it's rather less familiar to most Brits than its southern neighbour.

While the area was part of the Austro-Hungarian Empire prior to the First World War, football came to Slovenia via Germans and Hungarians, rather than directly from Britain. In Ljubljana, the Germans founded Laibacher Sportverein in 1900. In 1901, they defeated the Germans of Celje 4-1. Hungarians in Lendava also established a club in 1903.

Football became popular in schools. There are references to ball games as early as the 1860s but it is not until 1906 that it is clear that some of these games are association football. Grammar schools in Maribor and Ljubljana mention the game, and by 1908 students in Ljubljana seem to have been playing four hours of football a week. In Ljubljana, the students founded Hermes FC, which went on to become NK Ljubljana.

By 1914, there were football clubs in many Slovenian cities, but they were often short-lived. Any British influence on developments came largely from students and teachers picking up the game from Vienna, Budapest and Prague, where British links were far stronger.

Slovenia emerged from the First World War as part of the newly formed Yugoslavia. It played its football as part of a Slovenian sub league rather than a national Yugoslav one. In 1921, Slovenia played an international match in Ljubljana against France, losing 5-0 in front of Jules Rimet.

After the Second World War, of course, Yugoslavia became a significant footballing nation. Yugoslavia were Olympic champions in 1960 and runners-up in 1948, 1952 and 1956. In the Euros they were runners-up in 1960 and 1968.

While Slovenia undoubtedly contributed something to the national Yugoslav effort, there were only three Slovenian teams – Olimpija, Maribor and Nafta – regularly playing in the top level of Yugoslav football.

As an independent country, Slovenia qualified for the World Cup in 2002 and again in 2010, which was quite an achievement for somewhere with a population of only 2 million.

Slovenia's women also played a part in Yugoslavia's success in qualifying for two European Championships. Since independence, however, Slovenia hasn't been able to qualify for a major women's championship. There has been an eight-team league running since 1992 and this has been dominated by Krka and Pomurje, who have each won the title eight times.

Solomon Islands

Britain was the colonial power for a long time in the Solomon Islands, a group of hundreds of islands in the Pacific located to the north-east of Australia, but actual control was often patchy and they were comparatively little changed during the British period. There was also huge disruption caused by heavy fighting in the area during the Second World War.

Since independence from Britain in 1978, the nation has had a wide range of problems with which to deal, including a period of ethnic violence that mostly ended in 2003.

It is perhaps, therefore, not hugely surprising that football here is not as far developed as in a lot of other countries. However, a football league was formed in the capital, Honiara, in 1957, during the British period, and the club now known as Solomon Warriors FC, perhaps the country's best known, was founded for seven-a-side football in 1981. The Solomon Islands Football Federation was formed in 1978 and joined FIFA in 1988.

Scot George Cowie and Englishman Alan Gillett have both managed the Solomon Islands national team. The men's team has had some success in the OFC (Oceania Football Confederation) Nations Cup, and similarly the women's team has had some success in the OFC Women's Nations Cup.

Somalia

If you were watching the news in the 1990s, you will be aware that Somalia has had an occasionally pretty chaotic history in recent times. However, the complexities didn't start during the time of *Black Hawk Down*, and some of them are reflected in the story of the country's football and how it started.

Somalia is one of those African countries where there is a history of two different European colonial powers operating in two different parts of the country.

Somalia is shaped a bit like a number 7. From 1887, Britain controlled most of the flat bit at the top of the 7. It became known as British Somaliland, or the Somaliland Protectorate.

Apart from a period of occupation by the Italians during the Second World War, Britain controlled this part of Somalia until 1960. And during that period it, of course, introduced football. As elsewhere, Britain founded educational establishments to train the most talented locals to be teachers, minor officials and administrators. British sports, including football and hockey, were part of the curriculum.

Starting in the late nineteenth century, however, the colonial power in the rest of Somalia, including the capital, Mogadishu, was Italy. British governments did not take a lot of interest in British Somaliland. By contrast, the Italians, with far fewer imperial possessions, took quite a lot of interest in Italian Somaliland and spent quite a lot of money and effort trying to make it more Italian. These efforts included importing Italian colonists and building art deco architecture in Mogadishu – and football and football clubs. There were Italian teams, like the Italian navy team, but locals also started forming their own clubs, like Amaruini, some of which became an element in the Somali struggle against colonialism.

After Italian forces in the area were defeated in the Second World War, there would be a period of British military administration in Italian Somaliland, followed by another period of Italian administration, this time under UN authority, and finally, there would be independence in 1960. Soon after British Somaliland and Italian Somaliland became independent they were joined to create the borders of modern Somalia.

There are still some traces, however, of the colonial heritage in modern Somali football. The Mogadishu team Jeenyo United FC, for instance, was at one stage known as Lavori Publici (Public Works in Italian) because it had connections with the Ministry of Public Works.

More significantly, in 1991, local authorities in what had been British Somaliland declared independence of their area from

Somalia, as Somaliland. That independence has not been recognised by the international community, but Somaliland does now have its own football team. In 2017, Peckham Town took them on in a charity friendly and beat them 4-0.

The Somalia national football team has not had massive international football success either, but considering what the country has been through that's not hugely surprising.

South Africa

The 'rainbow nation' has, of course, hosted both rugby and football World Cups. In 1995, the Springboks lifted the rugby union trophy on home soil. They won again in Japan in 2019. In the 2010 FIFA World Cup, the Bafana Bafana, (Zulu for The Lads, The Lads) won one game and drew another before being eliminated. Brits introduced both games to South Africa. While rugby has thrived among the wealthy, football has had a more difficult journey, one that has often been badly affected by appalling and blatant racism.

The first game of football was played in 1862 in Port Elizabeth when a team of white players born in South Africa took on a team of new settlers. The game was played before the FA was formed and the rules used are unclear. In 1882, the oldest existing club, Savages FC, was formed in Pietermaritzburg and a Natal Football Association was soon formed. This featured Savages and three other whites-only clubs, Natal Wasps, Durban Alpha and Umgeni Stars. In 1883, the league grew to ten clubs. By 1892, there was sufficient support to establish a whites-only South African Football Association, affiliated to the FA in London.

Also in 1892, Scottish philanthropist Donald Currie gave a trophy for a football competition between the provinces of South Africa. Originally open to both football and rugby clubs, it has become South Africa's main rugby competition.

The Corinthians, the prestigious British amateur club, toured South Africa in 1897, playing games across the country. The tourists returned undefeated, including in matches played against a South Africa national side. The Corinthians made further tours in 1903 and 1907. After the final tour, they concluded South Africa had made 'great strides', and Corinthians had suffered five defeats.

In 1906, a whites-only South African side toured South America, losing only one game. South Africa's position as one of the leading football nations was confirmed in 1910 when they became the first country outside Europe to join FIFA.

Rugby was the game of the British urban upper class and had also been adopted by Afrikaner farmers. For status-conscious South Africans, football was often seen to be a game for the masses. It was also a game for soldiers. The Royal Artillery won the first three league championships in the Western Province, in 1891–93, and Army teams won all nineteenth-century Western Province Championships.

The future of the beautiful game in South Africa lay with Black Africans, and the British Army played a significant role in introducing football to them. To the disgust of many white South Africans, many Army units were happy to play the game with non-whites.

In the 1880s, football clubs for non-whites began in Durban and Johannesburg. In 1899, a Black South African team from the Orange Free State, led by Joseph Twayi, arrived for a tour of Britain and France. The team played forty-nine games in England, Scotland, Ireland and France, visiting famous stadiums like those of Tottenham Hotspur, Aston Villa and Newcastle United. The games were popular, although staged more as a show than competitive sport.

Twayi's only victory was in France. Twayi went on to be treasurer of the African National Congress, and football would contribute to the end of apartheid in South Africa by boosting the self-confidence of its many ethnic communities and allowing them to express their identities.

Gandhi appreciated the political value of football, and in 1903 he helped found the South African Association of Hindu football. The Association launched the Sam China Cup for teams of Indian origin, with Transvaal winning the first competition.

Inter-community football began in South Africa in 1935. The Suzman Cup, established in the Transvaal, allowed African, Indian and teams with more than one ethnic heritage to compete. Competitions like the Bakers Cup and the Godfrey South African Cup attracted large crowds and encouraged new teams like the Orlando Pirates to be formed. The club was begun by a boxing instructor, Andries 'Pele Pele' Mkhwanazi. The boys may have had to play barefoot but at least they could play.

In 1961, the South African Soccer League started. It gave its players opportunities to develop their skills to the point where some could leave and play abroad. To supporters it was an opportunity to gather, enjoy themselves and fight oppression. One émigré, Kaizer 'Chincha Guluva' Motaung, returned from playing with the Atlanta Chiefs in 1970 to form the Kaizer Chiefs FC (not the rock band).

Apartheid ended during the period 1990–94, and in 1994 Nelson Mandela became president. Since 1996–97 the Chiefs have been Premier League champions four times and runners-up five times, while the Pirates also have four titles and six consolation prizes.

Women's football started slowly but a professional league was established in 2019. The national side qualified for the World Cup in France in 2019 and has been runners-up in the Africa Women Cup of Nations five times: 1995, 2000, 2008, 2012 and 2018.

Steven Pienaar is one of the South African footballers who have contributed their talents to the game in Britain.

South Sudan

It's a young country that has seen tough times. After decades of Sudanese civil wars, South Sudan became independent in 2011.

Football was introduced to the area by British colonial administrators in the early twentieth century. In the 1930s, football clubs were being formed in Juba. And in the period after the Second World War, some of the major clubs of South Sudanese football were formed. For instance, in 1946 the Al-Malakia Sports, Social and Cultural Club was formed in Juba, and in 1956, fans of major Sudanese club Al-Hilal formed Al-Hilal (Juba).

There was a lot of conflict in the area in the six decades prior to the independence of South Sudan and the years since haven't been easy either, with civil wars plaguing the young nation. Not surprisingly, therefore, South Sudan has not had huge success in international football, but having national football teams at all is something of which many South Sudanese are proud. The men's team did beat Djibouti 6-0 in 2017, while the women's team beat Zanzibar 5-0 in 2019.

Spain

'Always keep the ball in movement from one player to another. Always help a player in a difficult position. A good attack is the best defence.' Three of ten pieces of guidance given by a Barcelona manager to his players. The advice is unsurprising, but what *is* surprising is that this was not Johan Cruyff or Pep Guardiola, but a little-known Brit, Alf Spouncer, and the date 1923, nearly a century ago. Brits took football to Spain and have continued to influence its development since then.

The first game played was in 1870 in Jerez de la Frontera, where the local press reported a cricket match and a bit of football, though it is slightly unclear what football rules were being used.

It was miners, engineers and railway workers, many of them Scots, who pioneered the game in Andalucía, as the British Rio Tinto company exploited Spanish copper resources. In 1874, Captain Adams of the British garrison in Huelva recorded a game between his soldiers and railway workers. Football became popular entertainment for the expat community and attracted Spanish interest.

The earliest football club in Spain still playing, Club Recreativo de Huelva, began in 1889, founded by Scotsmen Charles Adams and Dr William Mackay. Mackay took up football while training at Edinburgh University. In 1882, he moved to Huelva to work for Rio Tinto. He was interested in the health benefits of football and spent time teaching locals to play as well as attending to their ailments. The club was a mix of Spanish and Brits, and early opponents were engineers, miners or, yes, visiting sailors.

Local rival Sevilla Football Club emerged in 1890. This too was a mainly British-led venture, with Edward Johnson as president and Hugo MacColl as captain, although Spanish residents were also involved. In March 1890, Sevilla took on Huelva, winning 2-0.

Seville rival Real Betis was founded in 1907. Its green and white colours may be a reference to the colours of Andalucía, but there is also a link to Celtic, as one of its founders had studied in Glasgow.

Andalucía was where Spanish football really got started. OK, the clubs may not now be quite as famous as some other Spanish clubs, but they have had success. Real Betis, led by Irishman Patrick O'Connell, won the Liga in 1935 and Sevilla are the Europa League maestros, winning five times this century.

In the north, Bilbao's early industrialisation attracted British shipbuilders, miners and investors. Students watched British sailors playing football and asked them for a game. The sailors won and in 1898 the students set up Athletic Club to play football. A rival team, Bilbao FC, was formed two years later by different students.

The two teams combined in 1902 to send a team named Bizcaya to Madrid to participate in a football cup to celebrate King Alfonso XIII's coronation. The team may have borne a Basque name, but there also was a strong British contingent. Bizcaya won the Copa de la *Coronación*. The following year, the Copa Del Rey (King's Cup) started. Flushed with success, Bilbao's two teams merged to form Athletic Club de Bilbao. Bilbao played winning football and by 1916 had collected five Copas.

The first club in Catalonia was established in 1898 in Palamós, between Barcelona and the French border, by a student, Gaspar Matas i Danés, who had studied in England. Palamós FC made a winning start, defeating a team of British sailors 2-1.

Hans-Max Gamper (known in Barcelona as Joan), founder of FC Basel in Switzerland, started FC Barcelona with a group of Anglo-Swiss enthusiasts in 1899. The original blue and maroon strip may have been based on the sports shirts worn by pupils at Merchant Taylors School, in Crosby, Liverpool, as suggested by descendants of the English Witty brothers. The brothers played for Barcelona in the early years and had been pupils at Merchant Taylors. Perhaps coincidentally, Gamper's FC Basel share similar colours.

Pride in Basque identity has helped Athletic Bilbao and pride in Catalonian identity is deeply entrenched at Barcelona. The red and yellow stripes of Catalonia feature on its crest. St Jordi (St George), who also features, is the patron saint of both England and Catalonia.

In Madrid, it was the wealthy who started playing football. The first Madrid club, in 1897, was Sky (no connection to the broadcaster). One of its founders was the Count de La Quinta de la Enrajada, who had been educated at Oxford. In 1902,

Madrid FC emerged when Sky split, and it became Real Madrid in 1920, when it received royal recognition. For a decade after 1910, Madrid was managed by the Brit Arthur Johnson. Real's Madrid rival, Atlético, was formed in 1903 by Basque students as a branch of their Bilbao club.

Spain got a football association in 1909 and a national league in 1929. The early power lay with the clubs and regional leagues rather than the centre. The foundations of so many major elements of Spanish football were already there – passionate local derbies, political tension between Basques, Catalans and Madrid, and wealthy patrons, but also English influence.

The national team won silver at the 1920 Olympics in Amsterdam – a huge achievement, as these were Spain's maiden internationals. Defeated by Belgium in the quarter-finals, they got a second chance when Czechoslovakia walked out of the final complaining about unfair refereeing. A mini-tournament was arranged for the silver medal and Spain defeated Sweden, Italy and the Netherlands to claim the prize. In 1929, they became the first country from continental Europe to defeat England.

One of the coaches who guided Spain to victory over England was himself English. Fred Pentland played for Blackburn Rovers before moving to manage Athletic Bilbao in 1922. In his first spell in Bilbao, Athletic won the Copa del Rey and, in his second, Athletic won four consecutive Copas. He also won La Liga twice, including a 12-1 victory over Barcelona. Pentland's friend, England international Steve Bloomer, led Basque side Real Irun to their only Copa del Rey triumph in the 1920s. Irun defeated both Barcelona and Real Madrid to claim the trophy.

With Barcelona, it was the little-known Brit Jack Greenwell who helped shape one of their first great teams. He won the Copa del Rey twice and Catalan Championship four times. This was before La Liga started. English managers were often the stars in the 1920s.

British involvement has continued in recent years. John Toshack led Basque side Real Sociedad to success in the Copa del Rey in the 1980s before taking charge at Real Madrid and winning a title for them. Terry Venables worked at Barcelona in the 1980s. He won La Liga and laid some of the foundations for Johan Cruyff's 'dream team'. Bobby Robson won a Copa Del Rey and Cup Winner's Cup with Barça in the 1990s. Both managers played a part in the development of tiki-taka football.

Brits have starred on the pitch as well, with, for instance, Gary Lineker and Mark Hughes playing for Barcelona and David Beckham and Gareth Bale for Real Madrid.

The Premier League now has the Catalan maestro Pep Guardiola demonstrating the art of football management. Meanwhile, David Silva at Manchester City and Diego Costa, Cesc Fàbregas and César Azpilicueta at Chelsea have all brought a Spanish flavour to the home game.

The twenty-first century has been a golden age for Spanish football. Their skill and flair is admired worldwide. Spain won the World Cup in 2010 in South Africa, defeating the Netherlands in extra time. Between 2008 and 2012, they also won two European Championships and were the best team in the world. At club level, Real Madrid collected three consecutive Champions Leagues and reached five finals in less than twenty years. Barcelona have collected a further four Champions Leagues with their impressive play. It is no surprise that Spanish clubs have won more European titles than any other nation.

The Royal Spanish Football Federation recognised the women's game in 1980, but the first games had been played as early as 1914. A Spanish Girls Club was formed in Barcelona. It played a fundraiser for a tuberculosis charity and also staged games in Valencia, Reus and Tarragona before the First World War stopped play.

In Galicia, in the 1920s, the remarkable Irene González played in goal for men's team Orillamar. She went on to set up her own team, Irene FC, but died of tuberculosis in 1927. There must be a potential film script in there.

In the 1970s, there were attempts to popularise the women's game. Two Madrid teams, Mercacredit and Sizam Paloma, were formed and played a match. The star was young teenager Conchi Amancio, who scored five goals. Conchi left Spain to play in Italy, winning ten league titles before ending her career with Arsenal aged 40.

Since women's football has been recognised, the story has been somewhat more predictable. A national league was started in 1988 and the most successful club has been Barcelona with six titles followed by Athletic Bilbao with five.

The national team's first game was against Portugal. The women reached the semi-finals of the Euros in 1997 and have been quarter-finalists at the last two competitions.

Sri Lanka

Sri Lanka is probably better known for its love of that other game from England, the one with the bats and wickets, but there is also plenty of passion on the island for football.

The sport came to what was then Ceylon with the British military in the late nineteenth century. It is said that, in the 1890s, British soldiers were kicking a football in the capital Colombo, stripped to the waist because of the heat.

Between them, the British military, police, administration and planters then spread the sport across the island, with a lot of the locals enthusiastically joining in when given the opportunity.

In 1918, Saunders Sports Club, which would go on to be one of Ceylon/Sri Lanka's greatest football clubs, was founded in Colombo. Crystal Palace FC Gampola is another club on the island with a very English name.

In the 1920s and '30s, football leagues were formed and the game was put on something of a more formal basis. An influential figure in the process was Scot, and long-term resident of Ceylon, Sir John Allen Tarbat.

The national football federation was formed in 1939 and, after the country became independent from Britain in 1948, it joined FIFA in 1952. In 1995, the men's national team won the South Asian Football Federation Championship (then known as the South Asian Gold Cup). In 2012, Sri Lanka hosted the SAFF Women's Championship,

Sudan

It's a country that figured large in the late Victorian mythology of the British Empire, at a time long before the First World War, when British forces were fighting opponents with much less technologically sophisticated weaponry than the Germans.

There was, of course, Gordon of Khartoum, who features in that well-known painting of a Briton in a fez, calmly about to meet his death through the spears of his much more excited adversaries, and there was the subsequent Battle of Omdurman, in which a British–Egyptian force, including young Winston Churchill, used modern rifles, Maxim guns and artillery to slaughter thousands of much less well-armed locals.

And, interestingly enough, Gordon's name makes an appearance in the story of how we gave Sudan football.

After the Battle of Omdurman, Sudan was controlled by an Anglo-Egyptian condominium, which effectively meant it was run by Britain, and part of this administration was, of course, introducing British sport.

In 1902, as a flagship element of local education reforms, Gordon Memorial College in Khartoum was opened to train students who would become leaders of local administration. It was a prestige institution, known as 'Winchester by the Nile' or the 'Eton of the Sudan', that would educate a large number of key figures in Sudanese history. And football was a major part of the curriculum.

In 1908, students from Gordon Memorial College who were based in Omdurman, on the other side of the Nile from Khartoum, teamed up to form the sports club that would, in 1927, take the name Al-Merrikh SC and go on to become one of Sudan's leading football clubs. Later, in 1930, more Gordon Memorial College graduates would help form Al-Hilal Club, another of the country's great teams, and one that would become ferocious rivals of Al-Merrikh.

In 1936, British administrators assisted the creation of the Sudan Football Association, and the same year, the Khartoum District League was founded.

Another institution that helped spread football across Sudan was the railway. A key rail town was Atbara (also site of a British victory prior to Omdurman that led to a work by notorious poet William McGonagall), and British authorities encouraged football among the rail workers for team-building purposes. However, the authorities would find in Atbara, as elsewhere, that football and football clubs, rather than creating placid workers, tended to create local and national pride that sometimes turned against Britain.

Sudan became independent in 1956. The Sudan national side was one of the giants of the African game in the 1950s and '60s, and, in 1970, Sudan won the Africa Cup of Nations. Since then, the country's record has been a bit more mixed.

In 2019, a women's football league was established in Sudan, and in 2021 a team went to the Arab Women's Cup.

Suriname

It's located on the north-east coast of South America. Not perhaps one of the classic South American football nations, you might think, but it has exported an amazing array of talent to Europe.

Suriname's history is unusual in South America in that, rather than being colonised by the other European empires that seized so much land in the region, it was mainly colonised by the Dutch instead. We did occupy some territory in the area originally, but the Dutch seized those bits during the Second Anglo-Dutch War, and, in the peace deal of 1667 that ended the war, they kept what they'd seized there while we kept New York, which used to be New Amsterdam. Consequently it seems most likely that football mainly came here, not directly from Britain, but indirectly, via the Netherlands.

The early twentieth century saw competition for local control of football between the Surinamese Football Association and the Dutch Guyana Football Association. After it joined FIFA in 1929, the Surinamese Football Association eventually won out.

There may, however, have been some British influence on the development of Surinamese football since its main opponent in international football in the early years was neighbouring British Guiana, and a few early Surinamese clubs and players do seem to have British names. There was also the interestingly named MYOB (Mind Your Own Business) football club and also the Fearless club.

Suriname's main foreign footballing connection has continued to be with the Netherlands. And what a connection it has been. Ruud Gullit, Frank Rijkaard, Patrick Kluivert and Jimmy Floyd Hasselbaink are a few of the footballers of Surinamese heritage who have helped make the Dutch national team successful.

And, of course, British teams too have benefited from the talents of players from Suriname or those with Surinamese heritage. Dean Gorré, for instance, who went on to be coach of the Suriname national team, played for a number of Dutch clubs before crossing the Channel to play for a few clubs here. And Gullit, Kluivert and Hasselbaink are also well known for their time playing over here.

Suriname's own international football record has been pretty patchy.

Sweden

It's definitely not just flat-pack furniture that is coming over from there, several Swedes have made a major impact on the Premier League. For instance, at Manchester United, Henrik Larsson helped Utd to be champions in 2006–07 and Zlatan Ibrahimović scored seventeen goals for the club in his thirty-three Premier League appearances. Freddie Ljungberg was one of Arsenal's 'Invincibles' in 2003–04. Olof Mellberg made loads of Premier League appearances for Aston Villa, and Sebastian Larsson made hundreds of Premier League appearances split between Sunderland, Arsenal and Birmingham. Yes, British football has benefited from Swedish influence, but, of course, Brits have also played a major role in developing football in Sweden, both directly and via Denmark.

A Swedish version of football developed in the 1870s, which was a mixture of rugby and soccer. There were clubs in a number of major cities, all with their own rules.

Sweden was also developing a passion for gymnastics and developing a national network of sports clubs based on this. Some of these clubs had members who had experienced the fun of football during their studies in Britain and who then introduced the sport to other members.

The Danes were also keen to export football to the Swedes. In 1890, Halmstad Ball invited Copenhagen Academy Ball Club to a game. The Danes won but it is unclear what rules were used. The following year, Malmö Cycle Club invited Copenhagen Ball Club to play an exhibition match. One thousand spectators turned up to watch the game, which was played under Football Association rules, and the Danes left a couple of footballs to encourage the Swedes.

Further north, in Gothenburg, the Scots were to play a major role in spreading football. In 1887, Wilhelm Friberg helped to found a sports society, the Örgryte Idrottssällskap. In 1892, the club also took up football. Gothenburg was open to considerable British influence, with regular visits from sailors and Scottish textile workers at the local mills. The Scots, led by John Lawson, taught Örgryte Idrottssällskap how to play football.

In 1892, when Örgryte Idrottssällskap took on Idrottssäll-skapet Lyckans Soldater (Fortunate Soldier) there were six Scots included in the team and, according to the local press, the Scots were the key players in driving Örgryte Idrottssällskap to victory. This match is commemorated by a plaque where it was played and is usually seen as the first Swedish football game.

From these early beginnings, football began to spread steadily. By 1896, there were sufficient clubs to organise a knock-out championship, the Svenska Mästerskapet, which was won by Friberg's Örgryte Idrottssällskap. In 1904, the Swedish FA was founded and in the same year Sweden was one of the founding members of FIFA.

In 1904, the famous amateur side Corinthians toured Sweden, defeating Uppsala University 11-0 and a Stockholm XI 15-1. They left a trophy – the Corinthian Bowl – as something for which the Swedes could compete.

Interest in football spread and eventually the country would produce a formidable footballing culture.

The Swedish national side has enjoyed some major successes, and some of that has been down to British help.

Sweden won the gold medal at the 1948 Olympics and bronze four years later. They also finished second in the 1958 World Cup and third in 1950. All these successes were achieved under the English coach George Raynor. Raynor made the Swedish short passing game more aggressive, and as he prepared for the 1948 Olympics, he got his players to train with Swedish athletes. He was sufficiently confident of victory over Yugoslavia in the final that winners' shirts were ready for all his team.

Many of the Swedish stars who had won in the Olympics went to play as professionals in Italy and were not available for the World Cup in 1950. Undeterred, Raynor set up a national coaching programme to develop 'stars of the future' and as such his coaching may have had more impact on the game in Sweden than the Olympic victory.

Raynor's preparations for the 1950 World Cup are now standard but at the time were revolutionary. His players had special boots, balls were imported from South America so players would be used to them and each player had an individual training programme. By 1950, it was possible to suggest that Sweden were the best side in Europe.

Raynor left Sweden in 1953, but then returned for the 1958 World Cup, which was staged in Sweden. His triumph was in persuading the Swedes to be pragmatic and select Swedish-born professionals who were playing in Italy rather than in Sweden. Hence, Swedes playing at Lazio and both Milan clubs were selected. The Swedes defeated the Germans in the semi-final but couldn't handle Pelé and the Brazilians in the final and went down 5-2.

While the Swedes have subsequently come third in the 1994 World Cup in the USA and reached the quarter-finals in Russia in 2018, they have yet to surpass their record under an English manager.

The Swedish women's team has more recent origins than the men but they have still had major international success. Although women have played football in Sweden since early in the twentieth century, most of those early games were charity affairs or kick-arounds. It was not until 1973 that a women's team played an international match. However, they won the inaugural European Championship in 1984 and they won silver at the Olympics in Brazil 2016 and Tokyo 2020. In the Women's World Cup, they were runners-up in 2003 and finished third in both 2011 and 2019.

Football is the second most popular sport for women in Sweden and, like their fellow Scandinavian countries, they are a major force in the women's game.

Switzerland

Today Switzerland is the home both of FIFA, in Zürich, and UEFA, in Nyon. Admittedly, like many other international organisations, FIFA and UEFA liked Switzerland due to its location and neutrality, but, to be fair to Switzerland, it did enthusiastically embrace the beautiful game early, once we had given them football, and actually did a lot to spread it around Europe and the wider world.

Lausanne Football and Cricket club was founded in 1860 by English students and teachers at private schools in the area. The club was probably the earliest football and cricket club established in mainland Europe. It is not clear exactly when it started playing football, or even what type was being played, as 1860 was three years before the FA published its rules and in 1879 the club appeared to be playing rugby. By 1895, however, it was definitely playing football.

The oldest football club still playing is St Gallen FC, started in 1879. It was founded following an appeal in the local newspaper, the *St Gallen Tagblatt*, for anybody interested in playing to meet at the Hornli restaurant. It is not clear how many Brits responded to the advert in St Gallen, but the club did have three English coaches between the wars: Jack Reynolds, William Townley and Norman Smith. St Gallen would be a founding member of the Swiss Football Association.

Grasshopper FC of Zürich, one of the country's most successful clubs and another founding member of the Swiss Football Association, was founded in 1886 by an English student, Tom E. Griffith. The club had a blue and white kit based on that worn by Blackburn Rovers and their equipment was sent out from England. The club is unusual in that it won its first Swiss Championship in 1898 and its most recent in 2003.

When the Swiss Football Association was founded in 1895, it was also quite a British institution. While the president, Emile Westermann, and secretary, John Tollmann, were Swiss, the vice president, Thomas Kilham, and committee members J.W. Seymour Holey and Edmund Davies, were all Brits. As well as Lausanne Football Club, Grasshoppers and St Gallen, founding members included Neuchâtel Rovers and the Anglo-American Club Zürich. Young Boys of Bern were not founder members, but were playing before 1900 and continued the tradition of English names. Even those clubs lacking an English name had English players. Villa Longchamp Ouchy was an offshoot of a private school of pretty much the same name, which was popular with English students.

While Brits did much to start Swiss football, the Swiss did much to develop the game and spread it. By 1900, there were twenty-six Swiss football clubs and a functioning league. Hans Gamper, who had helped found FC Zürich, went on to play a key role in founding FC Barcelona. Swiss players in Milan broke away from the Milan Football and Cricket Club to create a new club. Milan Football and Cricket Club is now AC Milan and the

Swiss team is Internazionale Milan, Inter Milan. In neighbouring Turin, Alfred Dick from Switzerland left Juventus to found their rivals, Torino. Swiss influence even spread to South America, with Oscar Cox leaving Lausanne to set up Fluminense in Brazil.

Switzerland was neutral in the First World War, but it did play host to soldiers from both sides, including wounded men recovering and prisoners being exchanged. No doubt plenty of football was played.

Switzerland has yet to win a major international tournament. It came closest at its first attempt, the 1924 Olympics in Paris. The squad did not contain any Brits but the Swiss did have an English manager, Teddy Duckworth. Teddy had played for Blackpool during a short career at the turn of the century. He served during the First World War before starting a coaching career in Switzerland with Servette FC. He led the Swiss to the final, defeating countries like Lithuania, but also Czechoslovakia, Sweden and Italy en route. In the final, the Swiss met Uruguay and were beaten by the fast passing and moving of the South American team. Uruguay won 3-0.

While Switzerland has qualified for the World Cup on numerous occasions, the adventure has never gone beyond the quarter-finals. One of these adventures in 1994 in the USA was under the British leadership of Roy Hodgson. He led the Swiss through qualifying in a group that included Italy and Portugal. However, in the round of sixteen the Spanish eliminated them 3-2. While the tournament was in the end a disappointment for Switzerland, Hodgson did raise the Swiss FIFA ranking to third, which remains their highest so far.

There has been a women's league in Switzerland since 1971, with Zürich Frauen being the most successful team, followed by YB Frauen. At international level, the women qualified for the 2015 World Cup but were eliminated at the group stage. They qualified for the Euros in 2017 and again in 2022.

Brits gave the Swiss football and in return they have given us some star performers. Granit Xhaka and Philippe Senderos have both won FA Cups with Arsenal, while Stéphane Henchoz and Xherdan Shaqiri have both won the Champions League with Liverpool.

Syria

A lot of readers older than a certain age, and even a few younger readers, will have seen Peter O'Toole whipping his white robes around him, while charging around the desert as Lawrence of Arabia. The 1962 movie won seven Oscars, but probably wouldn't be quite as popular today.

Nonetheless, it did (and to the extent that anybody still watches it, still does) make people think about one of the British Army's less well-known exploits in the First World War. At the same time as the slaughter continued on the Western Front, British and Commonwealth forces fighting the Turks were advancing from Egypt towards Jerusalem, and then on northwards, while Arab forces under Faysal, with a number of Allied advisors including Lawrence, were also giving the Turks a lot of headaches.

In October 1918, as the war reached its final stages, both Allied and Arab forces ended up in a Damascus newly liberated from the Turks. The two forces were not going to be friends for long. Faysal would be declared Arab king of Syria, but the British and French governments had already privately carved up the region, giving Syria to the French, and Faysal would be forced to flee. Eventually he would be made King of Iraq.

However, in the meantime, we had helped give the Syrians something that would last a lot longer than either Faysal's rule or the French Protectorate in Syria; yes, a love of football.

The wealthy and aristocratic Nuri Ibish is said to have returned to Damascus with a love of football prior to the British arrival. However, the first official recorded major football match in Syria took place in 1919 on the outskirts of Damascus between a Syrian team, trained by Ibish and under the patronage of King Faysal, and a team from the British Army. The Syrians apparently won and each got a gold watch from the king as reward.

Syrian football fans are as keen as any others. However, it would be fair to say that Syria is sadly known around the world these days much more for the war it has been going through than for goals scored in international matches.

Taiwan

Most Brits will know this place as Taiwan but its complicated diplomatic status means that it is officially known to FIFA as Chinese Taipei. Taipei is the capital of Taiwan or, as it prefers to call itself, the Republic of China. It is not currently recognised by the UN due to objections from the People's Republic of China, which claims sovereignty over the island. It is, however, a member of FIFA under the name Chinese Taipei.

British missionaries came to Taiwan in the nineteenth century, when it was ruled by the Chinese government, and set up schools. A Japanese victory in the first Sino-Japanese War in 1895, however, left Taiwan under Japanese rule.

Football perhaps first arrived in 1914 when Edward Band became principal of Chang Jung High School. Band had degrees in maths and theology from Cambridge University. He had also captained the football team. He started Taiwan's first football club, Chang Jung, in 1916. He was an enthusiastic coach, making sure pupils attended practice after school rather than taking a nap. Band's move probably wasn't very popular at first – until, of course, they realised the full excitement of the new game.

Chang Jung eventually played other schools in a Southern League, established in 1929. Thomas Barclay, a Scottish missionary, helped out by donating the Barclay Cup as a trophy.

Rivalry between Chang Jung and the Japanese Tainan First Senior High School was intense and sometimes violent. In 1940, Chang Jung, as Taiwan School Champions, had the opportunity to play in the All Japan High School Soccer Tournament and represent their country.

Control of Taiwan returned to Chinese hands after the Japanese defeat in the Second World War. However, the Communist victory in the Chinese Civil War in 1949 resulted in the defeated nationalist leader, Chiang Kai-shek, and his KMT forces fleeing to Taiwan. This created the political separation between Taiwan and mainland China that still persists today.

Since then, increased American influence in Taiwan has led to baseball being far more popular than football. However, Taiwan joined FIFA in 1954 and it does have an eight-team Premier League, although the teams are only semi-professional.

Chinese Taipei has yet to qualify for a World Cup and has had limited international success. English-born coach Gary White, who played his football in Australia, helped Taipei to their highest FIFA ranking in 2018. One of his improvements was to search for eligible players abroad. Subsequently, two Brits, Tim Chow and Will Donkin, were given opportunities to appear for Taiwan.

The Taipei women's team, the 'Mulans', has had slightly greater success. They were Women's Asian Cup winners three times between 1977 and 1981.

Tajikistan

The country is situated to the north of Afghanistan. The Russians seized control of the area in the nineteenth century, incorporating it into the Russian Empire, as a move in the so-called Great Game, as Britain competed with Russia for control of Central Asia. However, as Britain found out in the nineteenth century and has seen again recently, getting entangled in Afghanistan is neither great nor a game.

Football, of course, is a great game, although it probably didn't reach Tajikistan directly from here. After Brits helped introduce football to Russia, imperial troops may well have kicked balls around in Tajikistan before the 1917 revolution. Certainly, after Tajikistan became incorporated into the Soviet Union, football became popular there.

The sport was already being played in the 1920s, and in 1936 the Tajikistan Football Federation was formed, with a proper championship starting in 1937 and the Tajik Cup following in 1938.

The club Dynamo Stalinabad played a dominant role in early football in Tajikistan. Stalinabad is not, as you might think, a moral condemnation of the Soviet dictator (a moral condemnation that could have got you shot in Tajikistan in the 1930s) but is in fact the official Stalin-era name of Dushanbe, the capital of Tajikistan.

Tajikistan became independent in 1991. There is plenty of passion in the domestic game, but its national sides have had somewhat limited success in international football. The men's team did beat Guam 16-0 in November 2000.

Tanzania (and Zanzibar)

Tanzania has a complicated history that is, in some sense, reflected in the fact that there are two major football organisations within the country, the Tanzania Football Federation and the Zanzibar Football Federation.

Zanzibar is a collection of islands off the coast of mainland Tanzania, and its main city is also called Zanzibar. Long before the arrival of Europeans, Arab traders were conducting extensive commercial operations on the islands and the nearby mainland, and in the eighteenth century the Sultanate of Oman took control of Zanzibar. In the nineteenth century, when European powers arrived in the area they looked on the affluent Omani and Zanzibari territory with some envy.

By the 1870s we were taking a particular interest in Zanzibar and were starting to develop extensive influence and trade there. And yes, we brought football, too. As in some other countries, the arrival of telegraph cables proved vital in bringing the game to Zanzibar. Britain's Eastern Telegraph Company was laying a submarine cable from Aden to Africa. The company workers brought their footballs with them and played the game in their leisure time, arousing the interest of some of the locals.

Again, major local educational facilities also proved key to spreading the game, with football being on the curriculum by 1891 at the UMCA, Universities' Mission to Central Africa school.

In 1896, after a dispute over succession to the Sultanate of Zanzibar, Royal Navy ships bombarded the palace and after less than an hour, in one of the shortest wars ever, we seized more direct control of Zanzibar.

The sport of football already had solid foundations and continued to grow under British rule. The Zanzibar Football Association (later Federation) was founded in 1926.

In contrast to the situation in Zanzibar, in the late nineteenth century, Germany became the colonial power in what is now mainland Tanzania. No doubt some football was played there. However, after the First World War the area became a British colony under the name Tanganyika.

In 1930, the Tanganyika Football Association was formed. In 1935, the football club that would become Young Africans SC was formed in Dar es Salaam, Tanzania's largest city, and in 1936 a football club was formed that has been known by various names, including Dar Sunderland and its present name, with its lion logo, Simba SC. Young Africans and Simba are two of Tanzania's most successful clubs, and huge rivals.

In 1961, Tanganyika became independent, and then, in 1964, Tanganyika and Zanzibar were joined to become Tanzania.

Tanzania has had some success internationally. The women's team did qualify for the African Women's Championship (now Africa Women Cup of Nations) in 2010, and the men's team have won the CECAFA (Council for East and Central Africa Football Associations) Cup on a number of occasions and have twice been to the Africa Cup of Nations.

The Zanzibar Football Federation is not a member of FIFA, but Zanzibar were the 1995 CECAFA cup champions.

Thailand

Chaophraya Thammasakmontri is known as the father of modern education in Thailand. He also, as it happens, is the father of football in Thailand. But he did have a bit of help from Britons.

Thammasakmontri was a nobleman who trained as a teacher, and in 1896 came to London on a scholarship to continues his studies at Borough Road College, which was later to become part of Brunel University. He wasn't only interested in the intellectual side of education, he was interested in the sports side as well. While in London, he found out about football and its role in schools and colleges in Britain. Among the teachers at Borough Road at that time, was also Joseph Gettins, who was a talented footballer and who had played for both Millwall and Middlesbrough.

On his return to Thailand, Thammasakmontri was keen to introduce the youth of his country to football and, in March 1901, a match was organised between a team representing Bangkok and one from the Department of Education. Most of the players in both of the teams were, in fact, British, and the result was a 2-2 draw, but it was a giant step forward in the history of football in Thailand.

Later that very same year, the Competition for the Silver Shield of the Department of Education was launched as the first knock-out football competition in the country. And soon adult football clubs started to form, too. For instance, the Royal Bangkok Sports Club established its own football team, and in 1915 was the venue for an international match against a team of Europeans. By 1916, the army had its own football club, too. The same year King Vajiravudh formed the 'Football Association of Thailand under Patronage of his Majesty the King'.

Internationally, Thailand has become the most successful footballing nation in south-east Asia, with both the men's and women's teams winning a bunch of regional championships, and the domestic game is lively, too.

We can't end the Thailand chapter without noting the contribution of the late Vichai Srivaddhanaprabha to Leicester City. Under the ownership of his Thai company, King Power, Leicester rose from the Championship to be Premier League champions and FA Cup winners.

Timor-Leste

It's one of those countries where you are not quite sure whether to call it by the name used by the locals, Timor-Leste, or by the English version (and the one more familiar to a lot of readers in Britain) East Timor. Both names mean the same and the fact that Timor-Leste has Portuguese origins gives some clue to the beginnings of football in the country.

When European colonial powers carved up the region in the eighteenth and nineteenth centuries, the Portuguese got what is now Timor-Leste and the Dutch got the western part of the island. Therefore, football came to Timor-Leste via Portugal rather than directly from Britain.

Portuguese officials first started playing the game there and the locals joined in. Football clubs were being founded in Timor-Leste in the 1930s, including Sporting Clube de Timor, based in the capital Dili, which was started in 1938 and has had a long history since.

As in other Portuguese colonies, there were close links between local clubs and those in Portugal. The name, lion emblem, and green and white shirts with black shorts of Sporting Clube de Timor reflect those of Sporting Clube de Portugal, and the two clubs retain links.

In 1949, the Dutch withdrew from Indonesia and in 1975, after Portugal withdrew from Timor-Leste, the Indonesians took power there. A long guerrilla campaign against Indonesian control ensued, and in 1999 a referendum showed a majority of the population in favour of independence. In 2002, Timor-Leste was internationally recognised as a sovereign independent nation.

Timor-Leste's performance in international football has been patchy and at times controversial. However, there is plenty of passion for football in the country. It is Timor-Leste's most popular sport and is widely played.

Togo

The country is a fairly long and narrow (for a country) strip of land to the east of Ghana. Germans were there before the First World War, but France eventually became the colonial power.

Some football seems to have been being played in the capital, Lomé, as early as 1907, and it may well be that the Germans introduced football to the country. However, Lomé is very close to what was then the British Gold Coast colony and is now Ghana, where British-influenced football was already very well established by 1907, so some influence from there is not out of the question.

Major clubs were being formed in the 1920s and '30s. Togo became independent in 1960, and the Togolese Football Federation was founded the same year. The men's national team qualified for the World Cup in 2006, and has reached the Africa Cup of Nations a number of times, reaching the quarter-finals in 2013. Featuring in both campaigns was none other than Emmanuel Adebayor, who has played for, among other teams, Arsenal and Manchester City.

Tonga

Tonga has long had close links with Britain. It's a huge rugby nation; football, not so much.

The Tongan Rugby Football Union was founded in 1923, while the Tonga Football Association wasn't formed until 1965. Kolofo'ou No. 1 took the league title in 1969–70 and the two subsequent seasons.

The national team has had a few wins against opponents such as American Samoa and the Cook Islands, but generally, it would be fair to say that it has struggled somewhat in the international arena. In 2001, Australia beat them 22-0. In the 2007 OFC (Oceania Football Confederation) Women's Nations Cup, Tonga did come third. There were, however, only four teams competing.

By contrast, the Tonga national rugby union team beat France in the 2011 Rugby World Cup.

Trinidad and Tobago

It's traditionally one of the powerhouses of Caribbean football.

In 2006 the Soca Warriors (plenty of US influence in the Caribbean, and soccer rhymes better with warriors than football), in their red and black strip, went on an epic venture all the way to the 2006 World Cup in Germany. After a two-legged play-off with Bahrain, they became the smallest nation ever to qualify for the World Cup. There they scored a notable draw against Sweden, but lost to both England (after holding us scoreless for eighty-three minutes) and Paraguay.

Among stars to grace both pitches here and in Trinidad and Tobago are, of course, Shaka Hislop, Collin Samuel, Russell Latapy and the mighty Dwight Yorke, all members of the 2006 Soca Warriors.

The national women's team, too, has had some success in regional competitions.

There are records from some of the earliest Europeans to arrive in the area of the local Arawaks playing a game with a rubber ball. However, it was a Scot who seems to have been the first to introduce the modern game to the islands.

Thomas Boyd had played football in Scotland and decided he wanted to carry on in his new homeland, too. So, in 1893, equipped with a ball his family had sent him (along with two extra bladders and something to inflate them), Boyd organised a game. Jackets and caps (not jumpers) were used for goalposts but some of the players soon found the heat was too much. Nonetheless, football had arrived in Trinidad and Tobago and, despite the competing attractions of cricket, it wasn't going away.

Boyd had the ball, now he needed a club. The result was the British Rovers Club. And now he had a club, he needed some opposition. Soon they were playing matches against the Queen's Park Cricket Club, who had decided it was worth diversifying their sporting efforts a bit.

Next, various groups wanted their own clubs to represent their own identities. The Scots formed Clydesdale, the police produced players and so did two colleges. An Irish priest started a team called Shamrock, while an assorted group formed the Casuals. Perhaps they were a little too casual, as it turned out, since Clydesdale beat them 2-1 in the first game played after the Trinidad and Tobago Football Association was formed in 1908.

Then, in 1909, as a sign of the future of football in Trinidad and Tobago, a Black team was formed, called Majestic.

Football in Trinidad and Tobago today still shows some signs of Scottish heritage. Among the leading clubs are those with names like Morvant Caledonia United.

Tunisia

It's a country with a great football tradition, but evidence of direct British involvement in the early years of the sport there is pretty thin on the ground. Football mainly came to Tunisia from Britain via France.

The French invaded Tunisia in 1881 and it became a protectorate. The first football club in Tunisia was Racing Club de Tunis, established in 1906. Its first games were between its first and second XIs, as there was no competition.

However, by 1907, a championship had started with two other civilian teams, Football Club de Bizerte and Sporting Club de Ferryville, and two school sides, Carnot High School and Sadiki College. Racing won the first four championships. The teams were predominantly French, although Racing had a local goalie. All clubs had to be agreed by the French authorities and all the club presidents had to be French.

Football spread rapidly, new clubs were founded, football associations sprang up and leagues were started. The game also spread among Tunisians. In 1910, Club Khereddine fielded an all Tunisian line-up in a match against Ariana.

Two of Tunisia's biggest clubs, Espérance Sportive and Club Africain, were founded after the First World War, in order to enable Tunisians to play and to snub the French. Espérance was started in 1919 by Mohammed Zouaoui and Hédi Kallel. Its name, Espérance (Hope), came from the café where it was founded, but was also an aspiration. Club Africain were founded the following year. Both clubs were required to have a French president. Espérance were able to find one, while Africain simply refused, but were allowed to form anyway. Both Espérance and Africain have won the Tunisian League and cup numerous times. Both have also won African club competitions, demonstrating the strength of Tunisian football within the continent of Africa.

The other two big Tunisian clubs, Étoile Sportive du Sahel and Club Sportif Sfaxien, began slightly later. Étoile began in 1925 in the French-Tunisian School in Sousse and is the only Tunisian club to have won all the African club competitions.

The excellent quality of Tunisian players has led to some playing in the Premier League.

Tunisia gained independence from France in 1956 and football thrived. Tunisia have been to the Africa Cup of Nations numerous times and in 2004 they won it. In the World Cup they have been less successful, but have qualified on four occasions. In 1998 in France and again in 2018 in Russia they played England at the group stage. In France, goals from Alan Shearer and Paul Scholes helped England to a 2-0 victory. In Russia, England relied on two Harry Kane goals to scrape home 2-1.

A women's football competition started in 2004. AS Féminine du Sahel have won seven championships. In 2008 the national team qualified for the African Women's Championship (now Africa Women Cup of Nations).

Turkey

Turkey certainly has a passion for football, and, yes, we gave them the world's best sport.

Football was played around 1890 by sailors and merchants in Izmir (which the Brits then knew as Smyrna), the main trading centre on the Levantine coast. There is some confusion about the type of football being played as some games featured fifteen players. Indeed, the first club in Izmir, Smyrna Football Club, founded in 1894 by Herbert Octavius Whittall, was also known as Bournabat Football and Rugby Club.

Brits in Istanbul also started playing football in the 1890s. In 1899, Kadıköy Football Club was started by James Edward La Fontaine and Harry Pears. Yorkshireman Horace Armitage and some Greek football enthusiasts also got involved.

In 1904, the Istanbul Football Association was founded and a Constantine Football League was started. The league had four teams: Kadıköy, Moda FC, Elpis (which means 'Hope' in Greek) and HMS *Imogene* (the name of a 460-ton two-masted steam yacht that served the British Embassy in Istanbul). Pretty much all players were either Brits, Greek or Armenian.

The teams played on Sundays and HMS Imogene were the first champions.

A major instance of British influence in Ottoman football came in 1906. In Athens, the Olympic movement organised the Intercalated Games, a special event between the 1904 and 1908 Olympics. A four-team football competition featured Smyrna FC, who took the silver medal. Five members of Smyrna FC were Whittalls. It was very much a family affair.

The Turkish authorities were happy to let foreigners play football, but they were initially were reluctant to let locals play a game they associated with political danger. In 1899, Fuat Hüsnü Kayacan founded a Turkish team. He named it Black Stockings and, to hide his nationality, used the name Bobby. Despite the subterfuge, police raided the first match against a Greek side. Fuat Hüsnü Kayacan lost both game and club.

Attitudes began to change in the twentieth century. The 'big three' Turkish sides were all formed before the First World War. In 1905, Ali Sami Yen founded Galatasaray, drawing on students from the Lycée de Galatasaray with the aim of playing football like the Brits. Fenerbahçe began in 1907 with school graduates. It also included Fuat Hüsnü Kayacan and players from Black Stockings. Beşiktaş had been a gymnastics club since 1903 but took to football in 1911.

Turkey's defeat in the First World War led to the end of the Ottoman Empire. Following a short period in which British and French troops occupied bits of Turkey, Ataturk established the Turkish Republic in 1923. The occupation provided a chance for football between Turks and occupying forces. This included a humiliating defeat for the British Army in its farewell match in 1923. General Harington had provided a cup in expectation of victory.

However, British involvement in Turkish football did not entirely end there. The big three have all been managed by Brits at various times. Scot Billy Hunter, in 1924, and Malcolm Allison, in 1976, both managed Galatasaray. Beşiktaş had Charles Howard and Eric Keen in the 1940s, and John Toshack in the 1990s. Fenerbahçe had Peter Molloy in 1949–51 and Oscar Hold in 1964. Turkey's national team has also been managed by a number of Brits.

Turkish crowds brought passion to football, and there has also been success on the field. At club level, Galatasaray won the UEFA Cup in 2000. As a nation, Turkey came third in the 2002 World Cup and reached the semi-finals of the 2008 Euros. The women's game started in the 1950s and there is now a women's league with twelve teams. One of the stars of women's football in Turkey is a referee; Lale Orta has offici-ated at a UEFA Cup final.

Turkmenistan

We had a lot to do with the beginning of football in Turkey; it may well be we had a lot less to do with the beginning of football in Turkmenistan.

It is not that far across the Caspian Sea to Turkmenistan from Baku in Azerbaijan, where Brits were playing football in the early twentieth century. It's also not far from Tehran to the border of Turkmenistan, and again Brits were prominent in football in Iran's capital in the early 1900s, too.

However, it seems likely that football reached Turkmenistan indirectly via Russia, rather than directly from Brits, and that football mainly developed in Turkmenistan in the 1920s, when the country was part of the Soviet Union. The first football champion-ship of the Turkmen Soviet Socialist Republic took place in 1937.

The capital of Turkmenistan is Ashgabat and clubs from there have had plenty of success, both in the Soviet era and more recently.

Independent Turkmenistan joined FIFA in 1994. In 2003, they beat Afghanistan 11-0 and they have twice qualified for the AFC Asian Cup. In 2019, the Turkmenistan women's team made their international debut when they went to the Turkish Women's Cup competition.

Tuvalu

It's not a big country. In fact, it's a nation that consists of fewer than 12,000 people on a few islands in the Pacific. And the islands aren't that big.

The football pitch is next to the runway on the main island because of lack of space and has to be shared with rugby teams. However, there is at least a football pitch and people are playing football on it.

Britain used to be the colonial power there but Tuvalu became independent from Britain in 1978. Football was already established in the British period. In 1979, Tuvalu's national football team went to the Pacific Games, and they have played in that competition again a number of times in the twenty-first century.

There is a domestic league in which various clubs represent various islands. Each of the clubs now has women's teams in addition to the men's teams.

Uganda

Uganda's national team are known as the Cranes, after the national bird of the country that appears on its flag. In 1978, despite the country suffering at the time under the cruel and murderous dictator Idi Amin, the Cranes, then mostly amateurs with other day jobs, made it all the way to the finals of the Africa

Cup of Nations, beating teams like Nigeria en route. Sadly for the Cranes, their fairy tale ended in the final, when Ghana beat them 2-0. Uganda didn't qualify again until 2017, but then in 2019 they qualified again and this time made it out of the group stage into the round of sixteen.

Uganda's journey to the 1978 Africa Cup of Nations final began in the late nineteenth century when British missionaries, military personnel and rail engineers introduced the game to the region. Among the missionaries who were involved with football, it's worth mentioning, in particular, George Lawrence Pilkington for his work at Mengo School in the capital, Kampala, and Alexander Gordon Fraser, for what he achieved at King's School Budo. Among the military personnel involved with promoting football was William Pulteney, who would go on to fight in the Boer War and command III Corps on the Western Front in the First World War.

In 1909, Budo Old Boys became the first proper football club in Uganda. Other clubs soon followed. In 1922, Archdeacon Robert Walker led the creation in Kampala of the Arab and African Football Association.

In 1924, the Federation of Uganda Football Associations was founded and, that same year, Uganda played its first international, taking on Kenya.

In 1926, Uganda played Kenya again (and lost) in the first Gossage Cup. However, the Gossage Cup eventually became the CECAFA (Council for East and Central African Football Associations) Cup, and Uganda has a good track record of wins in that over the decades. The men's national team has also been to the Africa Cup of Nations seven times, and in 2000 the women's national team qualified for the African Women's Championship.

In domestic football, SC Villa were the big club of the 1980s and '90s, while KCCA (Kampala Capital City Authority) FC has had a better time of it in the twenty-first century.

Ukraine

It is in the news because of the tragic war there. However, it is, of course, a major football power; for instance, making it to the 2006 World Cup quarter-finals and co-hosting the 2012 Euros. And yes, we had a lot to do with the beginnings of football in Ukraine.

It is possible that British sailors were playing football in the Ukrainian Black Sea port of Odesa as early as the 1860s. However, it was at the end of the nineteenth century and the beginning of the twentieth that the world's greatest sport really took off in Ukraine. Some of that was due to Russian, Polish and Austro-Hungarian influence. In 1894, for instance, a six-minute match was played in Lviv between a local side and one from Kraków. However, some of it was definitely due to Britain.

In the 1860s, a telegraph line was being built through Ukraine that, in the end, stretched from London to Calcutta. It was a monumental technological achievement that was of key strategic importance to the British Empire.

In the late 1870s, British engineers maintaining the line, who were based in Ukraine, needed something to fill some of their spare hours, so they formed the Odesa British Athletic Club. By 1911, they had a proper league up and running, the Odesa Football League.

However, the Odesa telegraph workers were not the only Brits changing Ukraine in the late nineteenth century.

John James Hughes had been born in Merthyr Tydfil in 1814. He became a successful entrepreneur in the steel industry and in the naval armaments field, and soon he had his own foundry and ship-yard. By 1870, after the Russian Imperial Government had taken an interest in his naval skills, Hughes, and a contingent of Welsh workers and their families, was in Ukraine building iron works and collieries. The town they built was named after him, Hughesovka.

Hughes died in 1889, but the town continued to flourish. Such British sports as tennis had already been introduced there in Hughes's day. In 1911, the Hughesovka, or Yuzovka, Sports Society was founded with its own football club.

Later, Hughesovka would be renamed, first Stalino, and then Donetsk, as it is today. Shakhtar Donetsk used to play its home games there, but Donetsk is in the area now occupied by Russian troops.

Football rapidly became a passion among Ukrainians and it remains very much so today, both the men's and women's games. And Ukrainian players, including Andriy Shevchenko, Andriy Yarmolenko and Oleksandr Zinchenko, of course, have made their own contribution to football in this country.

United Arab Emirates

It would be fair to say that the word Emirates is well known to football fans here, but, equally, it would probably be fair to say that is rather more because of the Arsenal stadium, than because of any long and glorious British involvement with football actually in the United Arab Emirates. Nevertheless, involvement there has been.

Football first took off in the area in the period when British influence there was at its maximum. The oldest club in the UAE, Al-Nasr, was, for instance, founded in 1945.

The UAE FA was founded in 1971, in 1972 the national team played its first international match, and in 1973, the UAE Football League commenced.

For much of the early period of its existence, the UAE national team had some UK kit suppliers, and then in 1977, they got an English manager, Don Revie, as well. Roy Hodgson would also later spend a couple of years managing the team.

The UAE men's national team did qualify for Italia '90, where it lost all three group matches, but it does have a better record in regional competitions. The women's national team won the WAFF (West Asian Football Federation) Women's Championship.

United States of America (Plus US Territories)

Yes, it's the land where football isn't football, it's soccer instead.

The USA, of course, has its own distinctive version of football in gridiron. It's fun in its own way, but it's never going to take over the world like real football has. And while soccer may not be as popular as American football over there, the USA was, in fact, one of the first countries to adopt soccer and, yes, unsurprisingly there are strong British links.

America has a long history of football games of many different sorts. When the *Mayflower* arrived in the seventeenth century, the settlers are said to have found Native Americans playing 'Pasuckquakkohowog', meaning 'they gather to play football', or something similar. The new settlers also brought with them their own versions of village football.

By the early nineteenth century, America's major educational institutions were beginning to develop new forms of the game, just as they were in England. As at Rugby, Eton and Harrow in the UK, these began as games between pupils within each school with their own rules, rather than games between schools.

The first soccer club was Oneida, founded in Boston as early as 1862 during the American Civil War. The club was founded by the 16-year-old Gerrit Smith Miller and the members were drawn from elite Boston secondary schools. The games were played on Boston Common and the opposition was other schools in the Boston area. The club was established before the Football Association rules were written and the games were played under

'Boston Rules'. The first team to score two goals won, the ball could be kicked or thrown and there were no goals, only a goal line to be crossed. The Oneida Club only lasted four years, but according to legend their goal line was never crossed.

Rules for football were published in America in 1866 and it would take some time for soccer, rugby and college football (gridiron) to become clearly separate. The 1869 game between Princeton and Rutgers is often seen as the first match to use a version of Football Association rules. However, the rules were modified by the two teams and this game is also claimed as the starting point for gridiron football. In 1873, there was a game between Yale and Eton. This was certainly the first time a match had been played between a British side and a team outside Britain, but it is less clear whether the game played was soccer. It did have a standard football and eleven per side, so it may have been recognisable as such.

By the 1870s, American colleges had largely moved away from soccer to develop their own form of football. The development of soccer was left to working-class migrants arriving from Europe, with the Scots being particularly influential.

As immigration increased, soccer grew in New Jersey, New York and Philadelphia, before spreading north to Massachusetts and Rhode Island. While many new arrivals took up baseball as they wanted to integrate, others organised local kick-abouts and teams. In 1884, this led to the formation of the American Football Association, making the USA one of the early countries to form its own association. The AFA introduced a cup competition. Scots from Kearney were influential in Clark Thread Company team, which won the AFA Cup in 1895, showing the influence of Scottish migrants.

There was even an attempt to set up a professional soccer league in 1894 when National League baseball clubs thought they could make money in the winter months using their stadiums to host a football league, the first professional one outside Britain. Team names ranged from the unusual Brooklyn Bridegrooms and Boston Beaneaters to the more familiar Baltimore Orioles, New York Giants and Philadelphia Phillies. Unfortunately, it only lasted one year and the amateur AFA banned any of its players from participating.

At the 1904 Olympics in St Louis, there was a football competition. It was an exhibition as football did not become part of the games until FIFA signed up in 1908. Sadly for home supporters in St Louis, it was the Canadian team Galt FC that were the winners.

The popularity of soccer was encouraged by tours from British sides. The Corinthians, for instance, toured in 1906. They were able to humiliate a New York side 18-0 but were defeated by Fall River. By 1913, football was sufficiently established in America for it to join FIFA.

The 1920s was a 'golden age' for soccer in the USA, and Brits, particularly Scots, played an important role. In 1921, a professional American Soccer League was started. Among the original teams, there was a Jersey City Celtics. The league was well funded by major manufacturers and consequently paid higher wages than were available in Europe. In 1925, the Scottish international Alex McNab was earning $25 per week playing for the Boston Wonder Workers. The league was popular and crowds were often large. It also had the money and prestige to attract tours from top European sides, and Sparta Prague and Hakoah Vienna toured in 1926, playing to crowds of up to 46,000.

The USA sent a team to the 1930 World Cup in Uruguay managed by Bob Millar, who had been born and brought up in Paisley. His squad also included five other Scots. There were the forwards, Bart McGhee from Edinburgh, Jim Brown from Troon and Jimmy Gallagher from Kirkintilloch. Behind them was Andy Auld from Stevenson, and at the back was Alex Wood from Lochgelly.

The Americans reached the semi-final, having defeated Belgium and Paraguay. All the Scots played in the semi-final against Argentina, where the Americans were heavily defeated, 6-1. The third-place finish remains the USA's best World Cup performance so far.

The 'golden age' gave way to the Great Depression and the ASL folded in 1933. There have been two subsequent attempts to revive an American soccer league.

In 1967, the North American Soccer League was established and it ran until 1984. This was the league that attracted international stars to play in America, and Pelé and Franz Beckenbauer played for the New York Cosmos. Four of England's 1966 World Cup heroes ended up playing in the USA: Bobby Moore for San Antonio Thunder, Alan Ball for Philadelphia Fury, Gordon Banks for the Fort Lauderdale Strikers and Geoff Hurst for the Seattle Sounders. The league was popular for a while, with more than 70,000 spectators watching the New York Cosmos play Ft Lauderdale Strikers in 1977, but the average crowd that year was less than 15,000.

Another attempt was made to establish a professional soccer league on the back of the 1994 World Cup, which was held in the USA. Major League Soccer started in 1996. David Beckham and Steven Gerrard have been among the latest in a long line of Brits heading to the USA.

Coming in the opposite direction in recent years have, of course, been a lot of US players, headed for British teams, like Brad Friedel, Brian McBride and Christian Pulisic.

Women's football appeared in the USA as early as 1893 in San Francisco. In 1922–23, the English team Dick, Kerr Ladies toured the USA. Opponents included men's teams and Dick, Kerr won six of nine games. They also beat the American Olympic team over a 4 × 100-yard relay race.

From these early beginnings, the USA women's football has turned into a superpower and on an international stage has won far more than the men. The women's team have won four World

Cups, in 1991, 1999, 2015 and 2019, and four Olympic Gold medals, in 1996, 2004, 2008 and 2012.

And before we leave the USA chapter, we need to mention briefly a number of other teams that come politically under the US umbrella.

American Samoa has been one of FIFA's lowest-ranked teams. However, American Samoa have actually managed victories against Tonga and the Cook Islands.

Guam has a population of less than 200,000. It joined FIFA in 1996 and in 2018 the 'Matao' won a World Cup qualifying game against Turkmenistan 1-0 in front of a capacity crowd of 2,000.

The Northern Mariana Islands are now part of FIFA and managed their first international victory in their own right in 2014 against Macau 2-1.

Spanish soldiers introduced football to Puerto Rico in the nineteenth century. It was also played by visiting sailors, some of whom may have been Brits or Americans. By 1914, there were at least four local clubs but the introduction of the American club Celtics FC in 1914 added a bit of ethnic rivalry to local derbies. Former Northern Ireland international Colin Clarke has played a part in developing football in Puerto Rico.

The US Virgin Islands did not join FIFA until the 1990s and it played its first international in 1998, the 'Dashing Eagles' defeating their close neighbours the British Virgin Islands.

Uruguay

Uruguay is a comparatively smallish country on the east coast of South America, sandwiched between Argentina and Brazil, but it has a very big football history.

It was this tiny republic with fewer than 4 million inhabitants that was to host and win the first World Cup in 1930. It also won Olympic gold medals in 1924 and 1928, and another World Cup in 1950 in Brazil. So it is a country that has punched well above its weight.

And, yes, it was the British rather than the Spanish, Italians or Uruguayans themselves who first introduced football to the country – although direct links between British influence and World Cup success are somewhat more debatable.

Uruguay was never part of the formal British Empire, although the British did invade in 1807 and returned in 1845. However, by the end of the nineteenth century it was part of an informal British Empire based on commerce, with about 2,000 Brits based in and around Montevideo. Some of these were middle-class merchants involved in exporting hides to Britain, while others were bankers and accountants helping build the rail network and organising public services. There were also plenty of manual labourers seeking adventure and work on the railways.

Montevideo Cricket Club had been founded by the British in 1861. However, it also played rugby, and like many cricket clubs elsewhere it took up football as a way of keeping players fit and active in the winter months. Montevideo Rowing Club, founded slightly later in 1874, also had a strong British presence.

The first recorded football match was in 1881 between Montevideo Cricket Club and Montevideo Rowing Club (although three years earlier, the Montevideo Cricket Club had played a game against a visiting Navy ship).

The combination of Montevideo Cricket Club and Montevideo Rowing Club was to give Uruguay its first international football match, when in 1889 they combined to play as a Montevideo Team against a Buenos Aires Team.

The first club formed solely to play football was Albion, started in 1891 by pupils from the English High School in Montevideo. The school was founded in 1874 by William Castle Ayre, who was keen on the value of sport in education. There is some uncertainty about whether the credit for founding the team belongs to the Cambridge graduate William Leslie Poole or pupil Henry Candido Lichtenberger (whose mother may have been Scottish).

While Poole played for Albion, it is as a referee and administrator that he had most influence. In 1900, he helped start the Uruguay Association Football League and was one of its earliest presidents. Poole is recognised in Uruguay as the 'father of football', and has a public space dedicated to his honour.

There is little doubt about British influence on Albion. In 1896, they became the first Uruguayan team to tour Argentina, and in 1899 they built the first stadium designed to be used only for football, which could seat 1,000 spectators. Albion was a driving force in nineteenth-century Uruguayan football, winning eighteen of nineteen fixtures in 1896, but by 1908 the club had faded and been relegated to the second division.

The driving forces of Uruguayan football today are Peñarol and Nacional, both of which had their origins in the nineteenth century. Peñarol began life as CURCC, the Central Uruguayan Railway Cricket Club, formed in 1891 by workers of the railway based in Peñarol. The British invested heavily in the railways in Uruguay and most of the founding members of the club were British. The railway link was reinforced by Peñarol's yellow and black strip, supposedly a reference to Stephenson's *Rocket*.

The engineer John Woosey, who had been a founding member of Albion, introduced football to the activities of the CURCC and their first match was a victory against the English High School. In 1913–14, the club changed its name to Peñarol. In 1900, both Albion and CURCC were founder members of the first Uruguayan football league. CURCC became the first champions.

Britain also had a role in establishing an international football competition between Uruguay and their neighbours Argentina. In 1905, the tea magnate Thomas Lipton, who was born in Glasgow, started the Copa De Caridad Lipton (Lipton Charity Cup). The opening match was a draw but rather than a penalty shoot-out the cup was given to Uruguay as the away side. Such sportsmanship.

The locals were quick to take up football, and they seem to have admired the British clubs. The pioneers also seem to have included the locals. William Poole was keen that football was for everyone and the CURCC had a Uruguayan captain as early as 1895. The locals also founded their own clubs, for example, Nacional, but some of the clubs had English names, like Britannia.

At the start of the twentieth century, the standard of football was poor, with a Southampton side defeating a Uruguay XI 8-1 in Montevideo in 1904. However, within twenty years they would go on to win the gold medal at the Paris Olympics.

While this was largely a Uruguayan triumph, there are some Brits who can claim to have had an influence on it. A Scottish railway engineer, John Harley, joined CURCC in 1909 and is sometimes given credit for introducing the short passing game to Uruguay. He was a centre half who could link forwards and defenders to make a more cohesive team. Despite his Scottish origins, he seems to have played seventeen games for Uruguay and became manager of Peñarol. Some 40,000 spectators turned up to honour him at a match in 1951, so the locals seem to have appreciated his efforts.

The most lasting evidence of the importance of Britain for the development of football in Uruguay is in the team names. Albion still play and there is also a Liverpool FC, which shockingly plays in a blue strip, and Montevideo Wanderers.

Returning the football favour, a number of Uruguayan players have contributed their talents to football over here, including Diego Forlán, Gus Poyet, Edinson Cavani and Luis Suárez.

While Uruguay has long been passionate about men's football, the women's game has taken longer to develop. The Uruguayan Football Association did not adopt the women's game until 1996. The biggest achievement so far for Las

Celestes, as the women's team is called, was third place in the 2006 Women's Copa América.

Uzbekistan

While Britain was extending its empire in the nineteenth century, so was Russia. In 1865, their troops seized Tashkent, the capital of what is now Uzbekistan. In 1868, they entered the city of Samarkand, home to the mausoleum of Timur (Tamerlane), and in 1876 they took control of Kokand.

In the early twentieth century, football had already established firm foundations in Russia itself, with the help of assorted Britons, and soon it was spreading across the Russian empire, too. In the early twentieth century, the locals in Kokand would watch Russian troops kicking a ball around in their spare time. It is said that a shoemaker was asked to make an imitation of the balls that the Russian soldiers used, but eventually the locals got their hands on a genuine one and then there was no stopping them.

In 1912 came the foundation, under the chairmanship of Scot Arthur MacPherson, of the All-Russian Football Union, the official body for football across the Russian Empire. The same year also saw the foundation of the football team that was to become FK Kokand 1912, or FK Qo'qon 1912. Other clubs soon formed and by 1914 they were battling each other for the championship of Fergana Valley.

Football subsequently expanded massively in Uzbekistan during the Soviet period and since independence it has continued to be something of a regional football power in Central Asia. Pakhtakor Tashkent FK, which has a cotton bud (not that kind, the plant bud kind) as its symbol – suitably enough since Pakhtakor means Cotton-Grower – is one of the domestic football superpowers.

The men's international team has had some success, as has the women's. In 2018, the women's team won the first Central Asian Football Association Championship.

Vanuatu

A small Pacific island nation, Vanuatu is in an unusual situation in terms of its colonial history. For much of the twentieth century until independence in 1980, the New Hebrides, as they then were, had not just one colonial power but two. Britain and France ran the territory as a condominium. To make matters even more confusing, for a while there was even provision for involvement from the king of Spain as a kind of independent arbiter. It is, therefore, hard to be entirely sure who introduced football to the country.

The English names of early football teams, like Golden Star FC and Shepherds United FC, might suggest maybe it came a bit more from Britain than France. On the other hand, there is also an Amicale FC, which is much more in the French tradition. Not much sign of Spanish influence on team names though, which might disappoint the Spanish royal family.

What became the Vanuatu Football Federation was originally formed in 1934, and the national team has achieved fourth place in the OFC Nations Cup four times so far. For a long time in the 1980s and '90s, Terry O'Donnell was the national coach. The women's national team has competed in the OFC Women's Championship.

Vatican City

Yes, the Vatican is a country. It's not your typical country (but then are any countries typical?) and it is not a member of the

United Nations, but it does have observer status, and in many senses it is like lots of other sovereign nation states. And yes, it plays football.

In fact, it has played various types of football for a very long time. For instance, on 7 January 1521, Pope Leo X was in the stands as the Papal States went at it in a Florentine football match.

It's not entirely clear who first played modern football in the Vatican. It is hard to believe that some of the British men in Rome's seminaries and ecclesiastical colleges were not occasionally kicking a ball around in the nineteenth century. Or perhaps football first came to the Vatican as it spread across Italy.

By 1947, the Vatican was ready to hold its first home football competition with four teams made up of employees. Or perhaps it wasn't entirely ready, since the competition had to be stopped when a fight started between the players and spectators. The domestic league has become more stable and settled since then.

In 1978, of course, a footballer became pope. Karol Wojtyla, who became Pope John Paul II, had often played football as a goalkeeper in his youth.

By 1994, the Vatican had its own national men's side, kitted out, of course, in papal yellow and white, playing occasional internationals (often against San Marino or Monaco) and in 2019 the Vatican national women's team took to the pitch for the first time, too. Italian first division side Roma beat them 10-0.

Such is the passion for football in the Vatican, however, that in addition to the domestic league and international matches, there is also the Clericus Cup. This is a regular football competition for the priests and seminarians who have come to Rome from across the world. England fans will be glad to know that in the very first match of the very first Clericus Cup competition, the Venerable English College soundly beat the Pontifical Beda College 5-2.

Venezuela

Considering Venezuela is a major South American nation, this is going to be a surprisingly short chapter.

Venezuela's comparatively thin footballing history can perhaps (as can be said of a lot of events in South American history over the last 150 years) be down to it being quite close to the United States.

We did our bit. As early as 1876, we introduced them to football. There are records of British workers from the mining and rubber industries giving displays of football. And there is a statue in La Plaza Futbolista Venezolano, in El Callao, with a plaque that records an 1876 match there between English and French immigrants. However, unlike in so many other places, the locals did not quickly grasp the full fun of football.

American oil interests brought baseball into the country and that rapidly became the most popular sport there.

However, we kept on trying. In the early years of the twentieth century, Brits working on steam engines had the idea of assembling a football club. Because of the lack of local players, a lot of the first members were from outside Venezuela, but soon, in 1902, the San Bernardino Sports Club was founded.

Despite all this, the Football Federation of Venezuela was not even formed until fifty years after that first match played between the English and French. And it took them until 2008 to put up the statue in El Callao.

Recently, however, Venezuela has finally shown some evidence of realising how important football actually is. For instance, they hosted the Copa América in 2007 and reached the quarter-finals. Its U-20 side reached the final of the U-20 World Cup in 2017 for the first time.

The women's national team has been to the Copa América Femenina a number of times and came third in the 1991 competition.

It's been a long time since 1876, but maybe, at last, Venezuela is about to really show us all it can do with the sport from Britain.

Vietnam

On 23 March 1975, the international football team of the Republic of Vietnam, or South Vietnam as it is more widely known, played its last match. Malaysia beat them 3-0. Just a few weeks later, on 30 April, as North Vietnamese troops and the Viet Cong occupied Saigon, President Minh unconditionally surrendered the south and the Vietnam War was finally over.

It's hard, for those of us old enough to have seen news of the war on our TV screens, not to think of it when we think of Vietnamese history, but, of course, Vietnam had plenty of history before the war, and has had quite a few decades of it since then, and part of that story is football.

At the time when football was first spreading across the world, Vietnam was part of French Indochina, so it is not surprising to find the French heavily involved in introducing this great new sport to the area. However, as in so many other countries, we were involved, too.

HMS *King Alfred* had a fairly chequered career. An armoured cruiser, launched in Barrow-in-Furness in 1901, she ran aground once and spent quite a lot of the First World War searching unsuccessfully for German raiders, before being torpedoed and eventually scrapped. In 1905, however, she had turned up to make Vietnamese football history, by landing a British team to take on a French military team drawn from a Marine Infantry regiment, in Saigon, in the first match on Vietnamese soil.

Brits were heavily involved, too, as football took off among the city's European civilian population. In 1906, the first football club in Saigon was formed, the Cercle Sportif Saigonnais, which had Swiss players as well as French and English. It did not take long for the passion for this new sport to spread to the local inhabitants. Soon after CSS, Vietnamese teams were on the ball.

At about the same time, football was also being adopted in the north of Vietnam, in the port city of Haiphong. In 1909, Olympique Haiphong took on a team from nearby Dap Cau. Olympique won 2-1 in the first match, but the Dap Cau team won 8-1 in the second.

And despite the years of war (so many) that would follow in the twentieth century, the Vietnamese have never lost their passion for the world's greatest sport. In 2018, the Vietnam U-23 team made it all the way to the final of the Asian Football Confederation U-23 Championship, only for Uzbekistan to beat them 2-1 after a goal late in extra time. And the women's national team has an impressive record, with multiple wins in the AFF Women's Championship and SEA Games.

Yemen

Tragically, these days, when people think of Yemen, they tend to think of bombed out buildings, heavily armed militiamen and hungry children. Having said that, despite the appalling civil war that has torn the country apart in recent years, people have kept on playing football.

Some footballers have been kidnapped, some have had to escape the war by boat, others have joined the fighting, but during these terrible years, the Yemen national side has even had the occasional success on the international stage.

And yes, football came to that land from here. Along with occupying forces.

In 1839, Britain seized control of Aden. It was a useful anti-piracy base for the Royal Navy and, after the opening of the Suez Canal later in the nineteenth century, it would become an extremely important coaling station for British ships on the long voyage from the Suez Canal to India.

Already by the 1880s, British soldiers and sailors were kicking a ball around in south Yemen. Soon the locals would take up the sport, too, and in 1905 what would become the Al-Tilal football club was founded. By 1934, at the latest, a proper football championship had started.

Until the First World War, the area of the Yemen to the north was still under Ottoman control, and football arrived there more slowly. However, people travelling from the south brought footballs with them, and in the 1930s, the Italians would lend a hand, with assorted doctors and others teaching football skills to some of the young lads in the capital of Yemen, Sana'a. The oldest football club there was founded in 1937.

In the early 1960s, some locals began an armed campaign against British control of Aden, which was known over here as the Aden Emergency. It was a bitter struggle, which accelerated our departure from the region.

Britain left Yemen but football never did, since it is part of the genius of football that, however it reached a country, once it has arrived there, it becomes as much an integral part of the local culture, with its own unique flavour, as if it had been invented there in the first place. And one day, when the fighting there stops, Yemen may finally achieve the results on the football pitch that the passion of its fans deserves.

Zambia

Although you might not have guessed it, one of the key questions about the beginning of football in Zambia is exactly how keen on football was famous nineteenth-century missionary David Livingstone.

Livingstone was, of course, a hugely famous figure in Victorian Britain, and even today, he is a familiar name to many, if only because of the supposed greeting from American explorer Stanley when finally encountering him after a long trek, 'Dr Livingstone, I presume.' Yet, few people think to ask themselves, 'What exactly was Livingstone's view on the offside rule?'

Yet, there are those who reckon Livingstone did indeed bring football to Zambia. As we have already seen in other African countries, missionaries often did encourage the locals to play football, and, apparently, Livingstone did indeed take a rubber ball with him to Africa. It is not clear that he intended to use this ball as a football, but then equally it is not clear that he did not. It is, after all, one of the facts that has made football the unique global phenomenon that it is that you can play it (and people have played it) with anything from a new hi-tech football to a bag full of rubbish formed into a ball.

However, whatever its origins, the people of what is now Zambia grew to love the sport from Britain. In the 1920s, the mining area of Broken Hill (now Kabwe) saw the creation of a number of proper, organised football clubs. And few Zambians loved football more than Kenneth Kaunda, the man who led his country to independence from Britain in 1964.

Even before independence, he had realised that football could be a force to unify a new nation. But he was clearly passionate about the sport itself and, as president, he put the resources of the state into making Zambian football great. The national side became known as the KK 11. Zambia Railways ran the impressive Kabwe Warriors team. The Zambian Army soon had its own elite team, the Green Buffaloes. Both are still major Zambian teams today. Kaunda even regularly got his first cabinet out on the pitch playing matches. Sometimes he would appear on pitches as the referee, a perhaps risky venture for any politician wanting to remain popular.

In the end, after a long period of one-party rule, Zambia's love affair with Kaunda would finish, but its love affair with football would remain. The men's national team have qualified for the Africa Cup of Nations many times, and in 2012, they won it. The women's national team has been to the Africa Women Cup of Nations three times and in 2020 they played in the Olympic football in Japan.

And traces of Zambian football's British heritage can still be found, for instance, in names of clubs like Mufulira Wanderers, one of Zambia's most famous.

Zimbabwe

What was perhaps the first ever football match in the land that is now Zimbabwe was played in September 1890 between a police and a pioneers team.

It does not seem to have been a very elaborate affair, and may indeed have been played in a dry river bed. However, by 1897, a police team was winning the First Bulawayo League Cup. By 1899, the country was a British colony called Southern Rhodesia, and Harry Allen from there was playing for Derby County against Sheffield United in the FA Cup final.

As in a lot of other places in Africa in the early twentieth century, football in Southern Rhodesia suffered from racist attitudes among the colony's white community. However, again as elsewhere, local Africans took to the game with enthusiasm, nonetheless. Workplace clubs were formed, and Bulawayo, for instance, became a major place for African football at this time. In 1926, Lions Football Club, now Highlanders FC, was founded there by two grandsons of Ndebele King Lobengula.

After a long guerrilla war against white rule in Rhodesia, Zimbabwe came into being in 1980.

The Zimbabwe men's national team has qualified for the Africa Cup of Nations five times, and won a number of regional cup titles. In 2000, the women's team came fourth in the African Women's Championship (now the Africa Women Cup of Nations).

Over the years, a number of talented players from the country have added to British football. The most famous of those is, of course, Bruce Grobbelaar.

Index